Noteworthy Women of
Oswego County, New York

Noteworthy Women of Oswego County, New York

Natalie Joy Woodall

excelsior editions

Cover Credit: (Top to bottom): Virginia L. Radley (courtesy SUNY Archives and Special Collections), Emma Eunice Adams (courtesy Town of Oswego Historical Society), and Rhea LaVeck (courtesy Author's Collection)

Published by State University of New York Press, Albany

Excelsior Editions is an imprint of State University of New York Press

For information, contact State University of New York Press, Albany, NY
www.sunypress.edu

Library of Congress Cataloging-in-Publication Data

Name: Woodall, Natalie Joy.
Title: Noteworthy women of Oswego County, New York / Natalie Joy Woodall.
Description: Albany : State University of New York Press, [2025] | Series: Excelsior
    Editions | Includes bibliographical references and index.
Identifiers: 9798855800401 (ebook) | ISBN 9798855800395 (pbk. : alk. paper)
Further information is available at the Library of Congress.

*This book is dedicated to the memory of
Margaret Jane and Keitha Mae,
my noteworthy women.*

Contents

List of Illustrations   ix

Acknowledgments   xvii

Preface: Where Are All the Women?   xix

Introduction: "Someone's Wife or Mother"   1

1. The Noteworthy Women of Oswego County, New York   19
    Harriet Rundell   19
    Ellen M. Bruce   26
    Armonella Marshall Devendorf   32
    Mary Victoria Lee, MD   38
    Julia McNair Wright   46
    Elvira Rainier, MD   54
    Charlotte "Lottie" Blair Parker   60
    Harriet Elisabeth Stevens   69
    Emma Eunice Adams   78
    Charlotte Lund   88
    Lida Scovil Penfield   101
    Una Clayton   108
    The Sisters Taylor: Isabel, Grace, Harriette, and Jane   116
    Those Mott Women: Ruth, Alice, Dorothy, and Bailey   132
    Helen Gay Purviance   158
    Grace E. Lynch   170
    Muriel Leola Jobst Allerton   175
    Virginia Louise Radley   182

2. Vignettes 193
    Cora M. Ballister 193
    Jessie Fairfield Gordon 194
    Ida Louise Griffin Keating 196
    Rhea Claire Wilder LaVeck 198
    Semantha "Almira" Reynolds McLean 201
    Mary Austen Oliver 203
    Caroline E. Waugh 208

Notes 211

Bibliography 259

Index 271

Illustrations

P.1   Charlotte Ambler Clarke actively participated in the abolitionist movement and Underground Railroad in Oswego City.   xx

P.2   Elmina Pleiades Keeler Spencer volunteered to accompany the soldiers of the 147th Regiment and worked tirelessly to assist the sick and the wounded.   xxi

P.3   Louise Irwin and her friends founded the Home for the Homeless so elderly and destitute women might have a safe place to live.   xxii

P.4   Louise MacFarlane was the guiding force behind the establishment of Oswego Hospital.   xxiii

I.1   Lucretia Mott's Declaration of Sentiments presented at the Women's Rights Convention in Seneca Falls, New York, in July 1848 exposed many sex-based legal and social inequities.   4

I.2   Dr. Ernest Manwaren flouted law and social norms by marrying Anna Murdoch without securing a legal divorce in New York from his first wife, Emma Louisa Thomas.   10

I.3   Darius Ballou deserted from the 147th Regiment and completely disappeared, leaving wife and child without any means of support.   12

I.4   A group of determined women established and ran the Home for the Homeless located on East Utica Street, Oswego, New York.   13

I.5   Dr. Mary E. Walker rejected the notion of "appropriate"
        female garb and wore "men's clothing" even though the
        practice led to public derision and frequent arrests.   14

I.6   Lottie Blair Parker was a "small town girl" who achieved
        success as an actress and playwright through determination
        and hard work.   17

1.1   Lieutenant Marshall Rundell died in the service of his
        country at the age of nineteen.   23

1.2   Harriet "Auntie" Rundell ministered to the sick in Mexico,
        New York, for over forty years.   24

1.3   Harriet Rundell is buried in Mexico Village Cemetery
        with her husband, William, and their two sons, George and
        Marshall.   25

1.4   Ellen Bruce spent her entire teaching career in the same
        school, located in Oswego City's Second Ward.   27

1.5   Ellen Bruce is buried in Oakwood Cemetery, Syracuse,
        New York.   31

1.6   Armonella Devendorf was among many officers' wives
        who joined their husbands at their military posts during
        the Civil War.   33

1.7   Samuel Arnold's scathing memoir about his time as a
        prisoner at Fort Jefferson met stiff criticism from
        Armonella Devendorf and others who had been there
        during Arnold's incarceration.   35

1.8   Armonella is buried with her husband, Henry Clay
        Devendorf, and her daughter, Emma Dygert Low, in
        Hillside Cemetery, Central Square, New York.   37

1.9   Dr. Mary V. Lee was a pioneer in women's athletics.   40

1.10   Dr. Lee was devoted to her students.   41

1.11   Dr. Mary Lee waged war against constricting clothes,
        including "fashionable" garters.   44

1.12   Dr. Mary V. Lee was a much beloved faculty member at
        the Normal School.   45

1.13   Lee Hall was named in memory of Dr. Mary V. Lee.   46

1.14   It has been estimated that Julia McNair Wright wrote more than two hundred books.   49

1.15   Laura Newkirk and Dr. Elvira Rainier lived together for nineteen years.   55

1.16   Elvira Rainier, MD, is buried in the Newkirk plot in Riverside Cemetery, Scriba, New York.   59

1.17   Lottie Blair Parker was, in her own words, legendary.   60

1.18   Lottie Blair's plan to become an elocutionist changed when a teacher encouraged her to become an actress.   61

1.19   Lottie Blair Parker kept her personal life very private.   68

1.20   Harriet Stevens was a faculty member at Oswego Normal for twenty-eight years.   70

1.21   Harriet Stevens was instrumental in placing this monument on the site of Old Fort George in Oswego City.   71

1.22   These two boxes, stored at the Richardson-Bates House in Oswego City, contain many types of notes Miss Stevens took pertaining to collecting data on every soldier and sailor from Oswego City who served in World War I.   74

1.23   Harriet Stevens's final report was considered a masterpiece of scope and detail.   75

1.24   Harriet Elisabeth Stevens is buried in the family plot in Rural Cemetery, Oswego Town. Her birth and death dates do not appear on the monument.   78

1.25   Emma Eunice Adams's early life was typical of the girls of her time.   79

1.26   Different sized dolls were displayed in the Adams family home.   83

1.27   Emma Adams used her doll-making business to pay off the mortgage on the family farm.   84

1.28   Esther Ruttan Doyle donated this large Columbian doll to the Oswego County Historical Society. The original dress has been replaced.   87

1.29 The Town of Oswego Historical Society possesses two
Columbian dolls.   87

1.30 Emma Eunice Adams is buried in Rural Cemetery,
Oswego Town, with her parents and sister, Cornelia.   88

1.31 Charlotte Lund was known for her lovely soprano voice
while still a very young woman.   89

1.32 Charlotte Lund's concert at the Richardson Theatre in
Oswego City was highly anticipated and well attended.   94

1.33 Andrew and Nell Byrnes Lund are buried in St. Paul's
Cemetery, Oswego City.   97

1.34 Charlotte posed with members of the Pacific Coast Singers'
Association at the 12th Sangfoerening in September 1917.   99

1.35 Madame Charlotte Lund is buried in Tappan Cemetery,
Tappan, New York.   100

1.36 Lida Scovil Penfield was beloved by students and peers at
Oswego Normal School.   103

1.37 Penfield Library on the SUNY Oswego Campus is the
second to bear Lida's name.   106

1.38 Lida Scovil Penfield, PhD, lies with members of her
family in Riverside Cemetery, Scriba, New York.   107

1.39 Una Clayton enjoyed an excellent reputation as a
vaudeville actress.   111

1.40 Una Clayton was a strikingly beautiful woman, a fact
frequently mentioned in reviews.   113

1.41 The Taylor family included five very talented daughters.   117

1.42 Adelia Cezarine Fish Taylor was committed to the cause of
women's suffrage and encouraged her daughters to become
involved.   117

1.43 Grace Taylor was a public school teacher for fifty years.   120

1.44 Harriette Taylor Treadwell was one of the official greeters
when suffragist Emily Pankhurst visited Chicago.   126

1.45 Harriette and Charles Treadwell are buried in the Treadwell
      family plot in Riverside Cemetery, Scriba, New York.   129

1.46 Jane Bliss Taylor was associated with amateur theatrics
      during her teen years in Oswego.   129

1.47 The Taylor family plot is located in the upper portion of
      Riverside Cemetery, Scriba, New York. A large monument
      lists many names. All are buried there except Harriette.   133

1.48 Ruth Woolsey Johnson's marriage to Luther Wright Mott
      was considered important enough to be reported in the
      New York Times.   134

1.49 Luther Wright Mott was elected to the House of
      Representatives seven times.   135

1.50 This poster reinforced Ruth Mott's belief that women
      should become active in the war effort in order to secure
      male support for women's suffrage.   138

1.51 Luther Wright Mott is buried in the family plot in
      Riverside Cemetery, Scriba, New York.   141

1.52 Ruth Johnson Mott is buried beside her husband in
      Riverside Cemetery.   144

1.53 Alice Wright Mott spent much of her girlhood in
      Washington, DC.   144

1.54 Alice and Edwin Charles Tifft were the parents of a son,
      Edwin, Jr.   146

1.55 Dorothy Mott was Ruth and Luther's youngest child.   147

1.56 Dorothy Mott enlisted in the Women's Marine Corps
      because she thought someone in her family should be
      actively involved with the war effort.   149

1.57 Dorothy Mott was the first full-time director of admissions
      at SUNY Oswego.   149

1.58 Dorothy Mott's gravestone pays tribute to her military
      service.   153

1.59   Thomas Smith Mott actively conducted his business affairs in Oswego City even though he was blind for the last twenty-five years of his life.   153

1.60   Bailey Mott did not permit her disability to curtail her career or leisurely pursuits.   155

1.61   Bailey Mott was an excellent student and graduated from business college after attending Oswego High School.   157

1.62   Bailey Elizabeth Mott is buried with her parents in the family plot in Riverside Cemetery, Scriba, New York.   158

1.63   Helen Gay Purviance's quiet pursuit of improving the lives of the poor in Oswego City resulted in increased respect among civic leaders for the work of the Salvation Army.   160

1.64   Helen Purviance fried doughnuts for homesick soldiers in France during World War I.   163

1.65   Lieutenant-Colonel Helen Gay Purviance is buried with members of her family in Mount Hope Cemetery, Huntington, Indiana.   169

1.66   Grace Lynch's love of history was recognized by the Oswego County Historical Society in its 1966–1967 publication.   171

1.67   Many of Grace Lynch's essays were compiled into two volumes after her death.   172

1.68   Muriel and Joseph Allerton, longtime opera buffs, were among the founders of the Oswego Opera Theatre.   177

1.69   Muriel Allerton was elected Fulton's first female mayor.   180

1.70   Muriel Allerton is buried in Mt. Adnah Cemetery, Fulton, New York. The inscription on her monument says, "Mayor of Fulton."   181

1.71   Virginia L. Radley made educational history several times in her career.   183

1.72   Virginia Radley's inauguration as SUNY Oswego's eighth president was full of pomp and circumstance.   185

1.73   Radley's office was on the top floor of Culkin Hall, affectionately known as "the tower of power."   188

1.74   Radley's first book was a biography of Samuel Taylor
Coleridge.   190

Vignettes

2.1   Cora Ballister was a buyer for Dey Bros. Department Store
in Syracuse, New York.   194

2.2   Jessie Fairfield Gordon is buried with her parents in
Riverside Cemetery, Scriba, New York.   196

2.3   Ida L. Griffin's election as the first female education
commissioner in Oswego County was big news and
reported in many newspapers.   198

2.4   Rhea LaVeck was in constant demand as a musician for
local weddings.   199

2.5   Rhea LaVeck was the first and only woman from Oswego
District to be elected grand matron of the Order of the
Eastern Star in New York State.   200

2.6   Almira Reynolds McLean lived for many years in Shaker
communities in New York State. She became an eldress
in the Harvard Community in Massachusetts.   202

2.7   Mary A. Oliver painted this portrait of her father-in-law,
Robert Oliver, Sr.   205

2.8   Mary A. Oliver was a well-known artist who specialized
in painting roses.   205

2.9   Mary A. Oliver and Kate E. Miller advertised their
Syracuse studio in local newspapers.   206

2.10   Mary A. Oliver is buried in Riverside Cemetery, Scriba,
New York, with her husband, Francis.   207

2.11   Caroline Waugh was "called" to teach former slaves in
southern states after the Civil War.   209

2.12   Caroline E. Waugh is buried in the family plot in
Hillside Cemetery, Scriba, New York.   210

Acknowledgments

To the persons and organizations named herein I tender grateful and heart-felt appreciation for advice and assistance in the production of this book: Richard Carlin and SUNY Press for the opportunity to tell the stories of these remarkable women; Mary Kay Stone, president of the Oswego County Historical Society, for permission to use photos of Charlotte "Lottie" Blair Parker, Jane Bliss Taylor, Ellen M. Bruce, Louise Irwin, and Harriet E. Stevens, and for access to Harriet Stevens's notes for compilation of Oswego City's World War I soldiers and sailors; Nancy Mott Frank, for information about and permission to use photos of Ruth Woolsey Johnson Mott, Alice Mott Tifft, Dorothy Mott, and Bailey Elizabeth Mott; Zachary Vickery, archivist, Penfield Library Special Collections, SUNY Oswego, for permission to use photos of Mary V. Lee, MD, Lida Scovil Penfield, Virginia L. Radley, Lee Hall, and Penfield Library on the SUNY Oswego campus; Shawn Doyle, president of Half-Shire Historical Society, for information on and pictures of Fanny Pearl Keyes "Una Clayton" and the Taylor sisters, for permission to use a photo of Darius Ballou, and for numerous, random acts of kindness; Steven T. LaVeck, for permission to use photos of Rhea Wilder LaVeck; George R. DeMass, Town of Oswego historian and president of the Oswego Town Historical Society, for showing me the Adams family home, the graves of the Adams family, and for permission to photograph the society's Columbian dolls and to use photos of Emma Eunice Adams and the Columbian doll workshop; Karen Marshall-King, grand secretary, for information on Eastern Star membership of Armonella Marshall Devendorf; Michael McCue, for permission to use the Findagrave.com photo of Charlotte Lund's gravestone; Susan Mitchener, national archivist, Salvation Army National Archives, for information concerning the career of Helen Gay Purviance and for permission to use photos of her; Janette Smith, for information on Rhea Wilder LaVeck's membership in Pulaski-Puritan Chapter No. 159, Order of the Eastern Star; Douglas McLean Wilson, for permission to use a photo of Semantha "Almira" Reynolds McLean; Diane LM, for permission to use the Findagrave.com photo of Ellen M. Bruce's gravestone; Robert Post, Sr., for permission to use the Findagrave.com photo of Helen Gay Purviance's gravestone; Sarah Pullar Gagne, for information about and permission to use photos of the Taylor family; Debra Allen, Oswego County historian, for information on Harriet E. Stevens's compilation of World War I military records; Maria Lore, Onondaga County Historical Society, for assistance with the story of Armonella Marshall Devendorf; Theresa Jones, museum coordinator, Friends of History in Fulton, New York, Inc., for pictures of Grace Lynch and Muriel Allerton; Edgar Manwaring, overseer of Riverside Cemetery, Scriba, for helping me find the grave of Jessie Fairfield Gordon; Tom Tryniski, for his fabulous website, Fultonhistory.com, which is the researcher's gold mine; and Joanne M. Paino, Darlene Woolson, Elaine DeLong, and Nancy J. Costello, all noteworthy women in their own right, for friendship and support.

Preface

Where Are All the Women?

"Where are all the women?" I innocently asked my high school European history teacher. I do not recall what he said or even if he replied. Being a man of the times he probably never thought about that vacuum. I did, however, and though I did not know it then, a feminist was budding in a tiny northern New York public school. As years passed, I watched the spectacle of the repressed 1950s, the sexual revolution of the 1960s, the women's liberation movement of the 1970s. I have seen reproductive rights granted and then denied. I have witnessed hard-won voting rights eroded by would-be demagogues who think only white, Anglo-Saxon males should be allowed to make decisions for everyone else.

Late in life I began a lengthy investigation into the role of Oswego County, New York in the abolitionist movement and subsequent Civil War. Once again I found myself asking "Where are the women?" And I found them—lots of them. They too were a part of the local Underground Railroad, such as Charlotte Ambler (see figure P.1), who together with her husband Edwin Winslow Clarke, was reportedly able to assist one hundred twenty-five fugitive slaves to escape to Canada.[1] They sent husbands, sons, fathers, and brothers to fight for the Union, knowing full well they might not return. Some, like Dr. Mary Walker and Elmina Spencer (see figure P.2), actively served in the war while thousands of others quietly held the fabric of society together by running the family business, tending to the family farm, rearing children, nursing the sick. They banded together to send barrels of medical supplies, books, tobacco, clothing, and food to the men at the front. They often made do with very little, since soldiers were paid infrequently. These home front heroes should include Maria Corey Alexander, Mary Celinda Montague Barnes, Catherine Casler Burr, Mary R.

Figure P.1. Charlotte Ambler Clarke actively participated in the abolitionist movement and Underground Railroad in Oswego City. Author's collection.

Smith Button, and Harriet Thompson Sampson, only a few Oswego County women who, however hesitantly, kissed their soldier husbands goodbye and never saw them again.[2]

If the Civil War had any positive result, it was the realization that women, those "weaker vessels," were as strong and resilient as their menfolk. With the passage of time barriers to education and the professions came down, making it possible for Mary Victoria Lee and Elvira Rainier not only to become doctors but also to command the respect of their male colleagues in Oswego County. Women's suffrage, so long in the making, was pushed along by brave, independent women such as Harriette Taylor Treadwell and Ruth Johnson Mott.

This book celebrates a tiny fraction of the women who were born, lived, or worked in Oswego County. I could have included many more.

Figure P.2. Elmina Pleiades Keeler Spencer volunteered to accompany the soldiers of the 147th Regiment and worked tirelessly to assist the sick and the wounded. New York State Military Museum.

The ladies who sat around Louise Irwin's (see figure P.3) tea table one day responded to a suggestion that some sort of refuge should be erected "for ladies of gentle birth who were destitute of means and home."[3] Working together with delegates from Oswego City churches they created an institution lasting 145 years, the Home for the Homeless, but how many people have ever heard of Mrs. Cheney Ames, Mrs. Delos DeWolf, Mrs. Robert Oliver, or Mrs. Mannister Worts?[4]

In a similar fashion, Oswego Hospital came into existence. Mrs. Carrington MacFarlane (see figure P.4), Mrs. Charles Bond, Mrs. Charles Pardee, Mrs. Edwin Stacy, and others saw a need and decided to do something about it. John Churchill paid tribute to their efforts but identified them only through their husbands' names. Learning their Christian names was an only slightly less than monumental task.[5]

Figure P.3. Louise Irwin and her friends founded the Home for the Homeless so elderly and destitute women might have a safe place to live. Oswego County Historical Society.

Figure P.4. Louise MacFarlane was the guiding force behind the establishment of Oswego Hospital. Author's collection.

It would be impossible in a work this size to include every woman who contributed in some way to the cultural, educational, or political circles of Oswego County. I have, therefore, selected thirty-one whose efforts were of such prominence that they practically demanded to be included. Perhaps my meager effort will spur others to enlarge upon this very significant yet generally marginalized group of Oswego County residents.

Natalie Joy Woodall
February 6, 2024

Introduction

Someone's Wife or Mother

The position of women until quite recently generally has been that of subservience, inequality, and legal powerlessness. Girls passed from the control of their fathers to the control of their husbands and had few if any rights as individuals. The system of patriarchy traditionally viewed daughters and wives as merely the vessels through which power and property were to be passed to the next generation of (male) children. To this day marriage between cousins is encouraged in some Middle Eastern countries as the best way to keep property "all in the family."

In England the first male born in a wealthy or titled family inherited not only the title but the entire estate as well. Families producing only females, such as the fictitious Bennett family in Jane Austen's *Pride and Prejudice*, faced the unpleasant eventuality that the family estate would pass to some distant male relative through a custom known as entail. Medieval heiresses who had no male relatives with a claim to their property and family title might make a marriage with a man who oversaw the property "with right of his wife."

The right of primogeniture involved more than property. Daughters born into royal families seldom ascended the throne even though they were the eldest children. King Henry VIII went through six wives in his determination to leave a male heir (or more) to inherit the throne. A German princeling, George of Hanover, became king of England following the death of the childless Queen Anne because his grandmother, Elizabeth Stuart, was the daughter of King James I, and he was the nearest male Protestant claimant through his mother, Sophia of Hanover, who died shortly before Anne's demise. Queen Victoria's eldest child, Vicky, was the heir presumptive only until her brother Albert, later King Edward VII, was born. More recently, Princess Anne, daughter of Queen Elizabeth II, lost position in the line of succession each time a younger brother was born. Not until 2013 did Parliament enact a law guaranteeing that royal daughters retained their lineal position no matter how many younger brothers might be born. Because of that law, Princess Charlotte of Wales, not her younger brother Louis, is currently her elder brother George's presumptive heir.

Other royal daughters are not so fortunate. Under the old French monarchy, women were legally forbidden to inherit the throne. The current heir to the Japanese throne, Aiko, is, by law, not permitted to inherit. As with entail in England the throne will pass to the emperor's brother and his son. The children of Prince Albert and Princess Charlene of Monaco are twins and, although Gabriella was born first, her brother Jacques is the heir apparent.

The position of married women has depended upon the culture. Although Greek and Roman women were considered legal inferiors to their husbands, they had certain protections in the form of the dowry provided by the wife's parents to help establish the new family. Husbands were required to use the dowry wisely and, in Roman families at least, were obligated to give their fathers-in-law an annual report on how they had handled the property or money. As an added protection for wives and children, husbands were not allowed to sell the dowry. If the marriage failed, the wife took the dowry with her.

Eighteenth- and nineteenth-century American women with whom this book is primarily concerned were saddled with an English concept known as coverture developed by Sir William Blackstone. According to this theory, which was eventually viewed as law, a woman lost her personal identity when she married. Blackstone posited that upon marriage the two contracting parties became one and that one was the husband: Mr. and Mrs. John Brown, Mr. and Mrs. Jacob Wilson. The wife was chattel, her husband's property. He had complete control over any and all real and personal property she brought to the marriage. He was legally permitted to sell her property without her consent. She could make no contracts, bring no suits, earn no money for her own use. If she worked outside the home the husband was legally entitled to all of her wages. Marital rape was an impossibility. Physical domestic abuse was condoned. The wife was for all practical purposes unable to obtain a divorce and if she was lucky enough to escape an abusive marriage, she would not be allowed custody of her children.

The views of well-known American founding fathers are representative of much of the male population in the late eighteenth and early nineteenth centuries. Thomas Jefferson, that great champion of (white male) freedoms, thought public morals would be corrupted if women participated in politics. A woman's role, he thought, was to soothe the wrinkled brow of her husband after he had returned from a hard day's labor in the political sphere. Female suffrage to him was unthinkable. John Adams's response to Abigail's "Remember the ladies!" was to laugh at her suggestion that women should enjoy equal rights with men.

Legislators were well aware of this inequity, but awareness did not equal action. The British Parliament did not attempt to effect a resolution to the problem until 1882. Some American legislatures, however, particularly in the northeastern states, took action much sooner. In April 1848, New York State, for example, pressured by a group of aggrieved women, passed the first Married Women's Property Act, according to which women retained control of property they brought to the marriage and henceforth would be able to control any property bequeathed or given to them by outside parties after the marriage. With few exceptions a woman's property could not be seized to pay a husband's debts. This law became the model for other states to use when enacting similar legislation.

When Lucretia Mott (figure I.1) and Elizabeth Cady Stanton called for the Women's Rights Convention that was held on July 19–20, 1848, in Seneca Falls, New York, they were aware of the new law concerning women's property:

> [Lucretia Mott] rejoiced at the great change in public sentiment, and at the passage of the law protecting the property of married women—it was a partial uprooting of a system of robbery. She read a remonstrance of 44 women in Wyoming and Genesee, presented to the Legislature, denouncing the present laws and usages of Society, by which women were degraded and made of no more account than children, lunatics and idiots, and the passage of such, as recognize her in all particulars as the equals of men.[1]

Their express purpose, however, was to expose the many, long-standing inequities between male and female citizens. Basing their Declaration of Sentiments on the Declaration of Independence, they affirmed that men *and* women were created equal. Their eighteen grievances were the products of

ages-old discrimination against one-half of the human population, although Mott worried that Stanton's insistence upon language dealing with suffrage would "make us look ridiculous." The finished document revealed a long-held rage against "the lords of creation":

> The history of mankind is a history of repeated injuries and usurpations on the part of man towards woman, having in direct object the establishment of an absolute tyranny over her. To prove this let facts be submitted to a candid world.
>
> He has never permitted her to exercise her inalienable right to the elective franchise.
>
> He has compelled her to submit to laws in the formation of which she has had no voice.

He has withheld from her rights which are given to the most ignorant and degraded men—both natives and foreigners.

Having deprived her of this first right of a citizen, the elective franchise, thereby leaving her without representation in the halls of legislation, he has oppressed her on all sides.

He has made her, if married, in the eye of the law, civilly dead.

He has taken from her all right in property, even to the wages she earns.

He has made her, morally, an irresponsible being, as she can commit many crimes with impunity, provided they be done in the presence of her husband. In the covenant of marriage she is compelled to promise obedience to her husband, he becoming to all intents and purposes her master—the law giving him power to deprive her of her liberty and to administer chastisement.

He has so framed the laws of divorce as to what shall be proper causes of divorce, in case of separation to whom the guardianship of the children shall be given, as to be wholly unjust and regardless of the happiness of woman—the law in all cases going upon the false supposition of the supremacy of man and giving all power into his hands.

After depriving her of all rights as a married woman, if single and the owner of property, he has taxed her to support a government which recognizes her only when her property can be made profitable to it.

He has monopolized nearly all the means of profitable employment and from those she is permitted to follow she receives but a scanty remuneration.

He closes against her all the avenues to wealth and distinction which he considers most honorable to himself. As a teacher of theology, medicine or law, she is not known.

He has denied her the facilities for obtaining a thorough education—all colleges being closed against her.

He allows her in church as well as state but a subordinate position, claiming apostolic authority for her exclusion from the ministery [sic], and with some exceptions, from any public participation in the affairs of the church.

He has created a false public sentiment by giving to the world a different code of morals for men and women, by which moral delinquencies which exclude woman from society, are not only tolerated but deemed of little account in man.

He has usurped the progressive of Jehovah, himself, claiming it as his right to assign for her a sphere of action, when that belongs to her conscience and her God.

He has endeavored, in every way that he could to destroy her confidence in her own powers, to lessen her self-respect and to make her willing to lead a dependent and abject life.

Now in view of this entire disfranchisement of one half the people of this country, their social and religious degradation, in view of the unjust laws above mentioned and because women do feel themselves aggrieved, oppressed and fraudulently deprived of their most sacred rights, we insist that they have immediate admission to all the rights and privileges which belong to them as citizens of these United States.

In entering upon the great work before us we anticipate no small amount of misconception, misrepresentation and ridicule, but we shall use every instrumentality within our power to effect our object.[2]

Mott was not finished. After the Declaration of Sentiments had been voted upon, she set about developing a framework for achieving the remedy to those eighteen grievances in twelve resolutions she presented the following day:

Whereas the great precept of nature is conceded that "man shall pursue his own true and substantial happiness"; Blackstone, in his commentaries, remarks, that this law of Nature being coeval with mankind, and dictated by God himself is, of course, superior in obligation to any other. It is binding over all the globe, in all countries, and at all times; no human laws are of any validity if contrary to this, and such of them as are valid, derives all their force, and all their validity, and all their authority, mediately and immediately from this original.

Therefore, Resolved, That such laws as conflict, in any way, with the true and substantial happiness of women, are contrary to the great precept of Nature, and of no validity, for this "is superior in obligation to any other."

Resolved, That all laws which prevent woman from occupying such a station in society as her conscience shall dictate, or which place her in the position inferior to that of man, are contrary to the great precept of Nature and therefore of no force or authority.

Resolved, That woman is man's equal, was intended to be so by her Creator, and the highest good of the race demands that she should be recognized as such.

Resolved, That the women of this country ought to be enlightened with regard to the laws under which they live, that they may no longer publish their degradation by declaring themselves satisfied with their present position, nor their ignorance by asserting they have all the rights they want.

Resolved, That inasmuch as man, while claiming for himself intellectual superiority, does accord to woman, moral superiority, it is pre-eminently his duty to encourage her to speak and teach as she has opportunity in all religious assemblies.

Resolved, that the same amount of virtue, delicacy, and refinement of behavior, that is required of woman in the social state, should be required of man, and the same transgressions should be visited with equal severity on both man and woman.

Resolved, that the objection of indelicacy and impropriety which is so often brought against woman when she addresses a public audience, comes with very ill grace from those who encourage by their attendance, her appearance on the stage, in the concert, or in feats of the circus.

Resolved, That woman has too long rested satisfied in the circumscribed limits which corrupt custom and a perverted application of the scriptures have marked out for her, and that it is time she should move in the way the Creator has assigned.

Resolved, That it is the duty of the women of this country to secure to themselves their sacred right to the elective franchise.

Resolved, That the equality of human rights results necessarily from the fact of the identity of the race in capabilities and responsibilities.

Resolved, Therefore, that being invested by the Creator with the same capabilities, and the same consciousness of responsibility for their exercise, it is demonstrably the right and duty of woman, equally with man, to promote every righteous cause by every righteous means; and especially in regard to the great subject of morals and religion, it is self-evidently her right to participate with her brother in teaching them both in private and public, by writing and by speaking, by any instrumentalities proper to be used, and in any assembly proper to be held; and this being a self-evident truth, growing out of the divinely implanted principles of human nature, any custom or authority adverse to it, whether modern or wearing the hoary sanction of antiquity, is to be regarded as a self-evident falsehood, and at war with interests of mankind.

Resolved, That the speedy success of our cause depends upon the zealous and untiring efforts of men and women for the overthrow of the monopoly of the pulpit, and for the securing to woman an equal participation with man in the various trades, professions and commerce.[3]

Although the Women's Rights Convention received considerable notice in the press, little changed in the lives of ordinary American women. At the time, it was not uncommon, as Mott pointed out, for women to be illiterate. My research into the lives of Oswego County Civil War soldiers uncovered numerous examples of war widows who could not even sign their names to their pension depositions. Many of these women had minor children whom they could support only through such occupations as nursing and domestic service. A lack of education foreclosed even the possibility of teaching. Their only practical solution to poverty-stricken widowhood was to marry another man. Sometimes these relationships worked out, and sometimes they did not.

Divorce in New York State was difficult to obtain since adultery and abandonment were the sole grounds and was originally granted only by the state legislature. Although coverture was meant to protect a woman because her husband was theoretically obligated to support her, the reality was that a man could simply walk away from his marital responsibilities with impunity. The case of Martin Pieter Van Buren and Catherine Pickens is illustrative of this situation.

After their son, William, died of yellow fever on July 7, 1864, at Key West, Florida, where he was serving as a soldier in the 110th Regiment, Catherine applied for a mother's pension, based on the claim that he had been her sole support before he had enlisted in the army. Catherine testified that Martin had abandoned her on or about May 1, 1858, and that he had absolutely refused to support her, forcing their son William to take on his mother's financial maintenance.

According to Catherine, "Her aforesaid Husband has abandoned her and totally refused to maintain her, that her said Husband is a libertine & is now living & cohabiting with another woman[,] that he is also a man of bad habits and is an inebriate and has neglected my said support for the past fifteen years and on or about the 1st day of May AD 1858 he removed our household goods to Olean, N. Y. & there had them put in a warehouse."[4]

Even more egregious was the practice of leaving a legal wife to marry another woman, after convincing her that he had obtained a legal divorce by waving around a piece of paper she could not read. Almira Meachem Weaver is a good example. Her husband, Henry Philip Weaver, a member of the 110th Regiment, died on March 18, 1864. Almira, the mother of three minor children, applied for pensions for herself and for the children. On January 11, 1870, she married Charles B. Philbrick and by this action deprived herself of her widow's pension. Philbrick was legally married to Adelia Tryon but he persuaded Almira that he had obtained a divorce by showing her, an illiterate, a document purporting to be his divorce decree. Only after Philbrick's death in 1890 did she discover the truth when she applied for a widow's pension based on his military service.[5]

Husbands desiring to be rid of their wives found another solution to their problem, self-divorce. They had only to cross a state line to be free of familial responsibilities, cognizant of the fact that local authorities were not eager to expend meager resources to locate and arrest delinquent husbands who had "gone west."

The case of Josiah Cooter and Lucy Elizabeth Parmiter is a prime example. Married on July 2, 1846, Josiah and Lucy had several children and apparently lived in relatively happy circumstances in Fulton, New York. In 1873, however, Josiah, another Civil War veteran, announced he was going to Nebraska to locate a place for the family to live. He subsequently wrote to Lucy, telling her to sell everything and join him. After living together in Nebraska long enough for Lucy to become pregnant, Josiah abandoned her, taking with him every dime still remaining. Lucy, completely destitute, was forced to appeal to family members in Fulton, New York, for funds to return home.

Cooter, in the meantime, was living with Georgia Ellis Frasier, by whom he fathered six more children. Georgia testified after his death: "He told me he had a davorsse and I did not no but he had." In 1899, Georgia's position was further negatively affected when the federal government passed the Abandoned Wives' Act, which provided that a deserted wife could claim half of her husband's pension, including any and all increases. For the next twelve years Lucy received part of Josiah's pension, and when he died in 1912, she, not Georgia, was eligible for a widow's pension. Georgia was understandably upset about this turn of events and made an unsuccessful appeal to the pension bureau, pointing out that she, not Lucy, had cared for Josiah in the role of wife. The official response was, "You are advised that if, as would appear from the evidence on file . . . under the Act of March 3, 1899, the beneficiary thereunder was the lawful wife of the pensioner at the date of his marriage to you and has so continued until the date of his death, she is now his lawful widow and there is no provision of law under which you could be entitled to a pension on account of his service."[6]

One of the most notorious cases of marital discord in Oswego County involved Dr. Ernest Manwaren (figure I.2), a prominent member of local society, well regarded physician, and past worshipful master of Oswego Lodge No. 127 Free and Accepted Masons. Manwaren was the husband of Emma Louisa Thomas, daughter of Almeron Thomas and Louisa Paine, respected residents of Mexico Village. Mr. Thomas was active in Mexico Lodge No. 136 Free and Accepted Masons.

Figure I.2. Dr. Ernest Manwaren flouted law and social norms by marrying Anna Murdoch without securing a legal divorce in New York from his first wife, Emma Louisa Thomas. Churchill's *Landmarks*.

Ernest and Emma married in 1879 and were the parents of two children, Lois and Ralph. In 1895, Manwaren suddenly moved to Illinois and remained there until late 1897, when he unexpectedly returned to Oswego and promptly married a young woman named Anna Murdoch, with whom, it was revealed, he had been having an illicit affair. When questioned by a local reporter, Manwaren confirmed that he had indeed married Anna but was entitled to do so because he had obtained a legal divorce in Illinois. He seemed unaware or unconcerned about the fact that his Illinois divorce was not recognized in New York State, where he was now viewed as a bigamist. His attorney advised him to leave New York State immediately. A few days after his leave taking, Anna also departed, reuniting with Manwaren in Chicago, where they were married a second time.

Meanwhile, the Masons were preparing to put Manwaren on trial for behavior "unbecoming a Mason and a gentleman." Manwaren hired an attorney to represent him, and at the end of the proceedings, Oswego Lodge expelled him, as did all concordant bodies to which he belonged. An appeal to Grand Lodge was rejected.[7]

If Manwaren had simply stayed in Illinois and sent for Anna he would have avoided all the negative press and the humiliation attendant upon his Masonic trial. His arrogance was his downfall. He and Anna did not return to New York State until after Emma's death in December 1902.

Some men simply disappeared. Darius Ballou, a resident of Parish, New York, was married and the father of a young son (figure I.3). He enlisted in the 147th Regiment in September 1862 but decided army life was not for him and deserted. After a couple weeks of playing cat and mouse with military authorities, he disappeared, never to be seen again, and forcing his wife to fend for herself.[8]

William Martin McKoon mustered out of the Second New York Provisional Cavalry on August 9, 1865. He apparently never returned to his wife, Sarepta, and their children. Absolutely no record of his life can be located after that date.[9]

Lewis M. Webb, a soldier from Mexico, New York, who served in the 147th Regiment, was captured at the Battle of Cold Harbor on June 2, 1864, and eventually landed in Andersonville. From that time until he was exchanged, his wife Emily did not know what had happened to him. He was discharged on July 8, 1865, but did not return home. Emily's obituary, no doubt composed to spare her and her children more humiliation, suggested he had died in the war: "Her husband enlisted in a New York regiment soon after the breaking out of the Civil War and did not return."[10]

Figure I.3. Darius Ballou deserted from the 147th Regiment and completely disappeared, leaving wife and child without any means of support. Courtesy Shawn Doyle.

The Civil War had an effect upon women no less profound than that upon men. Absent fathers and husbands forced women to assume responsibilities heretofore considered part of the male sphere. They not only had to care for minor children and elderly parents. Farms and businesses now depended upon their capabilities in order to survive. Women, only recently admitted to the medical profession, became military nurses and doctors. Dr. Mary Walker from Oswego Town persisted until she convinced authorities to give her a position as an army surgeon. Elmina Spencer, another Oswego resident, accompanied her husband Robert to war with the 147th Regiment. Although she initially faced stiff resistance from upper echelon military officers, she proved her abilities as a nurse and saved many soldiers' lives. Her organizational abilities ensured they received much needed food, medicine, and supplies.[11]

Despite these gains, women were compelled to navigate within a male-dominated society. When Louisa Irwin and her friends set out to establish a home for homeless women in Oswego City, their husbands, not they, were the incorporators.[12] The women ran the home (figure I.4), hired the staff, and organized fundraisers, but their husbands controlled the money. The same was true when Louise MacFarlane and her associates undertook to provide Oswego City with a permanent hospital. For years the women ran these facilities, but their husbands and fathers were considered the legal supervisors or overseers of the operation.[13]

Nowhere was there greater inequity between men and women than at the polling place. When the federal government instituted an income tax to pay for waging the Civil War, single women who were the owners of property were taxed just as their property-owning fathers and brothers were, even though the men were voting citizens and the women were not. Mott's complaint about taxation without representation was fully demonstrated through this measure. Dr. Mary Walker (figure I.5), a single female property owner, was subjected to open ridicule when she tried to vote in 1880: "Some pert young fellow in the crowd said if she was going

Figure I.4. A group of determined women established and ran the Home for the Homeless located on East Utica Street, Oswego, New York. Author's collection.

Figure I.5. Dr. Mary E. Walker rejected the notion of "appropriate" female garb and wore "men's clothing" even though the practice led to public derision and frequent arrests. Library of Congress.

to vote, they might as well dress up all their women in men's clothes and bring them down and vote them. 'I don't wear men's clothes,' retorted Dr. Walker, 'I wear my own clothes.' "[14] The situation was similar for others. Susan B. Anthony, for example, was arrested, tried, and convicted of illegally voting.

The passage of the Fourteenth Amendment to the Constitution guaranteed that all persons born or naturalized in the United States were citizens to be afforded equal protection under the law. Nevertheless, section two of that amendment specifically dealt with "male" citizens of voting age. When the Fifteenth Amendment was passed, the wording stated: "The right of citizens of the United States to vote shall not be denied or abridged by the United States or by any State *on account of race, color, or previous condition of servitude.*" Sex, therefore, still prohibited half the population from exercising the most sacred of all rights: the right to vote. Women were told that their mission in life was "the perpetuation of the race and by her function must be forever measured her capabilities in life."[15] Tammany Hall politician Richard Croker maintained that a woman's place was in the home. He predicted that if women became involved in politics the result would be the "complete demoralization of the world."[16]

It is not to be wondered at, then, that intelligent, educated white women were indignant at the fact that previously enslaved black men should obtain suffrage before they did. Space does not permit a full study of the struggle for female enfranchisement within the United States, but it is important to point out that the effort was lengthy, sometimes violent, and always persistent. Names such as Susan B. Anthony and Elizabeth Cady Stanton are familiar to all, but lesser-known names are equally significant for the struggle: Fannie Lou Hames, Ida B. Wells Barnett, and Jane Addams. Credit must also be given to the multitudes of women who quietly but earnestly pursued the vote by proving their worth in areas recently opened to them: medicine, law, and even theology. The Episcopal Church only lately permitted ordination of women, and the Roman Catholic Church still forbids women to become priests. Amy Eilberg became the first female rabbi in Conservative Judaism in 1985.[17] Not until 1930, after sixty-two years of trying, did the Presbyterian Church of New York State grant women the right to become ordained ministers, overcoming claims that ordaining women would "effeminate" the church and, further, that scripture was opposed to such an action.[18]

Women started businesses or operated them with male relatives. They attended college and became collegiate faculty members. They wrote; they discussed; they argued; they demonstrated. Seventy years of activism culminated with the passage of the Nineteenth Amendment to the United States Constitution: "The right of citizens of the United States to vote shall not be denied or abridged by the United States or by any State on account of sex." With one sentence, hundreds of years of official civil and legal inferiority ended for American women.[19]

That amendment did not, however, end discrimination against one-half of the population. Women contributed significantly to efforts during both World War I and World War II, yet once the fighting stopped, thousands lost their wartime jobs and were expected to return to the home. For years, women were regularly denied bank credit or access to credit cards. In certain locales, a woman needed her husband's permission to obtain something as simple as a library card. The women's liberation movement of the 1970s did much to eliminate such archaic behavior but failed to achieve full success through the passage of the Equal Rights Amendment. The question of reproductive rights, once ensconced in American culture as settled law with the Supreme Court decision of *Roe v. Wade*, continues to cause strife since being overturned in 2022. Women ask, How can my right to privacy be squared with government's assertion that it has the right to control my body? The fight goes on.

This book deals with women who did not permit current societal norms and expectations to deter them from their goals. Many have never been studied in any depth. My criteria were three in number: at some time in her life, the subject had to have resided in Oswego County; she had to have done something with her life in addition to marrying and bearing children; and she had to be deceased. I looked for women such as Helen Gay Purviance, Salvation Army soldier, whose dedication to Oswego's downtrodden has never been addressed.

Female politicians in Oswego County are a relatively new phenomenon, and I wanted to showcase their achievements. Nowhere could I have found a better example than Muriel Allerton, Fulton's first female mayor.

While women have traditionally been elementary and secondary teachers, their entrance into the ranks of collegiate faculties has been recent. Even more recent (and revolutionary) has been their entrance into the ranks of upper collegiate administration. The story of Virginia L. Radley, the first female president of a State University of New York college, is one of quiet courage and dignified strength in the face of years of strife, much of it sex-based.

Other women were as forthright in their chosen fields. Julia McNair Wright became a successful writer in a time when female authors regularly used pseudonyms to avoid having their works negatively regarded simply because of the writer's sex. Lottie Blair Parker (figure I.6) found personal satisfaction and financial security in the performing arts, despite the prejudice against female dramatists. Dr. Mary Victoria Lee championed the cause of female athleticism through dance.

The women catalogued in this book were intelligent, talented, tough, and resilient. They overcame personal tragedy, societal and familial disapproval, and legal inferiority to achieve their goals and thereby left this world a better place for those who came after them. They would undoubtedly agree with Dorothy Mott, who, when asked how she managed to achieve so much, simply replied, "I don't know. I just did it."

Figure I.6. Lottie Blair Parker was a "small town girl" who achieved success as an actress and playwright through determination and hard work. *Omaha Morning World-Herald.*

The Noteworthy Women of Oswego County, New York

Harriet Peck Ames Rundell

The place where Harriet Peck Ames was born, the future Oswego County, truly lay on the frontier of the United States in the early part of the nineteenth century. Heavily timbered, little explored, it was the home of bears and deer rather than humans. Only after the British evacuated Fort Ontario in July 1796 did permanent settlers begin arriving. Among them were Leonard Ames (April 25, 1776–February 18, 1843) and his wife, Minerva Peck (November 15, 1779–February 17, 1852).

Leonard and Minerva, natives of Litchfield County, Connecticut, together with several children were on their way to "Genesee Country" in western New York State with a team of oxen and the family cow "but when they arrived at a spring one mile west of Mexico hill, they encamped for the night. This spot seemed so pleasant to them that he built his hearth-stone there, made a farm of the then wilderness, and spent his days there."[1] The family settled on Main Street, Mexicoville, in 1804.[2] According to a letter Frederick Rhode wrote to George Scriba, "Ames did settle on his lot the 5th Inst." In a house built of logs, Harriet Peck Ames was born on October 4, 1812. Years later she was asked to describe her early life in a still remote, sometimes dangerous, and relatively primitive area:

> It is a long time to remember but there are some things so burned into my memory that I can never forget them. . . . First the

clumsy plow and the V-shaped harrow were the only implements used in the preparation of the ground for a crop. No cultivator, no drills on which men could ride. The seed was sown by hand and on foot. When grown and ready for harvesting the sickle was used. . . . The cooking was all done by an open fireplace; not even stoves at that time. But in a few years stoves were introduced but they were so imperfect that it was impossible to cook for such a family on them. Sometimes we used a tin oven, called a reflector, to bake before the open fire, but baking was usually done in a large brick oven, which was built on one side of the fire place. . . . My mother used to cook fresh salmon which were so delicious. They were so plentiful that my father put the same number of barrels of them that he did of pork. . . . Think of knitting for thirteen in the family, one stitch at a time; the garments, all to be made by hand, one stitch at a time, the cloth to be made, the flax and tow to be spun and wove, ready to be made up. Then the wool to be prepared, spun and wove, sent to the mill, dyed and dressed."[3]

Leonard Ames, a farmer and a blacksmith, in time became prosperous through his persistence and energies: "My father was a driving farmer, and if the work did not move, the chains broke."[4] Minerva Peck Ames was no less industrious, described as "a very sensible, intelligent and energetic woman" whose husband, Leonard, appreciated "the character of his excellent wife [and] entertained a very profound reverence for her religion."[5] Minerva's faith and dedication to the Methodist sect led to the establishment of the Methodist Church in Mexico. It was an institution in which Harriet would become intimately involved in the years to come. Sister Ames, claimed one informant, "was a friend of God."[6] According to the writer of her obituary, "She was a member and her house a sanctuary of the first Methodist society in this part of the State. Those were days of small beginnings of great events, for this mother in Israel lived to see the territory from which this society was gathered raise up and send out to other societies and to the Church triumphant, several still on the ground, with their ten or twelve preaching places and thousands of hearers. . . . She loved the cause, and liberally supported it in all its departments."[7]

Education was very important to the Ames family, as it was to many early settlers. Mexico Academy was formed in 1820 and incorporated on April 13, 1826.[8] Among its first students was Harriet Ames, who "was long a practicing homeopathic physician in the town, [but] was not allowed to study Algebra for fear that it would overtax her female brain."[9] At the semicentennial reunion held in August 1876, Dr. James V. Kendall, also a graduate, described her thus: "She was always an active and efficient person in whatever she engaged."[10]

How Harriet occupied the next few years is lost to history. Nevertheless, her life underwent a radical transformation when she married Rev. William W. Rundell on August 17, 1837.

William W. Rundell was born in Norwich, Chenango, New York, on April 3, 1794. A devout Methodist, he was ordained a minister at the age of twenty-five. For the next thirty years he served all over New York State and Canada, "where his name is still mentioned with great respect."[11] His first wife's name is unknown but she was the mother of William A. Rundell (January 22, 1831–January 2, 1894), who was born in Fulton County, New York. It is likely that Mrs. Rundell died in childbirth or shortly thereafter. How and where Harriet and William met is unknown, but since he was stationed at Fulton, Oswego, New York, at one time, they may have been introduced at a church function.

Harriet and William were the parents of two sons, George Albert (March 1840–January 3, 1842) and Marshall H. (1843–July 20, 1862). Marshall's birthplace in the 1855 New York census was listed as Tompkins County, and one of the places Reverend Rundell served was Dryden. Almost certainly that was where the boy was born.

Rundell's ministry came to an end at Scott, Cortland, New York, when "his health failed him."[12] The Rundells had moved to Mexico by 1850, and according to the 1855 New York census, they had resided there for six years. William became a member of Mexico Lodge No. 136 Free and Accepted Masons and of Mexico Chapter No. 135 Royal Arch Masons. Although officially retired, he occasionally performed marriage ceremonies.

As early as 1850 Rundell styled himself a doctor. According to J. H. Myers, "Brother Rundell's health being impaired, both he and his wife, under the advice of Dr. Dio Lewis, took up the study of medicine, and settled down to the practice of their profession together. Dr. Rundell's health continuing to fail, the practice devolved upon Mrs. Rundell, who carried it on with her characteristic enthusiasm and vigor for over forty-five years."[13] When the census was taken in 1870, Harriet openly claimed she too was a doctor: "She never attended a medical school but 'picked up' what knowledge she possessed and she was quite successful."[14] William Rundell was a charter member of the Homeopathic Society of Oswego County when it was formed in 1862 and was president in 1873. Harriet participated in the society's programs as early as 1870, when she delivered a talk on childhood diseases "and a case of her own of poisoning by the use of one of the popular hair dyes."[15] That her medical interests were wide-ranging was exemplified by a paper she delivered to the same organization concerning the treatment of stammering.[16] In 1877 Harriet was elected president of the organization, an honor that acknowledged her competency as a physician.[17] In 1876, James V. Kendall, MD, a graduate of Mexico Academy, remarked, "I learn that she has been in the active and successful practice of medicine in this village for many years."[18]

The outbreak of the Civil War in April 1861 was to bring personal heartache and grief to Harriet and William. Their only surviving son, Marshall, nineteen, volunteered for duty and with his cousin, Nelson Ames, raised Battery G, First New York Light Artillery:[19]

> It was during the gloomy days following our disastrous retreat at Bull Run that Lieut. Rundell offered his services to the government. He commenced raising a company. Young in years, slender in form, and of delicate appearance, it was supposed he would fail in the undertaking. But influential aid, combined with his great energy and tact, soon resulted in kindling a bright fire of military enthusiasm. His company was soon full and men to spare.[20]

The First Regiment was sent to Alexandria, Virginia, where, as with so many other units, the soldiers experienced harsh conditions resulting in serious medical problems. Harriet visited the camp for two weeks, ministering to the sick. A highlight was her opportunity to fire a cannon, "which was considered most remarkable for a woman."[21] Despite youthful enthusiasm, energy, and tact, Marshall Rundell lost his life on July 2, 1862, at Brooklyn City Hospital: "Lieut. Rundell was only 19 years of age, and was a young man of much promise. He was surrounded by many admiring friends and relatives, and was the only son of the most devoted parents, who are now overwhelmed at this their irreparable loss." The official cause of death was nephritis. He was one of the very few soldiers whose family could afford to have his body sent home for a funeral and a proper burial (figure 1.1).[22]

Harriet, a devout Christian, formally united with the Methodist Episcopal Church in 1831 and was a charter member of the church built in Mexico in 1833.[23] She was also a charter member of the Woman's Foreign Missionary Society in 1871.[24] This society was organized "for the purpose

Figure 1.1. Lieutenant Marshall Rundell died in the service of his country at the age of nineteen. Author's collection.

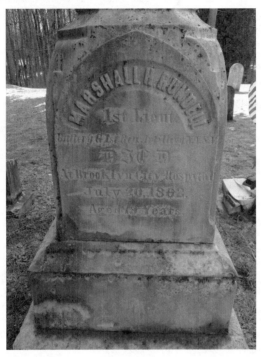

of promoting missionary work among heathen women, primarily in India and China," and over the years several women addressed the group about their efforts in those countries.[25] Harriet was the group's first president and in 1883 "she was elected president for life and held the position acceptably for 13 years."[26]

During the Civil War the women of Mexico organized a Soldiers' Aid Society, which sent boxes of food and books, among other things, to local servicemen. On May 12, 1864, Harriet, whose son had been dead for almost two years, was elected president of this group.[27] She was a member of the Social and Literary Society of the Methodist Episcopal Church and was an active participant in its programs. She also was a member of the Old Settlers' Association.[28] She was instrumental in arranging a reunion for Mexico Academy graduates in August 1876 upon the fiftieth anniversary of Mexico Academy's incorporation. She was one of the promoters of the affair and allowed a tent allegedly large enough to hold two thousand people to be erected on her lawn located next to the school.[29]

Reverend Rundell died on March 18, 1876, at the age of eighty-two. His eulogist noted, "As a preacher he was clear and calm, impressing his audience with deep sincerity. Integrity and tranquility were traits that characterized him through life and shone forth with increased strength and luster to the last."[30]

By the terms of William's will, Harriet was able to live comfortably for the rest of her life. She continued her medical career, "driving her own horse about the country in all kinds of weather."[31] She made a successful application for a mother's pension in 1878 based on Marshall's military service. Affectionately known as "Auntie," she was lauded for her "more than ordinary endowments" and her generosity toward the less fortunate (figure 1.2).[32]

Harriet's health began to fail in the 1880s. She was reported to have suffered several bouts of pneumonia, and in her last years was unable to attend church services. She died on August 4, 1896.

A long life of usefulness and activity was terminated Tuesday evening of last week. At about ten o'clock Mrs. Harriet Rundell passed peacefully away to her reward, at the ripe age of 85 years. Mrs. Rundell was almost a historic personage here. A

Figure 1.2. Harriet "Auntie" Rundell ministered to the sick in Mexico, New York, for over forty years. *Grip's Souvenir of Mexico.*

life long resident, familiar with the early history of the town, a brilliant conversationalist, well read and intelligent, far above the average woman of her day, she was one of our landmarks. She had an almost inexhaustible fund of wit and wisdom, incident and anecdote, at her command which made her society much sought after. Not to know "Auntie Rundell," as she was often called, was to lose the society of a very entertaining woman. As a physician she was very successful, and in cases of serious sickness her devotion to her patients was unparalleled, nursing them day and night during the crisis of the disease.[33]

Harriet's devotion to her church continued after death. As a provision of her will, she bequeathed her house standing next to the Methodist Church to serve as a parsonage.[34] In addition, she gave the Woman's Home Missionary Society fifty dollars to be used to furnish a room at Asheville Home, North Carolina, and "known as the Harriet Rundell Hospital Room."[35]

Harriet Peck Ames Rundell is buried in Mexico Village Cemetery with William and her two sons, George Albert and Marshall (figure 1.3).

Figure 1.3. Harriet Rundell is buried in Mexico Village Cemetery with her husband, William, and their two sons, George and Marshall. Author's collection.

Ellen M. Bruce

Educational opportunities for Oswego City children in the early 1850s were slim to nothing until dedicated teachers such as Miss Ellen M. Bruce came to town. For more than a half century she devoted her life to the little ones of the Second Ward.

Born in Oneida County, New York, she was the daughter of Phineas Bruce (January 7, 1793–March 20, 1867) and his first wife, Polly Converse (?–1828). Details about her childhood are lacking, but it is known that she graduated from Red Creek Academy. She then taught in local district schools for a short time.[36]

The year 1853 was significant for Oswego. Only five years earlier, the village had become a city, and the area was bustling with commerce, shipping, and trade. One area in need of improvement, however, was education.[37] Extensive schooling had been beyond the means of almost every family in Oswego, since students were required to pay fees and buy their own books and supplies. Edward Austin Sheldon's Orphan and Free School Association provided the first education opportunities for the community's poorer element in 1848: "The school opened with 120 children, most of whom had rarely, if ever, seen the inside of a school room before. It was continued for eighteen months, when it was proposed by some of those most actively interested in the school to initiate a movement to make all the public schools of the city free, and thus, in a great measure, obviate the necessity of this free school association."[38] Despite enthusiastic support from those favoring the plan, opposition to it temporarily frustrated the effort. Finally the New York State Legislature passed a local school act in 1853, and on May 11, 1853, Oswego formed its first board of education.[39] The following October, Ellen Bruce walked into Primary School No. 8 and was confronted with an enrollment of ninety boys and girls.[40] Many years later, she mused, "Had I been told when I first entered this building that I would continue here for the next half century I would have got out again a good deal quicker than I came in" (figure 1.4).[41]

The teaching profession was in its infancy when Ellen Bruce and others began teaching. Credentials might be as slender as graduating, as she did, from an academy.[42] The occupation definitely consisted of on-the-job training, and in Oswego City it was aided by the establishment of the Oswego Normal School in 1861.[43] Ellen M. Bruce was a graduate of the first teacher training class at Oswego Normal School, finishing her course in

Figure 1.4. Ellen Bruce spent her entire teaching career in the same school, located in Oswego City's Second Ward. Oswego County Historical Society.

OLDEST TEACHER IN THE STATE AND HER PUPILS.
[Miss Ellen M. Bruce, of Oswego, and the scene of her labors as an educator for nearly 50 years past.]

April 1862.[44] By that time she had taught in No. 8 School on the corner of East Ninth and Seneca Street for nine years.

Miss Bruce was a popular teacher, as evidenced by a parents' revolt in 1867. Upon learning that the board of education was considering moving her to a different school, Second Ward residents heartily and vocally opposed the plan:

> The undersigned, residents of the Second Ward, and patrons of the schools, beg to represent that we are informed that it is your intention to change Miss Ellen Bruce from her present school on the corner of Ninth and Seneca Streets in said Ward, to another School in the Fourth Ward, and we are also informed that it is her wish to remain where she now is, and having taught school in that locality a long time to the general satisfaction of its patrons, we humbly beg your honorable body to let her remain and teach where she now is, for which we humbly pray.

The petition, dated February 4, 1867, was signed by several prominent Oswego Second Ward residents, among them businessman Benjamin Doolittle and architect John Ratigan. Miss Bruce was continued in her present school.[45]

Teachers' salaries were always a topic of discussion and debate—as they are today. As principal of her school, Miss Bruce received more than her assistant, but the amount paid was at the mercy and whim of the current board of education since collective bargaining had not yet been invented. In 1876, for example, Ellen received $525 while Lizzie Dinsmore was paid $400. By 1879, Ellen's salary had been reduced to $426.31 and Lizzie's to $350. In 1880 Ellen received $380 and Lizzie, $300.

Despite everyday frustrations, Ellen Bruce maintained a sense of humor. In October 1882 a long missing gold watch was recovered. Some boys had found it lying in the bushes several years earlier and, disobeying their mother's order to put it back, had instead hidden it in a trunk. One of the boys had recently obtained a job in Syracuse and decided to sell it. The store owner promptly called the police, who arrested the boy and his companion. Several articles appeared detailing the affair, including one that alleged that Ellen had married a "Mr. Smith" and retired from teaching: "Ellen Bruce was the most popular schoolmistress in Oswego, when, five years ago, she decided to marry a Mr. Smith and take up the pleasanter occupation of making him happy."[46] Ellen, while apparently keen for her true marital status to be confirmed, nevertheless made light of the matter:

> Miss Ellen M. Bruce, the Oswego teacher, who a few days ago, through the efficiency of the Syracuse police, recovered her gold watch, lost about three years ago, saw a representative of this paper last Saturday to have several misstatements in regard to the affair corrected; and one especially which was published in the Times, somewhat affecting her social standing. The statement referred to represented Miss Bruce as "Mrs. Smith, formerly Miss Ellen Bruce." Miss Bruce says she is not aware that she ever married a "Smith," in fact, that she had no recollection of ever marrying anyone.[47]

On April 27, 1899, Ellen M. Bruce, aged sixty, suffered a stroke. How serious it was is unknown, but she returned to the classroom.[48] As a single woman with no one to take care of her, she had little choice. Social Security and medical insurance were unknown in her time.

In 1902 school officials established a committee to plan the celebration of the fiftieth anniversary of free public education in Oswego. One of the honored guests was Ellen Bruce, who was still teaching at the same building, affectionately called Bruce's School. When interviewed about her long career, she said, "I have been happy in my work. I have taught more than 3,000 boys and girls, and most of them have become good men and women. I have never seen a child who was not worth effort on the part of the teacher. I had faith in my first class, and it is undimmed today, as I look at the faces of the pupils of a later generation."[49] It was noted that only she and Isaac B. Poucher remained of the original 1853 faculty.[50] Called upon to speak of her experiences in a paper titled "Incidents of Fifty Years," she reminisced:

> I have sometimes dreaded the time when I must sever my connection with this school . . . Fifty years is a long time to be planted in one place; and in half a century one takes root deeply. . . . This house will ever be a dear spot to me, not only on its own account but there lives in my memory the unheard patter of the little feet that have passed to and fro along these aisles. . . . I can say, however, that these fifty years of school work have been a long, toilsome, wearying journey. A flinty pathway where many times tired feet have stumbled on alone and unhelped; a constant rowing up stream and against the tide until the aching arms well nigh hung down, but I have enjoyed my labors and loved teaching the little children.[51]

Her lengthy service, spanning fifty years, was widely reported, and it was truthfully said that she was the oldest active teacher in New York State.[52]

Miss Bruce's teaching career finally ended in 1905. The enrollment in her school, now called No. 10, had dwindled significantly, and the board of education planned to close it and send the students elsewhere.[53] In fact there had been discussions about closing the building since 1902. The physical condition of the school was bad. In 1898 an inspection committee had described it as "[a]nother wretched old style vault" where "the cold hall is used for hanging wraps and . . . [there is] no proper ventilation."[54] Miss Bruce herself confessed that the floor had been replaced twice.[55] At that time friends began a campaign to obtain her a pension, but apparently nothing came of it, forcing her to continue to work.[56]

On June 24, 1905, Miss Bruce handed over the keys to her school, thus ending a teaching career lasting fifty-two years. One reporter noted she had tears in her eyes.[57] Another reporter provided a more graphic description of her last day:

> With tears coursing down her wrinkled cheeks and sobs shaking her aged and bent form, Miss Ellen Bruce, for fifty-one years principal of the little brown school house at the corner of East Ninth and Seneca streets, surrendered the keys to the building to Truant Office W. J. Dempsey this afternoon and turned and left the school for the last time. The Department of Education had decided to close the building as a school house and there was no other position open for the faithful old teacher who had devoted more than half a century to the work of teaching the little ones their A. B. C's. . . . But this wonderful woman was not proof against the advance of time and old age. For the last three or four years the members of the Department of Education have had under consideration the closing of this school. There was hardly a handful of children to go there for instruction and Miss Bruce was growing old and hardly able to perform her duties. This morning Truant Office Dempsey was given the task of stripping the school of all its movable furniture. Miss Bruce was present during the work and as she saw what was being done she broke down and cried like a child.[58]

There was life after teaching, however, and Miss Bruce fully partook of it. She was a faithful attendant at services of Trinity Methodist Church. She served on a committee to raise funds for a monument in Riverside Cemetery honoring the memory of Edward Austin Sheldon.[59] She traveled and visited her siblings and other relatives. The end came rather unexpectedly:

> Since her retirement from active service she has lived quietly with relatives in the peaceful enjoyment of old age. She had a brilliant intellect, and her books were her choicest companions. A few weeks ago while making preparation for a visit to friends she met with a serious accident, breaking her hip, from

which she suffered much. Pneumonia set in, and it was more than the frail frame could bear. . . . She will be held in fond remembrance by a large circle of friends among whom are many prominent citizens who owe their early start in life to her painstaking efforts to lay the foundation of good character in those whom she instructed. . . . The funeral of Miss Bruce occurred this afternoon. The public schools are closed and also the Normal school and the attendance at the services at Trinity M. E. church was very large.[60]

Ellen M. Bruce is buried in Oakwood Cemetery, Syracuse, New York (figure 1.5).

Figure 1.5. Ellen Bruce is buried in Oakwood Cemetery, Syracuse, New York. Courtesy Diane LM, Findagrave.com.

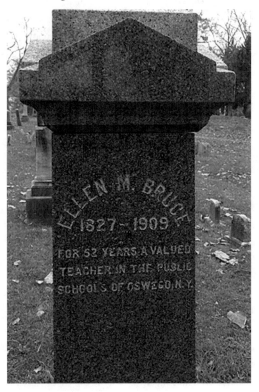

Armonella "Nell" Marshall Devendorf

Armonella Marshall Devendorf's life began in the small village of German Flats, Herkimer, New York, and ended in Hastings, Oswego County. In between she traveled extensively and contributed to no small degree to the civic and social fabric of the greater Central Square community.

Born on May 28, 1833, to Lorenzo Dow Marshall (July 18, 1804–August 10, 1840) and Emily Coolidge (1806–April 31, 1837), Armonella joined an older brother, James Lawton (August 12, 1830–June 7, 1900). By 1840 both parents were dead and she was sent to live with her aunt, Rebekah Marshall Devendorf.[61] Aunt Rebeka ensured that Armonella was well-educated, sending her to Clinton Liberal Institute, the first attempt by the Universalist Church to establish a school. Located in the town of Kirkland, it had divisions for both male and female students. Established in the 1830s "for the purpose of providing a literary seminary for the public instruction and education of youth," the Clinton Institute did not subject its students to any type of enforced theological training, although in the 1840s students might voluntarily attend classes in theology. Armonella learned her lessons well. She was a lifelong adherent to the tenets of the Universalist Church.

On April 10, 1853, Armonella married Henry Clay Devendorf (June 12, 1828–January 3, 1897), son of Peter Devendorf (December 22, 1800–July 16, 1881) and Rhoda Ann Sherman (December 19, 1804–September 9, 1838). Although he was Rebekah Marshall Devendorf's nephew and she was Chauncey Devendorf's niece, the two were not blood relatives.

Henry Clay Devendorf, born in Verona, Oneida, New York, began his adult life as a clerk in Oswego City. He would later operate a merchandise/grocery store in Central Square, New York. By 1855 he and Armonella were living in Hastings, Oswego County. He claimed to be a "merchant" when the 1855 New York State census was taken.

As it did for countless other young couples, life changed dramatically when the Civil War began in April 1861. Despite the initial belief that the war would end quickly, by 1862 most Americans in the north realized that the struggle to restore the Union was going to be both lengthy and costly. No one had more of a grasp on reality than President Abraham Lincoln, who in the summer of 1862 called for the raising of five hundred thousand troops under the threat of a draft. To the patriotic residents of Oswego County, such a possibility was anathema, and as a result of extensive canvassing and cajoling, the county raised the 110th Regiment, 1,037 strong. Among them was Henry Clay Devendorf.[62]

The 110th Regiment was one of the more fortunate Union regiments in that it saw little battlefield action, in contrast to other Oswego County regiments, such as the 24th, 81st, and 147th. Its greatest conflict was at Port Hudson, a fortified area on the Mississippi River. In February 1864 the 110th Regiment was ordered to Fort Jefferson, located on Cedar Key in the Gulf of Mexico. The soldiers would spend the rest of the war there guarding prisoners of all stripes. It was, according to contemporary accounts, a rather boring assignment.[63]

It was not uncommon for officers to invite their wives to join them.[64] In the summer of 1864 Armonella traveled from New York State to Fort Jefferson to be with her husband (figure 1.6). Exactly when she arrived is unknown but it was probably in late spring or early summer, based on a letter she sent to Sidana Hoyt, whose husband George had died on August 24, 1864: "When I just reached here George visited me, and I gave him all the good wishes you sent by me. He then looked as well as I ever saw

Figure 1.6. Armonella Devendorf was among many officers' wives who joined their husbands at their military posts during the Civil War. *Syracuse Sunday Herald.*

him, and seemed much pleased to hear from you and talk about home. *I think he continued so until the breaking out of this epidemic of fever that we have all suffered so much from.*"[65]

She was definitely there when Dr. Samuel Mudd, Michael O'Loughlin, Samuel Arnold, and Edman "Ned" Spangler, all convicted of conspiring to assassinate President Lincoln, arrived on a military vessel, the *Florida*, on July 24, 1865. The soldiers of the 110th Regiment were eager to be relieved of their duty and were on the lookout for their replacements. Therefore, on the morning of the 24th when a sail was sighted, Henry and Armonella both thought they would be leaving, and he hastened to the dock to confirm everyone's hope. Here let Armonella pick up the story:

> When he returned he said to me, "Nell, those Lincoln con-spirators are right outside." I was staggered, as 'twas the Major himself, for no one had any idea that those men would be sent to us. They had been sentenced, you remember, to the Albany penitentiary, and their coming to the Dry Tortugas was a great surprise. . . . My daughter and I were very anxious to have a close view of the men, and we finally prevailed upon Major Devendorf to let us bring our sewing into the office next morning and remain there while they appeared before him.[66]

Although the 110th Regiment finally was relieved and sent back to New York State, Armonella's recollections of her time at Fort Jefferson would resurface in 1902–1903.

After leaving the military, Armonella and Henry moved west. By 1870 they were living in Chicago, where he was employed as an agent for White's Express Company.[67] From there they migrated to Wayne County, Georgia, residing in Doctortown from 1871 to 1883. He was the local post master for ten years.[68] He claimed to be a merchant when the 1880 census was taken.

The exact date of the couple's return to Oswego County is unknown, but it was probably in April 1883, based on information contained in a local newspaper: "Major Devendorf has disposed of his property in Doctor Town, Ga. It is expected that himself and wife will arrive in our village [Central Square] soon to abide with us."[69] In the fall Henry, a Democrat, ran for state assembly.[70] He started a new business, described by Churchill as "the largest dry goods and grocery store in town."

Like most Civil War veterans, Henry became associated with the Grand Army of the Republic (GAR), founded in 1866. He was a charter member and first commander of Isaac Waterbury Post No. 418, chartered on November 9, 1883, and located in Central Square. In that same year the Woman's Relief Corps (WRC) was organized and Armonella became a charter member of Waterbury Post No. 55. She served as president in 1898.[71] The following year she was appointed chaplain at the annual state convention.[72] The scope of her duties as chaplain can be seen in the report she delivered at the annual convention in May 1900: "The report of the department Chaplain, Armonella Devendorf of Central Square, reviewed the work done by the corps in Memorial day decorations and services. The chaplain also gave an interesting report of work done in the south since the war."[73] Her interest in the WRC did not wane. As late as 1916 she installed new officers for Waterbury Post No. 55.[74] She also served as post treasurer.[75]

Major Henry Clay Devendorf died on January 3, 1897, "after a long and painful illness" and was buried with Masonic and GAR honors in Hillside Cemetery, Central Square.[76] In 1900 Armonella was living alone in Hastings. By 1910 she had moved into the residence of Dr. Hadwen P. Wilcox.

Armonella's memories of Fort Jefferson and the Lincoln conspirators were brought to the forefront in 1902 when Samuel Arnold's (figure 1.7)

Figure 1.7. Samuel Arnold's scathing memoir about his time as a prisoner at Fort Jefferson met stiff criticism from Armonella Devendorf and others who had been there during Arnold's incarceration. Library of Congress.

scathing memoir of his time spent at Fort Jefferson was serialized in the *Baltimore American.*[77] Among other topics, he complained bitterly about the food he and his fellow conspirators were served: "The rations issued at this time were putrid, unfit to eat, and during the three months of confinement I lived upon a cup of slop coffee and the dry, hard crust of bread. This is no exaggeration, as many others can testify to its truthfulness. Coffee was brought over to our quarters in a dirty greasy bucket, always with grease swimming upon its surface; bread, rotten fish and meat all mixed together and thus we were forced to live for months until starvation nearly stared us in the face."[78]

Reaction from those who had been there at the time was swift. Armonella was among several Oswego County residents asked for their recollections, and she categorically denied that the conspirators received harsh treatment of any kind while the 110th Regiment had control of the fort: "Now in regard to the food. To begin with, I can at once brand what Arnold said about the bread as a falsehood. It was as good bread as one could care to eat and prepared in as cleanly a manner as it could be anywhere. We had an excellent bakery at the fort, and the best Java coffee that could be procured."[79]

It is alleged that Armonella gave birth to a daughter, also named Armonella, in 1873, and if so, the child was probably born in Georgia. No confirmation of any type has been located. In 1900 she declared she had not given birth to any children, but that may not be true. Many women lied about the number of children they had borne, especially if some of them died young.[80] Nevertheless, she adopted and reared an orphan, Emma Dygert.

Emma, the daughter of Rudolf William Dygert (May 17, 1825–July 25, 1854) and Elizabeth Voorhees (March 4, 1827–March 28, 1860), was born on July 22, 1847. She and her brother Charles Rudolf (October 1851–January 7, 1920) lost their mother to tuberculosis, and probably their father too. Charles subsequently lived with Nathaniel and Maria Voorhees Hulson. Armonella, perhaps empathizing with the little girl, since she too had lost both parents at an early age, took Emma for her own. The daughter to whom she referred in the passage above was Emma.

Upon returning to Oswego County in late 1865, Emma married Avery Ten Eyck Low, MD (October 1841–May 2, 1911), who had been a soldier in the 110th Regiment. They were the parents of Armonella "Nell" Low (August 1872–July 11, 1942), who married Hadwen Purdie Wilcox, MD (1866–December 15, 1931), with whom Armonella was living in 1910.

Emma Dygert Low was a charter member and first worthy matron of Elizabeth Caldwell Chapter No. 141 Order of the Eastern Star in 1897, serving in that office for four years. In 1900 she was district deputy grand matron. Her daughter, Nell Low Wilcox, also served as worthy matron of that chapter.[81] Perhaps because of their encouragement Armonella Devendorf was initiated into Elizabeth Caldwell Chapter in March 1907.[82]

Armonella remained active in the last years of her life. She reportedly became involved in the Red Cross even though she was in her eighties.[83] Her extended family celebrated her ninetieth birthday in May 1923.[84] At the time she was the oldest member of the local Universalist Church.

A long and eventful life ended on September 23, 1927, when Armonella, aged ninety-four, died at Nell's home: "Possessing a charming personality, a gracious manner, kind, generous, charitable, she was of constant and valuable service to this community for more than fifty years."[85]

Armonella Marshall Devendorf lies with her husband, Henry Clay Devendorf, and her daughter, Emma Dygert Low, in Hillside Cemetery, Central Square, New York (figure 1.8).

Figure 1.8. Armonella is buried with her husband, Henry Clay Devendorf, and her daughter, Emma Dygert Low, in Hillside Cemetery, Central Square, New York. Author's collection.

Mary Victoria Lee, MD

Described as "one of the most lovable characters ever identified with the work of the Oswego Normal," Mary Victoria Lee was a pioneer in the field of women's athletics. Doing away with the myth that women's bodies were too frail to endure organized physical activity, she taught that exercise was good not only for the body but also for the mind.

Mary V. Lee was born on September 12, 1837, in Granby, Connecticut, the daughter of George Lee (February 1, 1802–December 26, 1870) and Adaline Hayes (June 15, 1807–January 25, 1890).[86]

As a young girl, free-spirited and precocious Mary disliked school, as evidenced by the following description.

> While the school life for ten or twelve years was for the most part utterly barren, the other life was fruitful. . . . The free, out-door life which the child enjoyed afforded splendid materials for school work—for all the common branches, as well as for botany, zoology, geology, political economy, industrial education, and the germ theory of disease—but there was no teacher big, wise and brave enough to use these materials; the girl who could never spell and hated at the age of nine, Smith's grammar, did not dream that in spite of schools, she was getting straight from God's big book that which she would never forget and always enjoy. It is easy to imagine that such a child, confined in an uninteresting schoolroom, might be an object of wonder, dread and even terror to the inexperienced young women and men who taught in that district. No one knew how to get the engine, which was under a full head of steam, upon a track.[87]

After leaving school at the age of seventeen, Mary had few occupational opportunities and became a teacher herself in East Granville, Massachusetts. She enrolled in the Connecticut Normal School in 1854, graduating in 1860, teaching in various school districts simultaneously in order to defray expenses.[88]

Mary lived and taught in Kensington, Connecticut, from 1860 to 1862. In the spring of 1862, David N. Camp, superintendent of public instruction, selected her to travel to Oswego, New York, to learn about Edward Austen Sheldon's use of the Pestalozzi Method for teaching young children.[89]

Johann Heinrich Pestalozzi (1746–1827) was a Swiss-born educator who believed that it was not enough to tell a child about something. He theorized that children learned best from observing, questioning, and thinking about a particular object or idea. He summarized his theory as one of hands, heart, and head. Education was, in his view, best conveyed when the student had to opportunity to touch an object, observe it, and ask questions about it. He used "object lessons" to teach students, that is, he presented them with an article or idea that they then thoroughly discussed, based on their level of reasoning. It was an inductive method, progressing from the simple to the complex.

Pestalozzi championed education for the poor and underprivileged. He was convinced that a sound training would result in an adult committed to individual thought and to civic responsibility. Therefore, it is little wonder that Sheldon decided to use this method in the "poor school" he established in Oswego and also in the free public schools that opened in the early 1860s. To Sheldon and his adherents, Mary Victoria Lee among them, the training of "hands, heart, and head" would result in well-educated, loyal, industrious citizens.[90]

Mary V. Lee, Class of 1863, was one of the first graduates of the Oswego Normal School that Sheldon founded in order to have a pool of trained teachers available for the Oswego City schools.[91] She subsequently opened the Davenport, Iowa, Training School for Teachers. By 1870 she was in Winona, Minnesota, working as an assistant to Professor William F. Phelps, the head of the normal school there.[92] She also taught in local Sunday schools and Sunday school conventions. She became familiar with Dwight Lyman Moody, the well-known evangelist and social worker, and spent a summer in Illinois teaching the Pestalozzian Method to Sunday school teachers.[93]

Although Lee enjoyed teaching, she had higher aspirations. She dreamed of studying to become a medical doctor but, as was usual in that time period, she had few role models. Her friendship with Charlotte Denman Lozier, MD (March 15, 1844–January 3, 1870), offered a renewed possibility of fulfilling her goal. Dr. Lozier was one of the first female physicians in the United States and was living in Winona when the two women met. Unfortunately, she died in New York City after falling from a ladder when seven months pregnant. Her baby, born two months early, survived, but Dr. Lozier succumbed to the effects of the early childbirth.[94]

Two years later, Lee entered Michigan University, graduating with a medical degree in 1874. She had realized that "women should be trained to respect and care for the body as the temple of the soul, and the conviction that a physician can speak with power because of the authority of knowledge, led her to begin serious work under two liberal minded physicians."[95] Upon her graduation she was hired as a professor of anatomy, hygiene, and physiology at Oswego Normal School (figure 1.9). In October of that year, she and Mary E. Little, MD, formed a medical partnership in Oswego City, something so rare it was front-page news.[96]

In 1880 Dr. Lee and her friends, Mary D. and Elizabeth Sheldon, traveled to Europe and the Middle East, visiting England, Scotland, Italy, and Egypt, among other countries. During the second year of the tour she studied physiology and biology at Newnham College in Cambridge.[97]

From her earliest residence in Oswego, Dr. Lee was in demand as a speaker. In March 1875 a newspaper advertisement announced that she would deliver a speech to "ladies of the school" about anatomy, physiology, and hygiene, to which the "ladies of Oswego are most cordially invited."[98] A lecture she gave to the Bible class of Grace Presbyterian Church was deemed so good by its auditors that they insisted it be published.[99] She frequently appeared as a speaker and instructor at teachers' conventions around the

Figure 1.9. Dr. Mary V. Lee was a pioneer in women's athletics. SUNY Oswego Archives and Special Collections.

state (figure 1.10). At a convention held in Lowville in October 1887 she gave a lecture titled "The Teaching of Reading."[100] In 1889 she delivered a lecture on temperance to Oswego County teachers. As paraphrased by the reporter, Dr. Lee stated,

> Every person's life is molded by an ideal. The greatest persons of history are those who have been helpers. We must either be helpers or hinderers of good or evil. Self-governance should be introduced into the schoolroom. We must not only preach temperance to children but train them to be temperate. The boy who has been properly trained in this direction will not choose the evil. The temperance cause is hopeless unless the youth of today are so trained.[101]

A firm believer in exercise for females, Dr. Lee became very interested in the Delsarte system of expression. François Delsarte (1811–1871) studied

Figure 1.10. Dr. Lee was devoted to her students. SUNY Oswego Archives and Special Collections.

Dr. Mary V. Lee reading to a group of students, 1888

the way people moved, how they acted and responded to various types of situations. He theorized that voice, breathing, and movement all played a part in how humans expressed themselves.

In 1871 Steele Mackaye brought Delsarte's ideas to the United States, where they became very popular across the strata of American culture: "Twenty years later, society salons, cultural clubs, public and private schools, seminaries [were] all flooded with 'Delsarte.' "[102] In Oswego Dr. Mary Lee became a proponent of the movement and determined to incorporate it into the physical culture program for her female students. She explained how and why Delsarte was so important for improving both body and mind in a paper delivered at the Normal School's twenty-fifth anniversary:

> As taught in our school, physiology and gymnastics are phases of the same subject. Physiology gives ideas of the structure, relation, and uses of the organs of the body; and it aims to give ideals. Ideals rule us; our ideals are our loves. What we love, we seek to attain. . . . Gymnastic lessons have for their object the creation of ideals and the giving of exercises that will lead to their attainment. The intellect, the feeling and the will are said to constitute the mind of man. In physiology there is play of the intellect; in gymnastics there is play of the will; between the two stands feeling—the child of one, the parent of the other. Without ideals nothing worthy can be accomplished in the gymnasium. . . . In the beginning of our experience, feeling was parent of expression; but now . . . expression becomes the parent of feeling. . . . So far as I know, no teachers of gymnastics, belonging to other than the Delsarte school—and but few belonging to that school—take cognizance of this fact that expression voluntarily assumed, rouses the emotion which naturally produces the expression.[103]

A newspaper reporter, invited to attend a gymnastics exhibition given by Normal School students, detailed his observations and admitted to being favorably impressed by their performance:

> Dr. Lee occupied the platform and gave the signal for the class to take their places in the center of the room, which they did, in open order, so that their hands and arms might enjoy the fullest

liberty of action. The first movement was a graceful inclination of the body forward, then a return to the original erect position, the eyelids slightly falling and rising with the swaying of each individual figure. Then followed a series of acts in which the fingers, hands, feet, lower limbs and all the muscles of the body were brought into requisition, naturally, gracefully, gently and, as one could but confess, beneficially to the entire person. We say gently and gracefully in contradistinction to the discarded system of school gymnastics which is more remarkable for its violent, awkward and unnatural features—its thrusts, jerks and distortions of the body—than for anything else, and especially any permanent beneficial effects growing out of it. Here, and by the recently adopted system, the pupil is taught to use his or her hands and feet, and all the parts of the body for that matter, as to feel that the possession of every one of them is a pleasure and not an encumbrance or badge of awkwardness. . . . The drill extended beyond the movement intended for the mere cultivation of strength, and which might be said to have called into play every muscle of the body of consequence and indicated its functions,—it went farther, we repeat, and dealt with the attitudes, postures, movements and expressions which the face, the limbs, the hands and other parts of the body participate in or undergo to indicate the varying emotions, such as joy, grief, surprise, fear, repulsion, anger or disputatiousness. All of these examples were exceedingly interesting and instructive.[104]

In 1886, Dr. Lee and Margaret Morley organized a children's gymnastics class that was held three times a week during one of the summer school sessions at the Normal School. To assure parents that their children would benefit from the training, they were invited to observe the initial class: "A number of ladies and gentlemen were present, among them mothers and fathers of the pupils, who watched the exercises with a keen interest. From remarks made it was plain to be seen that they were well pleased with what they saw done and that if they went there with any misgivings as to the value of this particular system of physical culture for children, they took no such misgivings away with them."[105]

As late as 1891, Dr. Lee was advocating for and demonstrating her version of Delsarte gymnastics. In April she agreed to give three lessons in gymnastics at a convention for Oswego County teachers. She had one prerequisite: "No one will be invited to join this class whose dress is not loose and free from articles that prevent bending at the waist."[106]

Among her many campaigns was that of dress reform. Dr. Lee abhorred corsets, ill-fitting shoes, and garters. Her students wore loose-fitting clothes in her physical culture classes. She opposed footwear with excessively high heels.[107] It was her edict concerning garters, however, that newspapers all over the United States found to be newsworthy (figure 1.11).

The fashion in 1890 was to wear garters fastened either below or just above the knee instead of those hitched to a belt worn around the waist. Dr. Lee rightly condemned them because they restricted blood flow to the lower extremities, and forbade her students to wear them. Some of the young women complained, but Dr. Lee held firm, although her stance provided much amusement to newspaper reporters, who took great delight in mocking her decision.[108] Most pieces were light-hearted and generally positive, but

Figure 1.11. Dr. Mary Lee waged war against constricting clothes, including "fashionable" garters. *New York Sunday Press.*

several southern newspapers took a less humorous view of her edict: "At this rate the doctor's protégés may wind up in trousers and Prince Alberts."[109]

For eighteen years Dr. Mary Lee devoted herself to the physical betterment of the students in her physical culture classes, and the beginning of 1892 indicated no lessening of her commitment to them or to the community at large. In January she presented a talk at the city mission on "common sense manners."[110] By April, however, her health had deteriorated to such an extent that she had to forego teaching. On several occasions the local newspapers published updated medical reports, such as the following: "Dr. Mary V. Lee, of the faculty of the Normal School, is very dangerously ill at the Normal Boarding house of rheumatism complicated with heart trouble. Dr. Rainier attends."[111] Several days later, another announcement was published: "The condition of Dr. Mary V. Lee, who is ill at the Welland, is decidedly improved today. Her physician is greatly encouraged."[112]

In June, Dr. Lee was well enough to take a trip to Rochester. Her condition again worsened and she died there on July 24. After a funeral in Oswego, her body was shipped to Granby, Connecticut, for burial in Granby Cemetery (figure 1.12). Her bearers included some of Oswego's most prominent men, including Judge John C. Churchill, Edward Austin Sheldon, and Professor Isaac B. Poucher.[113]

Churchill's tribute to her revealed how much she was revered in Oswego's educational circles:

Figure 1.12. Dr. Mary V. Lee was a much beloved faculty member at the Normal School. SUNY Oswego Archives and Special Collections.

During her connection with the school the members of this board and the faculty of which she was a part have had opportunity to observe her devotion to her work, her success in its accomplishment, and the results in the classes which have left the school year after year, greatly benefited by her instruction. She exalted her chosen profession as a teacher by her own high conception of its duties and responsibilities, and the evidence of the success of her earnest effort to impress upon her pupils her own estimation of the importance of their calling will be found in all parts of our country in teachers trained by her to adopt her own high conception of the noble and important character of their work.[114]

Dr. Lee's influence on the students at Oswego Normal School was to extend past her death. In a brief period of time, sufficient money had been collected to organize the Dr. Mary V. Lee Memorial Fund, the purposes of which were twofold. Students in need of financial assistance were eligible to apply for loans, and the entire college community was to benefit culturally from speakers and entertainers brought to the campus once a year.[115] One such speaker was Irish poet Seamus McManus, who was engaged to speak on Irish folklore.[116]

Other memorials were forthcoming. When the new physical education building was completed in 1914, it was named Lee Hall in her honor (figure 1.13). Inside the building was a copper tablet bearing the following

Figure 1.13. Lee Hall was named in memory of Dr. Mary V. Lee. SUNY Oswego Archives and Special Collections.

inscription: "Erected by her students in loving remembrance of Mary Victoria Lee, M.D., for eighteen years teacher in the Oswego State Normal and Training School. '*I have not worked so much as to impart information as to influence life.*'"[117]

Julia McNair Wright

A granddaughter of one of Oswego's earliest settlers, Julia McNair saw the tiny settlement grow into a city where she enjoyed the benefits of being born into a family made wealthy by the area's burgeoning population and prospering economy.

Julia McNair was born on May 1, 1840, the eldest child of John McNair (August 26, 1805–August 21, 1868) and Elvira Anne Seabury (August 7, 1816–July 21, 1856). Her paternal grandparents, Matthew McNair (1778–March 31, 1862) and Linda Reed (1787–March 23, 1851), were natives of Scotland. Among Matthew McNair's contributions to the tiny village was his interest in and support of the First Presbyterian Church, formed in 1816 and incorporated on February 10, 1824. McNair was a member of the congregation's first board of trustees.[118] The McNair family worshipped in this church until its destruction by fire on October 24, 1841, and later in the replacement building that opened in January 1844.[119] It was in the latter church that Julia would have received her initial training in Presbyterian doctrine.

John McNair, Julia's father, graduated from Hamilton College in 1823 and became a surveyor. He was responsible for surveying much of the land that gradually enlarged the boundaries of Oswego Village.[120] At that time, publicly funded schools did not exist in Oswego, and only those families with ample financial means could obtain any sort of education for their offspring. The names of the private schools Julia attended have been lost to time.

William Janes Wright (August 3, 1831–February 26, 1903) was born in Weybridge, Addison, Vermont. When he arrived in Oswego is unknown, but according to the 1860 census he was a teacher. He and Julia were married on March 21, 1859, and were living with John, now a widower, in 1860.

Wright was a graduate of Union College in Schenectady, New York. Shortly after he and Julia were married they moved to Princeton, New Jersey, where he attended Princeton Theological Seminary, graduating in 1863. Wanting to do his duty to the Union, he personally appealed to

President Abraham Lincoln for a commission as an army chaplain. According to Richard M. Wright, Jr. he "waited on the steps of the White House in Washington, DC, until he obtained President Abraham Lincoln's signature on his commission, dated June 10, 1863."[121] From July 10, 1863 to September 12, 1864, he served with the 76th Pennsylvania "Zouaves" Regiment. He was then deployed as chaplain at General Hospital in Springfield, Ohio, until mustered out of the army on August 10, 1865.

While her husband was attending seminary and later serving the Union cause, Julia was occupied with her literary career, which began when she was only sixteen.[122] Her works appeared in periodicals such as the *Ladies' Repository* and *Lippincott's Magazine*.

One early story was "The Life-Labor of Jean Garston," a "patient Griselda" tale detailing the many hardships and losses endured by Jean Garston, who several times eschews love on account of her overwhelming sense of duty. Each time an unworthy person commands Jean's assistance, she quietly and obediently abandons her own happiness and answers the call. Her stepmother, who abandoned her, contracts a "severe disease" and summons Jean to nurse her until she dies. Jean's long-absent father returns home a hopeless drunkard and demands that Jean care for him. He is finally sent to prison, where, upon learning that he has contracted smallpox, Jean goes to nurse him and many others. He finally commits suicide. Harry Osborn, the man Jean loves and to whom she is engaged to be married, falls in love with Lettie Graham and marries her instead. When Lettie abandons him, Harry begs Jean to live with them to care for his two small children. By now, Harry is hopelessly in debt and a heavy drinker. Both he and his son die, leaving Jean and the little girl alone and homeless. Temporarily finding shelter in the Osborn family household, they become the targets of Mr. Osborn's third wife, who jealously demands they leave. An angry Mr. Osborn wants to force his wife out, but Jean begs him to let her stay. She herself and the little girl "went to a quiet village," where Jean "labored there for her support." The money Mr. Osborn gives her she uses to pay Harry's debts. The author finally provides a modicum of happiness for her patient Griselda, Jean Garston, after a life spent denying herself in order to make life easier for others: "In a life of toil, beautified by good deeds, Jean Garston spent the years of her life's meridian and decline. She died in her adopted daughter's happy home, surrounded by those who loved her as few mothers are loved and who wrote over her tombstone, 'She walked with God, and was not, for God took her.'"[123]

From 1861 to 1865 Julia churned out at least ten full-length novels, in addition to the articles she submitted to periodicals. According to her grandson, Philip Whitcomb, she wrote 207 books in all.[124] Among them were *Mary Reed* (1861), *Blind Annie Lorimer* (1863), *The Cap-Makers* (1864), and, most famously, *The Little Norwegian* (1865) (figure 1.14).

After the war ended, Julia, William, and their two children, John McNair and Jessie Elvira, lived at various times in Ringoes, New Jersey, Pomeroy, Ohio, and Wellsburg, West Virginia, where Reverend Wright presided over local Presbyterian congregations. In 1873 the family traveled to England, where both parents studied at the British Museum, creating quite a stir among the British intellectual community: "While they were at the British Museum, where she studied with him, it was remarked by those in charge that they were the first husband and wife who had ever

Figure 1.14. It has been estimated that Julia McNair Wright wrote more than two hundred books. Willard and Livermore, *A Woman of the Century*.

Julia McNair Wright - about 1878

studied there on entirely different lines, he pursuing mathematics and she archaeology."[125]

Julia's intellect was the equal of, if not superior to, that of her husband. She was fluent in French and Italian. She had reportedly read the Bible in Latin and in Spanish nine times. According to Professor D. S. Gage, while studying at the British Museum, she "became known to its authorities as a pioneer among women for the extent and depth of her investigations."[126]

After returning to the United States, Reverend Wright accepted a position as professor of mathematics at Wilson College for Women in Chambersburg, Pennsylvania. In 1876 Julia also joined the faculty as a professor of history and literature.[127] During this period she published several novels having temperance as their theme. Among them were *John and the Demijohn* (1870); *A Million Too Much: A Temperance Tale* (1871, 1886); *A Strange Sea-Story: A Temperance Tale* (1877); *The Life Cruise of Captain Bess Adams* (1879).

The last-named book, while interesting for the author's relentless campaign to expose the evils of alcohol, is even more so for modern readers because of the character of Bess Adams, the chief protagonist. Born into a seafaring family, little Bess yearns to become a sailor and goes to sea with her father, Captain Philip Adams, to learn the business. Over the years her experiences enable her to advance in rank until she becomes the captain of her own vessel. Her sailors revere her for her knowledge and firm but just discipline. During a storm she displays great courage by remaining with her disabled ship even as she orders the entire crew to leave. In short, Captain Bess is the equal of any male who might find himself in identical circumstances and the author merely hints at the uniqueness of the situation. For her Captain Bess is just another chief executive officer doing a job.

This novel is interesting for a third reason. Not too far into the description of the hazards of the seafaring occupation the reader realizes that the author is drawing from real-life experiences. As a girl who grew up in the little lakeside village of Oswego, where "forwarding" or the transport of goods and people on the Great Lakes was an important industry, Julia McNair knew full well that fathers, brothers, husbands, and sons often did not return home from such expeditions. Her grandfather, Matthew McNair, was one of the first settlers to build a fleet of ships for such purposes, a fact that made the knowledge of the perils of water travel and commerce even more vivid to the young girl.

Julia may have stood on the banks of Lake Ontario watching with many others as ships attempting to enter the harbor at Oswego were tossed about in a winter gale. She was in all probability a witness, at age eleven, to the rescue of Captain Samuel Freeman, the lighthouse keeper, who risked his life in a terrible snowstorm in December 1851 to light the beacon on the pier so ships due to arrive might be able to navigate safely into the harbor. When his small boat was swamped and the crew thrown overboard, Captain Malcolm Bronson and several volunteers made a daring rescue just as the half-frozen men were about to lose their grip on the overturned boat and sink beneath the waves.[128]

McNair Wright, the descendant of Scotsmen who rebelled against the Roman Catholic Church and established the Calvinist Presbyterian Church, displayed in her novels an ingrained distrust and downright hatred of the Catholic Church and its standing in the United States. She loathed the idea that public funds were being expended on parochial schools; that the poor were allegedly systematically extorted of meager funds to build churches, buy organs, and enlarge the papal treasury; and that gullible young men and women were induced by deceptive practices to become nuns and priests. In *Almost a Nun* (1868), her wealthy Protestant protagonist is actually kidnapped by relatives who plot to force her to become a nun and transfer her wealth to the church.

While reviews of her works were generally positive, at times her views on Catholicism garnered a negative response, as is evident in this review of *Almost a Priest*: "Mrs. Julia McNair Wright has written several novels to show up the iniquities and dangers of Romanism. Fictions of this description and written for such a purpose are nothing if they are not extravagant. Mrs. Wright understands this, and in her present work—"Almost a Priest"—as in her former ones, she is exceedingly sensational. It is a mistake to assume that exaggerated fiction is an ally of truth. More evil than good results from it and Almost a Priest will not be an exception."[129] Despite her adherence to Presbyterian doctrine and her efforts to advance its tenets through her novels and articles, Julia was still considered an inferior member of her church. Nowhere was this more obvious than when female congregants in Carlisle, Pennsylvania, petitioned their minister to allow Julia to speak before a "promiscuous" assembly, that is, one composed of both men and women. The minister refused on the basis of Saint Paul's admonition that women must be silent in church. He did grant her the opportunity to speak before an all-female audience.[130]

Julia used her talent, time, and financial resources to advance the cause of foreign missionary work as a member of the Women's Home Mission Boards of the Northern Presbyterian Church: "In the organization of the powerful and widely useful Women's Home Mission Boards of the Northern Presbyterian Church, she and Mrs. Haines were the foremost workers and the famous Home Missionary of that Church, Dr. Sheldon Jackson, says that in the inception of this movement they were the ones on whom he relied to its success."[131] She was involved with the National Temperance Society and "one of its most earnest workers and most popular authors."[132] She praised the work of the Women's Christian Temperance Union not only for its efforts to reduce the suffering caused by excessive drinking but also for its "wonderful development of its members intellectually, morally, and spiritually."[133]

Two of Julia McNair Wright's works were especially well-received by the reading public. One was *The Complete Home* (1879). Advertised as "full of practical information," the 588–page book offers advice on "house-keeping, cooking, dress, accidents, sickness, children, company, marriage, religion, morals, money, family government, and a multitude of other topics fully treated."[134] Using the voice of a fictional Aunt Sophronia, who advises her three nieces, McNair Wright explores many household topics, including picking the correct spouse, household order and economy, responsibilities toward children, appropriate friendships for adults and children, and religion. Near the end of the book the author provides recipes using various types of fruits and vegetables. One particularly intriguing piece of advice concerns preserving dead game: "Take out the intestines, fill the inside with unground wheat, and place the fowl in a heap or cask of the same grain in such a manner as to insure its being covered. In this way fowls may be kept perfectly sweet for months. The feathers should be removed."[135] *The Complete Home* sold over one hundred thousand copies and was so popular that as late as 1973 people were still referring to it.[136]

Julia's second significant literary achievement was her series of nature stories written especially for children. The four books, *Sea-Side and Way-Side*, were published between 1888 and 1892. McNair Wright stated in the first book that her intention was to assist children to learn to read: "We bring no cat and dog stories, no tales of monkey antics; but we have endeavored to impress upon the little Heir of life, in one of its highest forms, a comprehension of, and a reverence for, life, even in some of its lower manifestations."[137] The first book uses very simple language to introduce the young child to crabs, wasps, bees, spiders, and shellfish. The second book deals with ants, worms, houseflies, beetles, barnacles, jellyfish, sea stars, and dragon flies. The third book introduces the reader to plants, birds, sharks, rays, and other members of the "fin family." And the fourth book uses relatively adult language to describe geology and geography to the student. It includes information on the stars, fossils, rocks, and early animals.

So popular and so accurate were these books that they were used as textbooks. Furthermore, Julia won a medal for them at the Chicago World's Fair in 1893.[138]

Julia and William traveled to Europe again in 1887, and upon their return to the United States, William became a professor of metaphysics at Westminster College, a position he held until his retirement in 1900 due to ill health. Julia became associated with the Presbyterian Publishing Company, having charge of the Home Department.

She continued writing until her death in 1903, her works including the well-received *Fru Dagmar's Son: A Survivor of the Danmark* (1891); *A Modern Prodigal* (1892); *The House on the Beach* (1893); *The Fourth Eclogue of Virgil* (1898); and *Three Colonial Maids* (1900). Her grandson, Philip Whitcomb, recalled in later years that he had spent the summer of 1903 with her when he was about eleven years old:

> As I remember it, Grandma died in the autumn of the year in which Grandpa had died in the spring. I had spent the summer alone with her, and she seemed perfectly fine to me. She still spent four hours in her study every morning, as she had done for about fifty years, reading methodically in Greek, Latin, French and Italian as a sort of obligatory exercise, and writing. The total number of books she wrote was 207, but I know of no way in which a list could be found.[139]

Julia McNair Wright suffered a stroke after her husband's death on February 26, 1903, and although Philip may not have realized it, his beloved grandmother's health was failing. According to D. S. Gage, "About three weeks before her death she became seriously ill, and died, gently and peacefully, on Wednesday, September 2, 1903."[140] Her death was widely reported in short obituaries across the United States.[141]

Although born in the tiny village of Oswego, New York, Julia McNair Wright became acquainted with some of the most prominent personages of the time, including Benjamin Jowett, the eminent Platonic scholar; Emily Faithfull, British pioneer in women's journalism and suffragist; Dwight L. Moody, American evangelist; John Pentland Mahaffy, Irish classical historian; and Frances Willard, American temperance worker and suffragist, to name only a few.[142] Her fifty years of research and writing proved that, given the proper educational opportunities, women were capable of producing significant literary and scholarly works. In a period which only grudgingly admitted that women even possessed an intellect, that was no small feat.

Julia McNair Wright is buried with her husband, William Janes Wright, in Hillcrest Cemetery, Fulton, Missouri.

Elvira Sarah Rainier, MD

A pioneer in women's efforts to enter the medical field, Elvira Rainier used her skill and knowledge to improve the health of Oswego City, her adopted hometown.

Elvira was born in Coldwater, Branch, Michigan, on November 2, 1847, a daughter of Stephen D. Rainier (1819–December 11, 1863) and Sarah H. Husker (May 5, 1816–June 12, 1894). She and three siblings were left fatherless when Stephen died at the age of forty-four.

Like many young women of the time, Elvira attended the normal school in Ypsilanti, Michigan, to train to become a teacher and was hired in 1869 to teach at Union School in Coldwater.[143] She had higher aspirations, however, desiring to become a doctor in an age when such ideas were not only novel but, to some, bizarre. She studied at the University of Michigan's Medical School from 1872 to 1874, then spent a year in the New England Hospital for Women and Children in Boston, Massachusetts. After a hiatus of one year she enrolled in the Women's Medical College of Philadelphia and obtained her medical degree in March 1877.[144] She began her career in a hospital in Philadelphia, Pennsylvania, but at the invitation of Dr. Mary V. Lee, a former classmate at Michigan University, she moved to Oswego, where she spent the rest of her life.[145]

Dr. Rainier quickly became accepted by the local medical community. In June 1878 the Oswego County Medical Society accepted her credentials and elected her to membership.[146] She served as the group's recording secretary or corresponding secretary numerous times.[147] She was also selected to be a delegate to state conventions.[148]

After residing at the Welland House for several years, Dr. Rainier established her residence and office in the home of Laura R. Newkirk (July

14, 1836–December 30, 1916). A daughter of Warden Newkirk (December 1, 1801–April 25, 1878) and Adelaide Rodman (June 21, 1806–October 22, 1878), Laura lived alone in the family home at 108 West Second Street after her sister, Adelaide Elizabeth (1847–December 25, 1916), married Reverend Joshua Law Burrows (1831–October 25, 1907) on October 9, 1883, and moved to Ashtabula, Ohio, with him. She invited Elvira to live with her, an arrangement lasting nineteen years. The two women were involved in many of the same endeavors, such as the Home for the Homeless and the Woman's Outlook Club (figure 1.15).

Elvira used her medical skills not only to heal but also to prevent illnesses. For example, she lectured at the normal school on how to care for a very sick patient.[149] She delivered lectures at the Fifth Street Mission titled "How to Keep Our Bodies Pure" on March 22, 1892, and "How to Keep Our Bodies Strong" on March 29.[150] She served on the county committee of the State Charities Association.[151] This group placed needy children in foster homes and served as the visiting committee to the County Almshouse in Mexico and the City Almshouse in Oswego Town. It also found positions for single mothers with infants.

Figure 1.15. Laura Newkirk and Dr. Elvira Rainier lived together for nineteen years. Author's collection.

A member of Grace Presbyterian Church, Elvira was a member of the King's Daughters, of which she was president in 1897 when the group raised funds to endow a bed at Oswego Hospital: "A vote of thanks was heartily voted Dr. Rainier for her efficient leadership of the union during the years of its existence. It is a recognized fact that without her wise counsel, her sympathy and her enthusiastic and untiring service, the efforts of the union would not have been so soon and so easily carried to a successful issue."[152] Elvira was also active in Grace Church's Ladies' Aid Society, serving as fourth quarter president in 1898 and helping to organize and execute a church fair in 1899.[153]

In 1897 the Woman's Outlook Club was created and counted among its membership some of the most prominent Oswego City women, such as Mary I. Alexander, Sarah Louise Wheeler Mott, and Mary Grace Skinner Wright. Its mission was both literary and practical. The group annually selected a theme for discussion and the members delivered papers or readings on the chosen topic. For example, in 1902, the general topic was the history of education and school laws in New York State. Speakers included Harriet E. Stevens, Amanda P. Funnelle, Lydia E. Phoenix, normal school faculty members, and Luther Wright Mott, a local politician.[154]

The group's civic focus was manifested in a work committee that undertook to ameliorate problems occurring in Oswego. One such problem was the amount of garbage being tossed into city streets. The work committee, headed by Dr. Rainier, encouraged the city fathers to place garbage cans in various places to combat the issue.[155]

A more significant undertaking was an inspection of the city schools that a committee, headed by Dr. Rainier, carried out in June 1898. In August the group met with the board of education commissioners and released a scathing report on the schools' condition. This problem was well-known to the commissioners, but either by errors of omission or commission, they had neglected to make necessary improvements.

Dr. Rainier and her committee members found overcrowding in the high school and stated that, among other recommendations, "the class room in the Northeast corner of the lower floor should be condemned on account of its close proximity to the water closet, all its windows opening to the odors of the closet and the same being exceedingly dirty." They found worse conditions in the elementary school buildings: "School building No. 12 is in every way a disgrace to the city. Five large windows are without shades. The old style vault is used by about sixty children and cleaned once a year. Water for drinking purposes is obtained by the pailfull from neighboring wells. A creek which is an open sewer for the region round about runs in an open channel beside the school house."[156] The women went farther in their campaign. Dr. Rainier and several committee members met with a special committee from the Board of Commissioners in September to address the problem again. After Elvira read a list of recommendations, she and the other women were surprised that "Mr. Hastings should consider the matter in a financial light and said that the health of the schools was at stake; that it was vitally important the changes be made at once."[157] When the city councilmen grudgingly agreed to a hold a special election asking the voters to pay for the improvements, the Outlook Club circulated flyers urging the passage of the proposals. They particularly appealed to women, pointing out that any woman on the assessment rolls was eligible to vote.[158] The special election was held on September 21, 1898, and, despite the determined efforts of the Outlook Club and its supporters, the proposition to levy five thousand dollars to improve the schools was defeated 168–812.[159] Money apparently was more important than children's health.

In 1899 the Woman's Outlook Club undertook another community project, this time acting as the liaison for an anonymous citizen who wished to buy an ambulance for the police and fire departments.[160] Certain stipulations were laid out in a letter signed by Dr. Rainier, Helen E. Hamilton, Isabelle C. Johnson, Mary I. Alexander, and Cora A. Page. Among them was the demand that the vehicle be kept in clean quarters free from vermin, dust, and mud.[161] The ambulance was displayed at the Deep Rock Inn in February 1900 and was accepted for use in March, following the announcement that it would be housed in Engine House No. 3.[162]

The quiet lives of Elvira and Laura were changed dramatically when Willard and Hazel Straight, the orphaned children of Henry Straight (July 20, 1846–November 17, 1886) and Emma Dickerman (January 20, 1850–March 28, 1890), came to live with them. Henry had been chair of the Natural Sciences Department at Oswego Normal School, and Emma, a Normal School graduate of 1871, taught literature and art in the same college. The couple left Oswego when Henry obtained a position as vice principal of the Cook County Normal School in Illinois. His career was cut short when he died of tuberculosis in 1886. Emma bravely attempted to support herself and her two children, even moving to Tokyo, Japan, to teach there. She, like her husband, contracted tuberculosis and returned to the United States, where she died in Yuma, Arizona.[163] Elvira and Laura brought the children to Oswego and became their legal guardians. In later years they were referred to as the children's aunts.

Willard Straight (January 31, 1880–December 1, 1918) graduated from Cornell University in 1901 with a degree in architecture. He had a distinguished career in business, diplomacy, and journalism. He volunteered for military duty in 1916 and was sent to France with the rank of major. He died in Paris, France, on December 1, 1918, from pneumonia complicated by influenza.[164]

Hazel Henrietta Straight (August 26, 1882–February 21, 1922) graduated from Vassar College. In 1910 she was teaching at a private school in Haverhill, Essex, Massachusetts. She married James Forrest Sanborn (September 5, 1876–November 12, 1949) on September 19, 1911, and was the mother of five children. According to family tradition, "Hazel died of pneumonia while practicing Christian Science. She was young and had small children at the time. As a result, James Forrest became very angry with God and the children were raised with 'issues' concerning religion."[165]

Dr. Elvira Sarah Rainier's life ended tragically. She contracted spinal meningitis in April 1902 and suffered for months before dying at her home on October 12.[166] Over the next few days obituaries and memorial resolutions appeared in the local newspapers: "During her residence of a quarter of a century in this city, Doctor Rainier had made for herself a large circle of warm personal friends who will learn of her death with sorrow. She was a woman of exceptional character and standing in the community and her lovable disposition and true womanhood won for her the respect and esteem of all."[167]

Elvira's life work was not forgotten with her death. In 1915 the local YMCA was soliciting donations to pay off the last of the building's mortgages. Willard contributed one thousand dollars to erect a plaque in memory of Dr. Rainier. It was unveiled when the mortgage was burned in March 1916.[168] Hazel Straight Sanborn's letter, read at the unveiling, epitomized the doctor's life and character:

> It is not always easy to remember that a creative thought, or a selfless act, can not die. We know that the memory of a personality lives on but we sometimes forget that to know a great soul is to share its immortality and we do not realize how vital a part of our lives has become the force that once expressed itself in living form. So we are fortunate indeed when it is our privilege to vitalize a memory in some tangible form that reminds us of the flowering of an inspired life. Here in this community

there lived and worked one whom we all loved, a soul with an enduring faith, a largeness of hope and love for those to whom she ministered, a wisdom clear-sighted and farseeing. She was a pioneer among women physicians; one worthy and capable of turning the difficulties of that opening field into glorious opportunities. Her creed was a conviction that only through sympathetic understanding of the life of a community and an intimacy with its members, born of cooperation, could the kingdom of heaven be realized. Her life was consecrated to this ideal; for the carrying of this vision into her daily life, she possessed rare sympathy, a will singularly forceful, and a powerful mind. To her was sent the vision; to us the privilege of sharing in the immortality.[169]

Dr. Elvira Sarah Rainier lies beside her long-time companion, Laura Newkirk, in Riverside Cemetery, Scriba, New York (figure. 1.16).

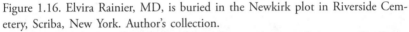

Figure 1.16. Elvira Rainier, MD, is buried in the Newkirk plot in Riverside Cemetery, Scriba, New York. Author's collection.

Charlotte M. "Lottie" Blair Parker

Charlotte "Lottie" Blair Parker was an acknowledged "true grande dame of the theater," but that appellation was hard won.[170] As a pioneer playwright she faced and helped break down prejudices and barriers that women experienced in the American theater (figure 1.17).

Born in 1853 to Captain George Blair (1829–August 15, 1895) and Martha Emily Hitchcock in Oswego City (1829–August 25, 1865), she was an only child.[171] Lottie, as she was generally called, was educated in the city schools. She subsequently enrolled in the Oswego Normal School, graduating in July 1872.[172] Her goal was to become a public reader "and during her time of study at the Normal School took many honors because of her ability as a student and a writer."[173] Lottie had a different opinion of herself as a girl. Speaking to a reporter in 1904, she confessed, "I was in no sense a phenomenon."[174] While attending the Normal School she was fortunate enough to have as a teacher Anna T. Fitch Randall, who was also interested in elocution and the stage. Randall gained fame as the author of

Figure 1.17. Lottie Blair Parker was, in her own words, legendary. *New York Dramatic Mirror.*

forty books, many on the subject of elocution. She was also the founder of the Fortnightly Shakespeare Club and the founding editor of the *American Shakespeare Magazine*.[175]

For the next three years after graduating, Lottie was a teacher in Bay City, Michigan, but she never lost sight of her interest in public speaking. She moved to Boston to study elocution with Wiseman Marshall, a former actor, who recognized her talent and encouraged her to become an actress (figure 1.18). Heeding his advice, she joined the Boston Theater Stock Company.[176] She reminisced about her decision when interviewed many years later: "After I left school I studied to become a dramatic reader. My family had old-fashioned notions about the stage and I shared them until my instructor, an old actor, persuaded me to adopt the dramatic profession. After mother had cried her eyes dry, she gave her consent and I became an actress."[177]

Lottie's acting career encompassed years of travel with various stock companies. Among the theatrical notables with whom she toured were Fanny Janauschek (July 20, 1829–November 28, 1904) and Lawrence Barrett (April

Figure 1.18. Lottie Blair's plan to become an elocutionist changed when a teacher encouraged her to become an actress. Oswego County Historical Society.

4, 1838–March 20, 1891), both well-established Shakespearean actors. She was a supporting cast member for several years before starring in *Hazel Kirke*, her culminating role.[178] Theorizing that her time on the stage was limited due to her age, Lottie decided to begin another career. She admitted that she was fascinated by the construction of plays and experimented repeatedly: "The number of people I created in those days, only to murder them ruthlessly, would surprise you. I honestly believe that in the first year of my work I began more comedies and dramas than Lope de Vega, who produced a thousand pieces, could have finished."[179]

According to Lottie, no one without stage experience could write a satisfactory play:

> I wouldn't want to discourage anybody, but it is the hardest thing to succeed at. It requires infinite condensation of expression, a faculty of putting things strikingly and spiritedly, the imagination and technical knowledge that is hardly within the reach of the general public. If one does take it up, though, I can only repeat the advice Mrs. Bloodgood gave a few nights ago through The Evening World to women aspiring to stage careers: "Work! Work! Work! And never be satisfied with you have done." That's my only recipe for winning success.[180]

Lottie achieved her initial success with a one-act play titled *White Roses* that she entered in a competition sponsored by the *New York Herald* in 1894. She spoke about it in an interview ten years later: "I wrote it for a newspaper contest and named it 'White Roses.' It did not receive a prize, but was mentioned honorably as a 'most excellent one-act play.' David Frohman consented to read it, and the result was that it was produced at his Lyceum Theatre . . . After its success, for strangely enough it was a success, I hadn't the slightest trouble having my plays read among managers. Production was another matter."[181]

According to Lida Penfield, Lottie's greatest play, *Way Down East*, had its genesis from bits and pieces of plays written by an unnamed "aged actor" whom Lottie and her husband, Harry Doel Parker, befriended during their touring days. When the man died, he left her a trunkful of material that she mined during a winter spent in Oswego.[182] Lottie worked on the play, initially called "Annie Laurie," for ten years. How it came to be produced was the subject of many stories told over the years.

In one version, Lottie used the pseudonym of Mrs. Fernandez and employed "a dramatic agent" to deliver it to William A. Brady, a prominent theater manager with whom her husband Harry Parker worked. Her reason for the false name was to ensure Harry would not be embarrassed if Brady rejected the manuscript.[183] Another version of the story had Harry himself asking Brady to read the play.[184] The latter version seems confirmed by an article in which Brady revealed how the play was developed: "A booking agent of mine, Harry Doel Parker, brought me a script called 'Annie Laurie.' I read it, and saw a chance to build it up into one of those rural things that were cleaning up everywhere. Parker told me that his wife, Lottie Blair Parker, was the author."[185]

A third version of the story held that the play was handed to Brady anonymously, "and strangely enough Mr. Brady handed it to Harry Doel Parker, who commended it as a fine piece of dramatic work. Later he was surprised to find that his wife was the author."[186]

While the exact details of the play's acceptance are lost to history, one fact is certain: Lottie (or Harry, acting on her behalf) sold the rights to Brady for ten thousand dollars. Therefore, while Brady and others gleaned millions of dollars from its long run and subsequent remaking in three movies, Lottie received nothing:

> I sold the play outright to Mr. William Brady years ago when it was first produced on Broadway. That was about 1897. It has made thousands, I suppose for everyone connected with it, but I have had nothing to do with that. I wrote the play and I sold it. Today I would know better and wouldn't sell that way. No author today would think of selling his work for a flat sum. But in those days it was different, especially for a woman playwright. I was one of the first women playwrights in America. Martha Morton had been writing plays before me, but I was among the first of them, and there have not been many since. We were not very much relished by the men back in those days.[187]

Way Down East was referred to as a "weeper" or "tearjerker" because of the pain the innocent heroine, Anna Moore, suffers at the hands of the men in her life. She becomes pregnant after going through a sham wedding ceremony with a cad named Lennox Sanderson. He abandons her, and she gives birth to her daughter alone. After the baby dies, she finds shelter as a servant in the home of Squire Amasa Bartlett only to be recognized and cast out of the house by him into a blinding snowstorm. She survives only because the squire's son, David, who has secretly fallen in love with her, rescues her. Audiences for years wept openly at the trials Anna Moore endured at the hands of unworthy men.[188] While the plot today may seem a bit far-fetched, similar behavior did actually occur. Consider, for example, the case of Anna Slauson Alger, a young widow residing in Fulton, Oswego, New York, in 1884. She found herself wooed by William E. Waugh, the son of the village mayor, who literally swore on a Bible that he was not married to induce Anna to marry him. When the truth was revealed that Waugh was not only married but the father of a young child, a terrible scandal, reported all over the United States, ensued.[189]

The play was considered daring in its day. For the first time in theater history, a character had used the word "baby" on stage.[190] It was also controversial because the author plainly pointed out the prevailing double moral standard. Innocent Anna paid the price for her mistake by being labeled a social pariah while her seducer suffered no such penalty. As Lottie herself pointed out, "Even in my time I was considered to have written an immoral play."[191]

In 1910 Lottie, having been asked to write about "my most successful play," composed her version of the genesis and development of *Way Down East*. She rejected the prevailing notion that the play was "rewritten" or "revised" after she sold it to William A. Brady, since that "implies the existence originally of defects in its theme or the manner of its development which it has been found necessary to correct." Indeed, she alleged that she was actively involved in what few changes were made, and when Brady and Joseph Grismer wanted to add a scene to the third act, she adamantly objected. After one performance Lottie was vindicated and the script was returned to its original form. The story that Grismer changed the title is refuted by Lottie's assertion that she herself submitted a list of substitutes, one of which was *Way Down East*: "A careful comparison of the original manuscript with the copy printed for copyright purposes shows that the great body of the play is today just what it was when first written. It is the same in every essential detail of its story, in its principal people, in their characteristics, in their relation to each other and their relation to the plot, and in its situations."[192]

Lottie's recollections of the creation and development of the play stand in stark contrast to William Brady's reminiscences, conveniently published after her death: "The play had the makings, and we finally agreed an outright purchase price of $10,000, he [Harry Doel Parker] giving me the right to call in a play doctor. I gave the job to Joseph R. Grismer, who rechristened the play 'Way Down East,' and took a year or more, with many performances in the sticks, to finish his job."[193]

Lottie's second important play was *Under Southern Skies*. Set in Louisiana in 1875, it too was controversial. Lelia Crofton, the main character, knows little about her long absent mother, who is presumed dead. When a male character taunts her about her mother's "tainted blood," Lelia concludes that her mother must have had Negro antecedents. Objection to Lottie's characterization of Lelia appeared in a letter published in the *New York Times* wherein the male correspondent declared that "no Southern girl of good family would entertain such a thought" and Lottie's response justified Lelia's concern based on the fact that no one will tell the girl what had happened to her mother. Lottie offered "to remove the objectionable complication" if "a majority of the Southern people who go to the Republic share the opinion of your correspondent."[194]

In addition to her pioneering efforts as a playwright, Lottie also laid claim to another milestone. In 1902 four of her plays were produced in New York City: *Way Down East*, *Under Southern Skies*, *Lights of Home*, and *A Colonial Rose*. Only one other person, Clyde Fitch, "can boast like honor and appreciation at the hands of the playgoing public."[195]

Lottie's other works included *A War Correspondent*, *Lights of Home*, and *The Redemption of David Corson*. The last named was based on a novel with the same name by Charles Frederic Goss. David Corson, a Quaker known for his faith and his oratorical skills, is the target of a huckster named Dr. Paracelsus Aesculapius who thinks David may be helpful in selling his fake wares. Traveling with him is a woman named Pepeeta, whom David believes to be the man's daughter but is in reality his mistress. David falls in love with Pepeeta, travels with the couple, and engages in a fight with Paracelsus when he discovers the truth. Thinking he has killed the man, he is so filled with guilt that he falls into a life of depravity. When he finally discovers that he has not killed the man but only blinded him, David permits Paracelsus to attack him without displaying any resistance. At that very moment, Paracelsus drops dead. The rest of the tale involves how David Corson finds redemption for his years of sin.[196]

Through the years Lottie gave many interviews and invariably was asked to describe her writing method. On more than one occasion she freely admitted she had none: "I haven't any regular hours for work. I utterly lack order and arrangement in my writing. I take up my pen when the mood seizes me. I have literary friends who tell me they go to their desks and write for certain stated periods daily whether they are in the mood for work or not. That's not my case. I couldn't keep literary office hours."[197] She elaborated in another interview: "I utterly lack order and arrangement in my writing. I take up my pen when the mood seizes me. As a matter of fact, I love to write and put in some time every day at my desk, but it is not schedule[d] time. I plan a lot and lay out a huge amount of work for myself, but I don't accomplish it."[198]

She was also honest in her assessment of her work, admitting to one interviewer that she actually hid on opening night: "I go and hide myself and stay hid until after the applause or censure has died out. Then, finally a day comes, when I steal into the theatre to hear for myself. HOW I suffer! As each sentence meant to be funny, as each phrase meant to be pathetic, falls on my ears I blush to think I could have written it. I wonder HOW I ever could have thought any of it worthy to offer a manager."[199]

Lottie theorized that women were sometimes better playwrights than men since they were "more emotional than men" and "write more from the heart and less from the brain." According to her, "The consequence is that, perhaps without quite understanding the cause themselves, they draw tears and provoke laughter with material from which a masculine author could get neither. . . . In my own work I have found that my best efforts have been results of impulse, of enthusiastic emotionalism, of inspiration and divination."[200]

Asked about the actors and actresses who brought her plays to life on the stage, Lottie confessed, "Naturally no actor or actress on the stage could come up to my ideal. I may say my disappointments have been as numerous as the characters in the plays. Their interpreters have been possibly, probably abler, but they have not been the creatures of my imagination."[201]

Lottie maintained it was easier to write novels than plays because of the freedom the author had in plot and character building. In 1901 she announced that she was engaged in writing a book: "I am writing a novel. I planned to finish it this winter, but I am only one third through with it."[202] In a later interview she revealed more about the story: "You must know what it is about? Well, it is a novel of rural life. I was born up-State and I know many interesting characters in the vicinity of my home. I am weaving these into the story and the plot is founded on real-life incidents. I shall not tell you my native village, because I don't want you to alarm folks up that way. It's somewhere in the neighborhood of Syrchester."[203]

The book, *Homespun*, which finally appeared in 1909, was unsympathetically reviewed: "'Homespun,' by Lottie Blair Parker . . . is written by the author of the successful plays 'Way Down East' and 'Under Southern Skies,' and presumably that is why it has been published, for there is no other discoverable reason apparent as you read it. . . . It is as moral as a Sunday school tale, and at the end pleases if not surprises the reader by the tableau of virtue triumphant and vice in the dust." After listing all the characters and plot elements, the reviewer sarcastically concluded, "What more, after all, does one want? Only the end, after all, and there is that, too."[204]

Although the details of Lottie Blair Parker's personal life are scanty, some facts are known. She married Harry Doel Parker (1860–April 19, 1921), a fellow actor, in Ray, Missouri, on December 2, 1882. At the time she was using the stage name of Justyn Van Dyke.[205] Harry left acting and became a prominent theater manager. The couple had a home in Great Neck, New York, and spent winters in Miami, Florida. One of Lottie's hobbies was polo, and she organized an all-female polo club. She also enjoyed sailing her own yacht.[206]

She loved dogs and at one time owned two Saint Bernards. An amusing story appeared in 1910 reporting that Lottie had complained to the North Hempstead Town Board about the overly zealous dog catcher and his assistants, who liked to hide in the bushes near her home hoping to capture her unleashed dogs when she took them across the road for a bath in Long Island Sound:

> This man and his assistants hide behind bushes in front of my grounds and wait for my dogs to come out so that they can catch them. I own property along both sides of the Shore Road and to go from one side to the other my dogs run the risk of being caught. Do you expect me to build a bridge over the roadway so that my pets can cross without molestation. . . . It is absolutely necessary for my dogs to swim every morning before breakfast. . . . It aids their digestion. If these pound keepers are permitted to skulk in the roadway they will catch my dogs before the dear things can get to the water.

Lottie's complaint got results. The town supervisor told her the law banning unleashed dogs would no longer be in effect after September 1, to which she replied, "Well, that's a comfort."[207]

She was interested in local politics, and one year campaigned for a school board candidate.[208] She was not in favor of female suffrage: "I am not a suffragette, indeed not. I cannot see what advantage it could possibly be for women to vote. It would mean that quite as many illiterate as educated women would have the privilege of the polls."[209]

She was a member of the Woman's Professional League and the Eclectic Club.[210]

In 1912 Lottie and Harry may have suffered a few minutes of anger and confusion when it was announced that the author of *Way Down East* had gotten married:

> Little Dan Cupid, about whose wiles and snares Mrs. Annie Laurie Parker, under the pen name of Lottie Blair Parker, wrote so entertainingly in "Way Down East" and "Under Southern Skies" two plays that made fortunes for their producers, has once more succeeded in piercing the heart of the fair authoress with one of his wing darts. In the offices of Justice of the Peace Bernard J. Flood yesterday afternoon, were said the words that united in marriage Mrs. Parker and Joseph Burkhard, a wealthy real estate operator of Los Angeles.[211]

Few details exist about Lottie and Harry's marriage (figure 1.19). They had no children but evidently were content in their relationship. He retired

Figure 1.19. Lottie Blair Parker kept her personal life very private. Wikimedia Commons.

in 1915 after a long and successful career in theater management. They were in Miami in 1921 when he suffered a series of strokes and died on April 19. His body was sent to Chicago and buried in Rosehill Cemetery.[212]

Lottie Blair Parker considered herself "legendary," and indeed her life was composed of events of which legends are made. When she died on January 5, 1937, at her home in Great Neck, obituaries appeared all over the United States and Canada, once more paying tribute to the author of *Way Down East* and *Under Southern Skies*.[213] Her body was taken to Chicago for burial.

Reporters also mentioned the fact that she had for years refused to give her age and that at her death it was finally revealed to be seventy-eight. Lottie, however, had the last laugh. She was actually eighty-three.[214]

Charlotte "Lottie" Blair Parker is buried in Rosehill Cemetery, Chicago, with her husband, Harry Doel Parker.

Harriet Elisabeth Stevens

Born in Granby, New York, in December 1856, Harriet Elisabeth Stevens was an acknowledged local historian. Among her achievements was the compilation of the names and service records of every soldier and sailor from Oswego City who served in World War I.

Harriet was a daughter of Alonzo Robert Stevens (March 7, 1818–February 2, 1889) and Harriet Adelle Farley (April 6, 1822–February 6, 1894). She was the fourth child in a family of seven, three of whom died young. Her father, a chair maker, had moved the family to Oswego City by 1860. Harriet and her siblings all attended the city schools.

After leaving the public schools, Harriet enrolled in the advanced course at Oswego Normal School, graduating in July 1872.[215] In September of that same year she was recommended for appointment as third assistant at Primary School No. 3.[216] The following year she was promoted to second assistant.[217] By 1876 she had been advanced to assistant principal, a position she held for several years. In 1896 she was the school principal.

Harriet was described as a teacher who "always kept up to the demands of modern educational methods."[218] To that end she enrolled in the critic course at Oswego Normal School, graduating in June 1899.[219] She also attended summer classes at Columbia Teachers' College.[220]

Following her graduation in 1899, Edward Austin Sheldon hired her to be the principal of the Primary Department and teacher of elementary methods at the Normal School. This position she held until her retirement in 1927 (figure 1.20).

Harriet was frequently invited to provide teaching seminars at local teachers' institutes. In 1904, for example, she was slated to give a talk titled "Methods of Teaching Primary Reading" at a weeklong convention at Pulaski, New York.[221] She presented a talk titled "Relation of Elementary and Advanced Reading" during another session of the institute.[222]

Harriet developed a great love for local history, born, perhaps from an interest in her own family's antecedents. She was a descendant of two Revolutionary War soldiers, one of whom was Captain John Stevens (1752–1801), who served under Colonel John Lamb in the Second New York Artillery in 1777. The other was Elihu Field (1753–1814), also a member of the Second New York Artillery. Harriet joined Fort Oswego Chapter, Daughters of the American Revolution (DAR), and was a particularly active member.[223] She served as chapter regent in 1922–1923 and in 1926 was granted honorary regent status.[224]

In 1906 Harriet led a discussion titled "Places of Local Interest" at a DAR meeting and afterward took her fellow DAR members on a walking

Figure 1.20. Harriet Stevens was a faculty member at Oswego Normal School for twenty-eight years. SUNY Oswego Archives and Special Collections.

tour around the city to visit locally significant sites, one of which was Fort George, an outpost built in 1754 by the British and destroyed on August 14, 1756, by General Louis-Joseph de Montcalm, thus restoring to France undisputed control of Lake Ontario during the Seven Years' War with Great Britain. Harriet was subsequently appointed chair of a DAR committee to investigate all such places in Oswego City and make a report as to the best way of designating them historically important.[225] The group determined that the site of Old Fort George should be marked with a boulder set with a large bronze plaque.[226] The unveiling of the boulder and plaque took place on October 14, 1909: "[I]t is a monument that will go down through the generations for it is an extremely heavy bronze tablet set in a boulder of enduring granite" (figure 1.21). [227]

Harriet was also instrumental in the creation and maintenance of Montcalm Park, located in the block between West Schuyler and Van Buren Streets:

Figure 1.21. Harriet Stevens was instrumental in placing this monument on the site of Old Fort George in Oswego City. Author's collection.

In the year 1911 when the cornerstone of the new Normal building was laid, we began to realize that the day was not so far distant when our school would leave behind the then-present site and its associations and take up our new abode on a hilltop farther west. The thought was not an altogether pleasant one for several reasons quite apparent, and leaving our wonderful school garden was one of the things we much regretted. From a stony, unsightly cow pasture at first the garden had developed into a spot of wonderful beauty and attractiveness. . . . What would be done with the plot when it could no longer serve as a school garden? As I stood watching the children returning one afternoon with their hands full of flowers, and their beautiful smiling faces, it seemed as if it must in some way be preserved for them during the coming years. Suddenly the thought came to me, why not a park? A park to carry out the patriotic idea embodied in the already-placed boulder a little further toward the lake? To some it was a well-known fact that this entire section was historic ground, and part of the enclosure around Fort George (or new Ft. Oswego) which stood about where the Castle now stands. But no effort had ever been made, except the placing of the boulder, to convey to coming generations these interesting facts of history. It would be nothing less than a crime to let this spot pass into oblivion. The thought of buildings elsewhere the sites that had already become state property because of such association suggested, "Why not Oswego?" and I determined to see what could be done about it. Tremblingly I wrote to our Representative in the Legislature, Hon. T. C. Sweet of Phoenix, and put the matter before him."[228]

Having secured Sweet's promise to introduce the necessary legislation, Harriet, together with other DAR members, quietly set about purchasing the desired properties adjacent to the Normal School garden. After the bill passed the legislature, Harriet addressed the Common Council, explaining the project and urging the city fathers to support the measure: "There was not a breath of opposition and the Council voted unanimously to approve this measure."[229] The following year the park, named after General Montcalm, was dedicated. The ceremony was to be part of the program of the New York State Historical Society, which was holding its annual meeting in Oswego in 1913.[230] On September 30, Harriet delivered the speech excerpted above as part of the day's activities. The event was considered significant enough that Assistant Secretary of the Navy Franklin D. Roosevelt attended and delivered a speech.[231] Montcalm Park remained under the care of the DAR until 1947, when the state reassumed control. Oswego City took over the park's maintenance in May 1952.[232]

Harriet's recognized ability to organize, together with her knowledge of and interest in, local history, led to a further honor in 1916, when she and Frederick Leighton were selected by Dr. Sherman Williams, president of the New York State Historical Society, to "become custodians for whatever documents of early or late historic value individuals may see fit to entrust to them." The materials were to be kept in a safe provided by the Oswego Historical Society and housed at the Normal School. The ultimate goal was to preserve any and all local records that might prove important should the complete history of New York State ever be undertaken.[233]

Harriet was heavily involved with the New York State Historical Association, serving as vice president a number of times.[234] She also belonged to the Central New York Historical Association and in 1926 was elected vice president.[235]

Membership in one historical society, however, eluded her for many years. When the Oswego Historical Society was organized and chartered in 1896, it was a men-only club.[236] The Fortnightly Club's male-only policy forced the Historical Society, which used its rooms on West First Street, to adopt such a rule as well.[237]

When the New York State Historical Society held its annual meeting in Oswego in 1913, several women joined that organization. Harriet, already a member, served on the planning committee.[238] This action caused the local group to rethink its long-standing policy, but nothing was done immediately. As time passed, the original members died or moved away, causing interest in the group to wane. Not until 1923, however, was any direct action taken to revise the rules concerning membership in an effort to revitalize the group. Current members met to discuss the future of the society late that year. Enough interest was expressed that in January 1924 any person, male or female, desiring to become a member was invited to an organizational meeting. Harriet E. Stevens was elected session secretary and took minutes that are still extant, "thereby attaining the distinction of being the first woman to be elected as an officer of the Oswego Historical Society." Permanent officers were then elected, including Harriet as corresponding secretary, an office she occupied for many years.[239] At that same meeting, she was selected curator of the society.[240] Other women who became members that night included Mrs. Frederick Leighton and Lida Scovil Penfield, for whose story see below.

The Oswego Historical Society probably needed Harriet more than she needed it. In 1919, Mayor John Fitzgibbons selected her to be Oswego's first city historian: "Upon the recommendation of the Oswego Historical Society, Mayor Fitzgibbons has named Miss Harriet Stevens of the Normal faculty to be local historian. The position is an honorary one and is in accordance with a state law. Miss Stevens' selection is very gratifying to her numerous friends."[241]

By 1919, World War I was history and steps were being taken to collect data on every soldier and sailor who served from New York State. Mayor Fitzgibbons charged Harriet with the task of collecting and recording the information pertaining to Oswego City residents. Two huge boxes, housed in the Richardson-Bates House in Oswego, give proof of the intensive research she undertook for this project (figure 1.22). They contain notes, snippets of a projected book (which never materialized), and even bits of poetry.

Figure 1.22. These two boxes, stored at the Richardson-Bates House in Oswego City, contain many types of notes Miss Stevens took pertaining to collecting data on every soldier and sailor from Oswego City who served in World War I. Author's collection.

When she finished her research, she used a separate page to record each soldier or sailor's career. Items such as company, regiment, rank, vessel (for navy men), place of induction, and discharge were noted. Those who died in service were recognized. The final product was a binder several inches thick. Due to a lack of funds, the plan to publish Harriet's work was never accomplished, although five copies of the finished product were made and distributed to various agencies (figure 1.23).[242]

The scope and extent of her research were phenomenal, going far beyond basic information:

> A mere recountal of the activities covered in Miss Stevens' remarkable compilation would fill columns. First attention was given to lists of the more than 1,000 service men and women from Oswego, those engaged in the armed forces or related bodies, with particular attention on the boys who gave "the last full measure of devotion," and the men cited for bravery. Then

Figure 1.23. Harriet Stevens's final report was considered a masterpiece of scope and detail. Author's collection.

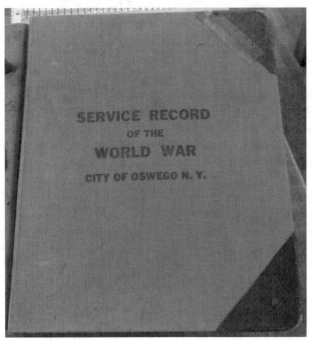

comes the self-sacrificing labors of devoted women in the Red Cross and welfare work; the War Chest and its related activities; the five Liberty and Victory loans to which Oswego did itself as proud; the war savings stamps; the Mayor's Smoke Fund, the City of Oswego medals, the General Hospital at Fort Ontario, the honor rolls and service flags at the various churches, schools, lodges and plants; the patriotic meetings, the great drives for various war relief and other funds; the fuel and food administration work; the part taken by the "Minute Men," by the legal advisory boards, by the numerous other voluntary boards and agencies. . . . The magnitude of the task did not daunt Miss Stevens, in fact, it is only when she recounts the results that it is realized the mighty work Oswego did in behalf of the nation during the great struggle.[243]

Harriet herself was singled out for her diligence and persistence in completing this task: "What endless labor it has entailed is not appreciated because few know the number of activities and the seemingly endless ramifications. Miss Stevens has sacrificed her leisure and encroached on her time without stint for the better doing of her task. No detail has been too small to overlook, no subject too formidable for her to overcome. Oswego is fortunate to have made such an excellent choice of historian. Other cities have had to expend thousands of dollars for the information and work which Miss Stevens has contributed without charge."[244]

Harriet's hard work was not unnoticed elsewhere. In 1925 she received a commendatory letter from state historian Alexander C. Flick: "Oswego County leads all others in the state in the matter of sending records of World War veterans to the Department of Archives and Records in Albany, with a rating of 91 per cent. The next highest is 73 per cent and the average for the state is 54 percent."[245] Flick also referred to Harriet by name when he came to Oswego to deliver a speech during the Oswego Historical Society's celebration of the 175th anniversary of the battle of Lexington. After urging Oswegonians to create a museum to house historically significant artifacts, he said, "One of your citizens here, Miss Harriet E. Stevens, has sent down to us at Albany one of the finest and most complete records of the activity of this part of the State in the World War that we have had from any part of the commonwealth."[246]

Harriet did indeed lead a busy life. In addition to her teaching and supervisory responsibilities at the Normal School, she was in demand as speaker. A few examples will illustrate her breadth and depth of knowledge.

She spoke on "Old Oswego" for a fathers' night banquet at the Normal School; she educated the Mothers' Club with a talk on child labor; she entertained her DAR chapter with a talk on the town of Constantia; and she lectured on Oswego's early history for the Women's Club of the Church of the Evangelists.[247]

Taking her role as city historian seriously, Harriet involved herself with many civic activities. In 1917, for example, soon after the United States had entered the war, many local groups desired to make the Memorial Day celebration in May 1918 especially eventful. Harriet was elected secretary of the planning committee that pledged to "make this year's celebration the biggest and best of any yet held."[248]

When Oswego was making preparations for an Old Home Week, Harriet undertook research pertaining to the two hundredth anniversary of the establishment of Oswego as a trading post in 1723.[249]

In response to a letter, Harriet compiled a list of interesting places to visit in Oswego County. Among others she named Spy Island at Mexico Point, Scriba Mansion, and Fort Brewerton, as well as the Oswego River and Fort Ontario. At the conclusion of her article she remarked, "I have exceeded already the number asked for and yet have not included several [which] others would include."[250]

When the Oswego Historical Society planned a display of relics pertaining to George Washington and Abraham Lincoln, Harriet took on the assignment to collect and display them in local store windows.[251]

She was one of the earliest members of Grace Presbyterian Church and "was at all times keenly interested in its welfare."[252] At one time she served as the chair of the Sunday school nominating committee.[253]

Her interest in politics related primarily to the status of teachers. In 1904 she was elected secretary of the new Oswego Teachers' Alliance formed in May, whose "avowed purpose is the advancement and improvement of teachers in this city." The group demanded better salaries, pointing out that teachers had received no increases for many years.[254] Harriet knew from bitter experience that teachers' salaries could and would be based on the mood of the current board of education. For example, in 1876 her salary as assistant principal was four hundred dollars. In 1879 the amount was reduced to three hundred and fifty dollars.[255]

In 1910 James B. Alexander, editor-owner of the *Oswego Daily Times*, held what can only be termed a popularity contest for young ladies in each of the districts where the newspaper was sold. The girl receiving the most votes in each district would win an all-expenses-paid trip to Europe. At the same time a contest was held to determine who would be the girls' chaperone.

Harriet Stevens won.[256] Soon thereafter the tourists sailed to Europe for a grand adventure that included London and Edinburgh. Harriet sent home several informative letters describing the places the group visited.[257]

After fifty-five years of teaching Harriet retired in September 1927. She was proud to have been a member of the Normal School: "After serving as grade teacher and primary principal for a number of years, she was invited by Dr. Sheldon to occupy the position she now holds. It has ever been a source of satisfaction to her that this appointment came through him."[258] Now, however, many of those with whom she worked, including Sheldon, were no longer alive. Younger professors were making their own Oswego Normal School history.

Harriet succumbed to heart disease on June 4, 1931, in the home she built at 30 Sheldon Avenue. Normal School colleagues eulogized her: "Miss Harriet Stevens represented the original traditions of the Oswego Normal school and was ever loyal to them. Her influence will long live through the lives of those she trained. Her sympathetic interest in the children and students will always endear her to them. We, her colleagues, feel it was a rare privilege to have been associated with one so kindly; one who gave herself unsparingly and one whose memory will ever be cherished in the hearts of those who knew her."[259]

Harriet Elisabeth Stevens was buried in Rural Cemetery, Oswego Town, in the family plot (figure 1.24).

Figure 1.24. Harriet Elisabeth Stevens is buried in the family plot in Rural Cemetery, Oswego Town. Her birth and death dates do not appear on the monument. Author's collection.

Emma Eunice Adams

Emma Eunice Adams lived in a quiet corner of Oswego County her entire life, but her artistic creativity put her hometown, Oswego Center, on the world map. She was the driving force behind the phenomenon affectionately known as the Columbian dolls.

Emma was born in January 1858 to William "Will" Adams (May 7, 1820–February 5, 1907) and Mary Ann Graves (December 24, 1832–August 30, 1905) and was the eldest of three daughters.[260] She was distantly related to John Adams.[261]

Her father, a native of Rodman, Jefferson, New York, settled in Oswego Town, where his parents had earlier moved. Her mother, born in Rochester, Monroe County, moved with her parents to Oswego County when she was young. Emma and her sisters were born and grew up on the farm located on Maple Avenue. They attended District 10 School in Oswego Center. To all outward appearances her early life was not unlike that of other girls of her time (figure 1.25).

Figure 1.25. Emma Eunice Adams's early life was typical of the girls of her time. Town of Oswego Historical Society.

Farming was then, as it is now, a hard occupation, and in 1864 Will Adams saw an opportunity to earn a little extra money. The Civil War, which had so far had no immediate effect on the Adams family, was about to envelop them. The year had been particularly bloody. General Ulysses Grant's relentless campaign against General Robert E. Lee resulted in battle after battle during the spring and summer months. Newspapers in the North and the South recounted details of battles fought at the Wilderness, Spotsylvania, and Cold Harbor, to name only a few. In July, President Lincoln called for five hundred thousand additional troops to replenish regiments depleted by death or expiration of term, and Oswego County was required to muster another new regiment, ultimately named the 184th. Part of the enticement used to encourage enlistments was the bounty system whereby each enlistee was eligible for payments from local, state, and national governments. Additionally, each soldier received a salary of sixteen dollars per month, although the money was in many cases only intermittently paid, due to battlefield conditions or other logistical problems.

Thus, like many others, William Adams saw military service as a way to earn extra income. According to *The Town Clerks' Registers* he enlisted on August 7, 1864, and was assigned to Company C. There is no indication in the record that he received any type of bounty.[262] The 184th Regiment was used primarily for guard duty during its ten months of service and saw little battlefield action. Its only real contact with the Confederate Army occurred on October 19, 1864, at Cedar Creek, Virginia, and Company C was not engaged in the fighting that day.[263]

While men were away at the front, the womenfolk cared for homes, farms, and businesses. Children, elderly parents, and animals all required attention. Field crops and family gardens needed tending, and no one could predict when the war would end. William Adams raised potatoes, strawberries, and apples on his property. Without doubt, while he was absent, it fell to Mary Ann to ensure that her little daughters, Emma and Cornelia, as well as other household members, were fed and clothed.

It was a happy occasion when Will, having been mustered out at City Point, Virginia, on June 29, 1865, returned home. Family life again settled down to much of its antebellum routine. Emma, who had attended Miss Wilmot's art studio after completing grade school, was noted for her artistic abilities and began to paint and draw commercially. In 1878 her collection of pencil drawings won first prize at the Fulton Agricultural Fair.[264] The next year she was asked to judge pastel drawings for the same fair.[265] She painted portraits using photographs as models.[266]

Cornelia attended the Oswego Normal School and graduated from the advanced course in June 1885. It appears that she subsequently obtained a teaching position in Utica.[267] Marietta, the youngest daughter, attended classes at a business school in Oswego City. She enjoyed bicycling and was a member of a cycling club.

Emma was actively involved in her small community. Her family worshiped in the Oswego Center Methodist Episcopal Church and she was a member of the Ladies' Aid Society. In 1894 she was the group's secretary.[268] She was a member of the Woman's Home Missionary Society.[269] She taught Sunday school, directed a children's choir, and led a youthful mission band.[270] Emma's love for children extended to forming a "society" known as the Band of Hope, comprised of twenty boys and girls, ages four to eight.[271] She found intellectual stimulation with a membership in the Chautauqua Literary and Scientific Circle.[272] One summer the local newspaper correspondent noted that she and Marietta were camping with friends at Demster Grove, situated near New Haven, New York.[273]

It was to please and entertain the little ones in her life that Emma began making rag dolls. In an undated letter preserved by the family addressed to a Woman's Exchange Store, Emma described how she got into the doll making business:

> The year 1891 and the first six months of 1892 I spent in Chicago with the exception of three months in Topeka, Kansas. While in this latter place, a friend purchased a rag doll from Marshall Field & Co. for a little niece of hers. On my return to Chicago, she was urgent in her appeal that I should make a doll and paint the face. She felt sure I could make one that would be more attractive, although she had paid two dollars for the one purchased (it was not dressed) and the child was delighted with it. Wishing to please my friend we purchased a pattern and I did the best I could with it, but my success was but a little better than a failure. I then proceeded to reconstruct the doll and becoming more and more interested in the work, spent several weeks in making dolls and finally succeeded in making one which all pronounced a success. The idea came to

Mr. Fine that I might make a profitable business and I took the doll to Marshall Field and Co. It was pronounced a novelty and a few were ordered immediately. I returned home and made several dozen for the coming holidays. . . . The following year I improved upon them and gained admittance to the Columbian Commission of the World's Fair. I named the dolls at this time and sold about 100 and received a Diploma of Honorable Mention.[274]

From this innocent experiment designed to make small girls happy grew an industry employing many people for almost twenty-five years. As Emma herself stated, "And when friends ask How did you happen to think of such a thing we say it was not a happen but a kind of providence that led us to this work."[275]

An unknown reporter from Toledo, Ohio, visited the Adams home in 1898 and was impressed by the activity taking place (figure 1.26):

While our friends were busily engaged hurrying to get some of their pretty dolls off to Marshall Field in Chicago, we were invited to "look around." In one corner was a large pile of arms, another of legs, all stuffed ready to put together, and on the sofa was a long row of heads, ready for the artistic brush of Miss Emma. The faces were exceedingly pretty, and the beauty of the dolls is, there is nothing about them to break, being stuffed with cotton and excelsior.[276]

Local reporters also took notice of the female-led business located in tiny Oswego Center:

The best words we could use to describe their work would be to call their home a child's paradise. For there you can see hundreds of dolls in every stage of making, baskets and boxes of arms, legs, bodies; tables filled with dolls all ready to paint the face upon them; long shelves filled with boxes of clothes of all sizes, as they make four sizes of dolls that sell from two to five dollars. These dolls are made entirely of cloth and the painting of the face and hands is the finest part of the work. Miss Emma Adams attends to that part herself, being an artist of no small

Figure 1.26. Different-sized dolls were displayed in the Adams family home. Town of Oswego Historical Society.

> skill. . . . They expect this year to increase the number made to twelve hundred. . . . But very few are sold in Oswego. The largest sales are made in Chicago[;] one firm in that city, Marshall Field & Co. took over $400 worth the last year.[277]

Emma might well have called the creation of the Columbian dolls providential because her elderly parents were having financial problems. According to Parrish, in January 1890, several months before William Adams applied for a military pension, he and Mary mortgaged the farm for twelve hundred dollars (figure 1.27). Emma alluded to the family's financial precariousness in her undated letter quoted above: "We have a pleasant and comfortable home but it is heavily mortgaged and for some time it had seemed as if everything would be lost. My father is nearly seventy years of age and although active could not meet the obligations resting upon him although we did all we

could to assist him. The success of the doll business has brightened our lives."[278] Thanks to the increasing popularity of the dolls, Emma was able to pay off the bulk of the debt in 1899.[279]

The dolls were available in various sizes, ranging from a fifteen-inch model dressed in a gown selling for $1.50 to a twenty-nine-inch version clothed in a white dress costing five dollars. A multipage advertising brochure described the dolls and extolled their virtues. For example, the dolls could be dressed and undressed. They were made of lightweight material and could be washed. Most importantly, they were unbreakable.[280]

More fame was to come to Emma in 1899 when Elizabeth Richards Horton, a wealthy Bostonian who collected dolls and exhibited them to raise money for children's charities, contacted her to acquire a Columbian doll for an upcoming International Collection of Dolls in early 1900.[281]

Mrs. Horton conceived of a novel way to raise funds for needy children in other places. She announced that she would send her doll, whom she named Columbia, on a trip around the world. Mrs. Horton also worked out a plan with the Adams Express Company and Wells Fargo to permit the doll to travel from place to place free of charge. Unfortunately, the doll originally scheduled to make the trip was stolen from the exhibition, and Mrs. Horton had to contact Emma to obtain a replacement.[282]

When the new doll was about to set out on her journey, the express office manager added a sash and American flag to her outfit and placed in her special trunk copies of local newspapers describing her proposed journey.[283] The doll's travels were widely reported in newspapers across the United States. After leaving Boston, Miss Columbia traveled to places such as Philadelphia, Chicago, Omaha, Denver, San Francisco, Los Angeles, and Skagway, Alaska. She then moved on to Hawaii, the Philippines, Japan, China, India, and Spain. Anyone wishing to see Miss Columbia was permitted to do so at no charge, but if the doll was exhibited for a fundraising event, the name of the organization and the amount raised were to be noted on a tag and pinned to her dress. A log book recorded places and people the doll encountered. Miss Columbia arrived in Los Angeles in July 1900 and, among other places, visited the News and Working Boys' Home and the Protestant Orphans' Home.[284]

Miss Columbia returned to Boston on December 25, 1902, two years and eight months after setting out on the grand adventure.[285] Unfortunately Emma was not alive to participate in the homecoming celebration.

In early July 1899 Emma was reportedly "quite sick," and although a subsequent article reported she was "better," her health was failing.[286] On July 26, 1900, she died unexpectedly in the house where she was born. A cerebral hemorrhage was pronounced the official cause of death. Her passing was noted across the nation, mainly with brief notices, many of which were practically identical.[287] The notice might contain somewhat misleading information: "She was the originator of Columbian dollars [*sic*] and had acquired considerable fame and fortune from their manufacture."[288] Emma definitely acquired some measure of fame but not any great fortune. Besides her mother and sister, many local women worked in the business, and they all were paid for their labor.

In Oswego Center the news of Emma's death was received with shock and grief, and a poignant obituary demonstrated how much she was loved and esteemed in the tiny community:

Some lives have been so lived among us that when they pass out from us they merit more than passing mention. Such was the life of our friend, Emma E. Adams, who has so suddenly been called up higher. Born and reared at Oswego Center, her life has always been identified with the people and place. Interested in every good movement she moved among us a gracious presence,—with us but not wholly of us. Her gifts were of no mean order. Her flute-like voice was always a delight to those who heard her sing. With a poet's soul, though perhaps never making a rhyme,—with an artist's eye and touch, all combined with a magnetic personality, she was one whom to know enriched one's life. . . . Her self-sacrificing, consecrated life is not ended even here. Its fragrant memory will still be an inspiration to her family and to her wide circle of friends.[289]

The story of the Columbian dolls does not end with Emma's death. Marietta Adams Ruttan (November 1869–May 15, 1944) carried on the business for another eighteen years, and her daughter, Esther, and granddaughter, Diane, have helped keep the interest alive. Esther Ruttan Doyle became something of an expert on the dolls and lectured widely on them.[290] Miss Columbia, the globe-trotting doll, is today exhibited in the Wenham Museum, Wenham, Massachusetts, together with her trunk and log book. In 1997 the US Postal Service created a stamp commemorating the Columbian dolls as part of its "Classic American Dolls" series.[291] Locally, the Oswego County Historical Society, housed in the Richardson-Bates House in Oswego City, has not only the doll contributed by Esther and her brother George in 1972 but also pieces of dolls and written material pertaining to their history and construction (figure 1.28). In 2000 an updated version of Miss Columbia made a journey similar to that of the original and spent time at the Richardson-Bates House, where it was exhibited next to the doll donated by Esther Ruttan Doyle.[292] Two more dolls can be seen in the Town of Oswego's museum, located in the old church where Emma prayed, taught, and sang (figure 1.29). An online survey quickly reveals that the dolls have maintained their popularity with collectors. The asking price for a Columbian doll on rubylane.com is $15,500. Another, for sale on eBay, is offered at $4,100.

Emma Eunice Adams is buried in Rural Cemetery, Oswego Town, with her parents and her sister, Cornelia (figure 1.30).

Figure 1.28. Esther Ruttan Doyle donated this large Columbian doll to the Oswego County Historical Society. The original dress has been replaced. Author's collection.

Figure 1.29. The Town of Oswego Historical Society possesses two Columbian dolls. Author's collection.

Figure 1.30. Emma Eunice Adams is buried in Rural Cemetery, Oswego Town, with her parents and sister, Cornelia. Author's collection.

Charlotte Lund

Unni Charlotte Lund, born in Oswego City to a Norwegian father and an Irish mother, was a musician, grand opera singer, painter, writer, and philanthropist. She is one of Oswego's musical treasures.[293]

Andrew Lund immigrated to the United States in 1857 and settled in Oswego City. He married Ellen "Nell" Byrnes circa 1863. A sailor, he first served in the US Navy from 1861 to 1862. In late 1863 he enlisted in Company C, 1st New York Light Artillery, mustering out at Elmira on June 15, 1865. In civilian life he was a foreman in the Kingsford Starch Factory in Oswego.

Nell Lund was a charter member of St. John's Roman Catholic Church in Oswego, and it was in this church that Charlotte grew up. Born on December 27, 1870, she demonstrated an interest in music early in life.[294] Although her first name was Unni, she always called herself Charlotte, primarily to distinguish her from her equally talented cousin, Unni Charlotte Lund (July 20, 1866–November 16, 1901). Unni, born in Norway, succumbed to pernicious anemia. At the time she was a professor of music at Syracuse University.[295]

By the age of seventeen Charlotte was the organist and choir director for St. John's Church, and it was said that hers was the finest choir in the city. On one occasion she organized and directed a chorus of one thousand voices.[296]

In June 1891 Charlotte completed the classical course and graduated from Oswego Normal School.[297] Her name was mentioned occasionally in the newspapers for the next several years (figure 1.31). In addition to her position as church organist she was engaged sometimes for special music. One such event was the funeral of Mrs. Catherine Looney for which she sang "Rest for the Weary": "It was one of the richest and most beautifully rendered solos ever heard in St. John's."[298] Charlotte and her father traveled to Europe in July 1895 and were away until August.[299] Upon their return Charlotte moved to Fairfield, New York, where she took charge of the Music Department of Fairfield Seminary.[300]

Figure 1.31. Charlotte Lund was known for her lovely soprano voice while still a very young woman. *American Scandinavian Review.*

MADAME CHARLOTTE LUND

In the fall of 1897 she was hired by the Oswego City School District as a teacher and district music director at a salary of four hundred dollars. Her talent as a music teacher was put on display in May 1898, when she organized and conducted a program at the Richardson Theatre featuring a chorus of eight hundred students from all grade levels.[301]

Her salary was increased to seven hundred dollars the following academic year, reportedly because it was thought she might take a position elsewhere: "Mr. Hastings said that he had a high opinion of Miss Lund's ability and he favored the increase because he was fearful that the music teacher might leave the Department's employ as she had been offered a $1,200 position in New York and was an applicant for the instructorship in the Syracuse schools which pays $1,700 a year. He was not sure, he said, that Miss Lund would consent to stay even at the increased salary."[302]

In the summer of 1898 Charlotte was hired as an instructor at the Summer School of Music at Hingham, Massachusetts: "Miss Lund is regarded as one of the best instructors of music in the State and the American Book Company recognized that fact in making the appointment."[303]

The following year she returned to Hingham and graduated with a bachelor's degree. As part of the graduation exercises she was chosen to sing Schubert's "Serenade."[304]

In the meantime, events were occurring in Oswego that would directly affect Charlotte's career. On January 1, 1899, a new state law was enacted, establishing the position of superintendent of schools in whom was vested the absolute power to hire and fire staff. George Bullis, secretary of the board of education commissioners in Oswego City, automatically assumed that position although he had not formally been appointed. Bullis pledged not to make any changes to the faculty. Nevertheless, he was determined not to pay Charlotte's seven-hundred-dollar salary. Promising not to cut the music program, he did admit "the salary of the teacher selected to have charge of it will not exceed $400 and may even be less than that."[305]

Bullis thought he could persuade Charlotte to resign in order to hire someone at a lower salary and sent her a letter requesting her to do so. He must have been quite surprised when Charlotte refused to resign, claiming he had no authority to demand such action because the law creating the position of superintendent would not go into effect until July 1, 1900.[306] Thus began a controversy that lasted through 1900. Charlotte maintained she was a faculty member and showed up for work in September. Although Bullis had warned principals and teachers not to admit her to schools or classrooms, the Democratic members of the Board of Commissioners sent their own letter supporting her. The parties argued for weeks until Bullis threatened not to pay any of the teachers unless the Democrats dropped their opposition. In October, faced with an increasingly hostile community backlash, they conceded, thereby admitting she was not a faculty member.[307]

Charlotte, undaunted, sued the school district in February 1900 for the money due her for the first semester. For months the local newspapers reported on the case.[308] Charlotte ultimately abandoned the suit, perhaps theorizing that continuing to fight would cost her more than the money she thought the district owed her, although as late as November 1900 her father insisted that she was continuing the effort.[309]

Yet behind that dark cloud of professional humiliation was a real silver lining. In 1900 Charlotte was a "special student" at Syracuse University, where she studied organ with Professor George Albert Parker and harmony and piano with Professor William Herwold.[310] It was probably due to the influence of these two men that she decided to travel to Italy to study music theory. Exactly when she departed Oswego is unknown but it is possible she departed during the summer because she was not in Oswego in November.[311]

The oft-told story was that Luigi Vannuccini, a famous voice teacher, conductor, and composer, heard her sing and encouraged her to study voice. She returned to the United States and for several years worked in various choirs in the eastern part of the United States, particularly in the Philadelphia, Pennsylvania, area, to save money for a return to Europe.[312] She was the soprano in the Christian Union Congregational Church in Upper Montclair, New Jersey, and a member of the church quartette.[313]

On May 30, 1906, Charlotte left New York City aboard the *New Amsterdam* "for an extended trip to Europe for further study."[314] Her destination was Paris, France, where she studied with tenor Jean de Reszke. She debuted in Paris on May 1, 1908: "According to reports received here [Oswego] Miss Charlotte Lund of this place, who for the past two years has been studying vocal music with M. Jean de Reszke in Paris, made a successful debut Friday night in Paris and received an ovation from the American colony. . . . She expects to make her debut in grand opera in Italy next season."[315]

A week later she performed in London: "Charlotte Lund, an American singer of much promise, faced a London audience in a concert at Bohemian Hall yesterday afternoon. I am happy to announce that she made good and left a very favorable impression."[316]

Charlotte fulfilled her goal of performing in grand opera when she appeared as Nedda in *Pagliacci* and in the starring role in *Marta,* but when de Reszke urged her to make her career in the United States, she heeded his advice and found success as a concert soprano.[317]

Few recordings of Charlotte's singing survive, but her voice was described as possessing "dramatic power and exquisite tonality" that ran "the gamut from the tenderly exquisite to the highly dramatic."[318] In the words of one critic, "Of Madame Lund's singing, too much can not be said. It was ideal. Her splendid training, her numerous public appearances, both in this country and abroad, have made her an artist of the first rank. Her voice, a rich, clear soprano, beautiful in quality, and big in volume, her pleasing personality, and her graciousness in responding to encores, endeared her to the hearts of all present."[319]

Another critic wrote, "Miss Lund has a voice of thrilling quality and large range which she can carry from the highest dramatic point to a point of the utmost simplicity and pathos. The charming personality of the singer, necessary for this form of recital, combined with her beautiful dramatic voice and thorough musicianship, made this third concert in the Highland Hall lecture-concert series one of great enjoyment."[320]

Charlotte once described how she prepared a song: "I want to live with it a while; I want to learn all the fine inner shades of meaning; I want to make it my own in a very real sense before I feel ready to give what I have learned of it to others."[321]

From 1909 until the late 1920s Charlotte was a fixture in concert recitals and grand opera. In 1911, for example, she undertook a tour taking her from Washington, DC, to New York City, then to Montclair, New Jersey, Montreal, Pittsburg, Wilmington, Delaware, San Francisco, Los Angeles, San Jose, Omaha, Dubuque, Des Moines, and Lafayette, Indiana.[322]

Among other venues in New York City, she performed at Carnegie Hall, the Metropolitan Opera House, the Princess Theatre, and Aeolian Hall. She specialized in French and Scandinavian music but was not averse to other genres. A recital performed at Aeolian Hall featured songs from twenty-one different composers. She could sing Irish and American folk songs with equal aplomb.[323] A performance at Recital Hall in New York City was a "charming afternoon of song," and Charlotte's voice described as possessing a "lovely quality" that "lent itself readily to every mood of the composers she illustrated."[324]

Ever the teacher, she began to host radio programs in the 1920s devoted to opera. Known as the "living libretto," she detailed operatic plots for her listeners and was a particular favorite with blind opera goers: "Madame Lund is said to be one of the only singers in the world who enable blind listeners to "see" the opera from which their numbers are selected. When she sings in concert the balconies are always filled with blind listeners, for she precedes each of her selections with a graphic, colorful description of the action and story of the opera in question, actually painting a verbal setting for the aria."[325]

In 1928 Charlotte, who was considered the first female impresario, founded the Charlotte Lund Grand Opera Company for Children, the aim of which was to introduce youngsters to an appreciation of opera.[326] Charlotte's technique was to talk to the children before the performance began to let them know what they were about to see. Included in the company's repertoire were *Hansel and Gretel, The Snow Maiden,* and *Cinderella.* She explained how she handled the acting and singing: "The idea, you see, was to give the children the best possible rendering of the music, while holding their interest by letting them see children like themselves in action."[327] Her achievement was noted in a hometown newspaper: "Madame Lund has an established reputation as an opera singer both in Europe and America but her greatest work and a field in which she stands almost alone is in her presentation of opera for children through the Charlotte Lund opera company. She is also a teacher and composer, and editor of the magazine *The Young Music Lover.*"[328]

She continued her campaign to educate children about opera in other ways: "Mme. Lund believes firmly in the desirability of paying equal attention to the poet and composer. She spoke of music as a necessity, not a luxury, and feels that all children should be acquainted with the best music."[329]

In 1932 Charlotte was appointed director of the opera department at the New York College of Music. She immediately set about producing her first performance, an "operalogue-ballet of *Thais.*[330]

Charlotte freely gave of her talent for worthy causes. She sang in a benefit for Midwest flood victims in April 1913.[331] A month later she performed for the benefit of the Fresh Air Fund at the Bergen Lyceum.[332] In 1917 she gave three separate concerts for the local War Relief Fund in Peekskill, New York.[333] During the same time period, she organized and directed the Oscawana Community Chorus in a benefit for the Red Cross.[334] She entertained soldiers during World War I.[335] One memorable concert took place at the Base Hospital in Toronto, Canada, when she entertained over three hundred soldiers, nurses, and officers: "Mme. Lund's singing of 'Keep on Hopin',' the great war song used by Clara Butt in the trenches in France, was received with unstinted applause so much so that the great singer was obliged to repeat it twice. After the concert, Mme. Lund spoke to the soldiers collectively and individually, [and] said how proud America was of their great stand in the big fight and the example it has been to American manhood."[336]

She performed the Christmas Message in Song at the Bowery Mission in December 1919.[337] Nor did she forget her roots. Charlotte returned to

Oswego on many occasions to perform. One such concert took place in October 1909 at the Richardson Theatre (figure 1.32):

> Never have residents of this city more clearly manifested their appreciation of rare musical talent than tonight [October 16] when an audience that completely filled Richardson Theatre greeted Miss Charlotte Lund, prima dona of this city, at her first public concert of the season. The audience, with the women exquisitely gowned and the men in evening dress, presented a metropolitan appearance. . . . When the curtain arose for the opening number, the audience greeted the artists with intense applause, showering many costly bouquets upon the prima dona, who has set Paris astir by her revelations in vocal accomplishments . . . the programme was varied in its composition and brought out the voice of Miss Lund in all its real beauty.[338]

Figure 1.32. Charlotte Lund's concert at the Richardson Theatre in Oswego City was highly anticipated and well attended. *Oswego Daily Times.*

The event, adjudged "the musical event of the season," was heavily publicized.[339]

Charlotte gave a recital to benefit the building fund of the Oswego YMCA in October 1913.[340] She performed arias from the opera *Thaïs* to benefit Grace Presbyterian Church in July 1932.[341]

She took an active role in Normal School alumni affairs. She gave a recital in December 1924 in Oswego to benefit the Sheldon Hall fund.[342] For several years she was second vice president of the New York City Normal School Alumni Association.[343]

On October 9, 1934, she took part in the celebration of Edward Austin Sheldon's 111th birthday, singing his hymn, "Calm Me, My God, and Keep Me Calm."[344] During the same trip to Oswego she gave a morning concert for faculty and the entire student body: "Miss Lund added to the interest of the program by relating anecdotes concerning the lives of the composers from whose works she sang. . . . In the afternoon she talked on music before pupils of the Campus school. She received many compliments from faculty members who found her work of considerable educational value among students and pupils."[345]

Charlotte was not only a singer but also a composer and writer. In her effort to educate American children about grand opera she wrote a series of twelve booklets. Each one centered on a separate opera, six French and six Italian: "In each case the story of the opera is told, who wrote the music and the book, and there is an analysis of the drama and the music, presented in easy, simple terms." In March 1911 she wrote an article about young women with aspirations to become opera stars. She bluntly described the sacrifices they would have to make, as she had done, if they wished to become respected and successful prima donnas. One of her songs, "Good Night," was published in 1905 and was used by Madame Lillian Nordica as an encore piece shortly after it appeared.[346]

In 1925 Charlotte revealed that she had been working on a novel for over a year: "I may have no friends left after it comes out," she remarks laughingly, "as I'm putting most everybody in it. Some of them may not like seeing the truth in print for once—but I'm having great fun writing it."[347]

She maintained that the critic was a performer's best friend:

> I do not understand why so many artists feel badly when they are scored by the critics. . . . Criticism is much more helpful than the deadly flattery of one's friends. If artists are really trying to achieve, they are glad to have defects pointed out, glad to

be told where they may improve. When a criticism of my work is made I immediately set myself to find out if the fault really exists. If it does I set out to correct it. It is one of the best ways of improving one's work that I know.[348]

Charlotte's interests extended beyond music. She took up painting:

Mme. Charlotte Lund, the singer, has come out in a new role, that of painter. A few months ago, when at the studio of her friend, Christine Lumsden, she said suddenly, "I feel as if I could do it." "Well," said Mrs. Lumsden, "take my brushes and that piece of academy board and begin." Mme. Lund tried, and began to copy, first, a little landscape by her friend. She kept at it all the afternoon and made quite a success of it. Since then she has gone on steadily, painting under Mrs. Lumsden, and now she is giving an exhibition of her canvases at the MacDowell Club, beginning today.[349]

Her paintings were good enough to sell: "At the recent exhibition of independent artists in New York 'Oscawana Woods' by Charlotte Lund, the soprano, was sold."[350]

She participated in educational seminars and delivered papers. One, titled "The Artistic Side of the Child," was presented at a meeting of the Chiropean Club at which the topic was education and child welfare.[351]

While Charlotte's career is well-documented, her private life is less well-known. One source related that her musical education began at the age of eight under Henri Lavigne, but no corroboration for that assertion has been located.[352] After her mother died on February 11, 1910, she and her father decided to leave Oswego permanently.[353] Andrew died in Charlotte's apartment on West 86th Street, New York City, on January 20, 1921. His body was returned to Oswego and buried next to his beloved Nell in St. Paul's Cemetery (figure 1.33).[354]

Charlotte's love life is shrouded in mystery. According to one tale, "she did not begin to study until after she had become widowed at the age of 20. Before that time, she had had no thought of entering any profession." In 1890, however, Charlotte was a student at Oswego Normal School and had never been married. A long article appeared in November 1900 that announced that Charlotte, "who came into unusual prominence on July 1, 1899, by reason of her dismissal from the schools at the instigation of Superintendent Bullis," was engaged to Mr. George King of New York City.

Figure 1.33. Andrew and Nell Byrnes Lund are buried in St. Paul's Cemetery, Oswego City. Author's collection.

The reporter alleged that relatives and friends had been informed and "it is expected that the formal announcement will be made public shortly."[355] At that time, Charlotte was studying as a "special student" at Syracuse University, a fact acknowledged in the announcement.[356]

George Milton King was born in 1869, the son of George W. King (1836–1930), a noted artist, and Emily Taft (February 17, 1836–April 10, 1885). At the time of the announcement he was allegedly working in New York City, although he had previously lived in Oswego, working for the R. W. & O. Railroad. His life after 1900 cannot be determined with any detail but it is possible that the man named George M. King who died on September 10, 1938, in Manhattan is the correct person. He is buried with his parents in Sand Beach Cemetery, Fleming, Cayuga, New York.[357]

Even more mysterious was Charlotte's relationship with Thomas Raleigh Raines (January 20, 1873–February 28, 1921). Raines was born in Hickory, Newton, Mississippi, the son of William Newby Raines (1821–1892) and Rebecca Ann Elizabeth Walling (1832–1906). If the following description is even partially accurate, he cut a fine figure:

There was a fellow at the Kimball yesterday who created a sensation wherever he went. The number of his key at the hotel tallied with the aesthetic name, T. Raleigh Raines, Mississippi. He was a tall, handsome young man, with extremely fair complexion, resembling that of a beautiful woman, and his eyes were of a deep brown color, with dark lashes. He wore a large sombrero of a hat, which made him all the more picturesque, but the most striking thing in his entire make-up was his abundance of long, black hair. It was long and wavy and brown—so long, in fact, that he "did it up" on the top of his head like a woman in the latest fashion wrinkle. Everything about him was picturesque, and he was all the world like a full-fledged Castillian of old, the only thing to disprove such a description being that he carried no mandolin.[358]

Raines, a lawyer, worked for the federal government in Washington, DC. According to Charlotte's entry in *Who's Who in New York City and State,* she and Raines were married in Washington, DC, in 1906. If that is true, the wedding had to occur before she sailed to France in May. So far as can be determined, there is no record of the marriage and no announcement appeared in the newspapers. It is unknown how or when they were introduced to each other. Raines was prominent in Washington social circles, but no information on female friends has been unearthed. He was a member of the Sons of the Revolution and the Mississippi Society. In 1902 he was the commandant of Anselm J. McLaurin Camp No. 305, United Sons of the Confederacy. When he died of a heart attack on February 28, 1921, he was described as unmarried.[359] Charlotte apparently suppressed any acknowledgment of her marriage to Raines but never obtained a divorce. Her entry in *International Who's Who in Music and Musical Gazetteer* (1918) makes no mention of a spouse.[360] Not until the 1930 census was taken did Charlotte admit she was a widow. She also claimed to be a widow in 1940. She filed an application for Social Security on January 11, 1946, under the name Charlotte Lund Raines. When *Who's Who of New York City and State*, volume 11, appeared in 1947, both of Charlotte's entries stated she was the wife of Thomas Raleigh Raines.[361]

Charlotte led a full and active life both on the stage and off. She once declared, "To give richly, one must live richly; have no regrets, take everything as a lesson, swallow hard and go on."[362] In addition to her work promoting opera for children, she strove to introduce grand opera to audiences all over the United States (figure 1.34). In the words of one critic:

Figure 1.34. Charlotte posed with members of the Pacific Coast Singers' Association at the 12th Sangfoerening in September 1917. *Musical America.*

It is not surprising that Charlotte Lund, in three years, has built up such a fine following for her opera recitals in New York. She and Mr. Pavey are unquestionably doing invaluable work in their opera recitals of the novelties and revivals presented each season at the Metropolitan. The fact that each successive season the attendance of these Princess Theater Opera Recitals has increased until they are now an established feature of the musical season, and that Mme. Lund and Mr. Pavey have many concerts outside of New York, in many cities where opera companies are never heard, prove that they are doing a great pioneer work for the development of appreciation of opera.[363]

She was the founder of the New York Opera Club and its first president; member of and president of the Musical Drama and Book Club; and member of the Grieg Society. She supervised the Boys' Club at Madison Square Garden. She had many private students and engaged in music therapy in the Women's Prison Association. In later life when she lived in Peekskill-on-Hudson during the summer she was involved in local women's groups.[364] She frequently performed recitals for individuals and private groups. In 1903 she sang at a session of the Federation of Women's Clubs in Carlisle, Pennsylvania.[365] She had her own radio show.[366] She was decorated by the French government for introducing French music, especially Debussy, to foreign audiences.[367]

Charlotte spent much of her later life in Orangeburg, New York, dying on July 8, 1951, at the age of eighty-one. Obituaries erroneously claimed she had died in Ogdensburg, New York.[368] In reality she died in Rockland State Hospital, where she had been a patient for almost a year. Her death certificate reveals that the official cause of death was arteriosclerosis and heart disease, with senile psychosis as a contributing factor.

This daughter of Oswego endured her share of heartache and misery in the early days of her professional life, but following her own advice she enjoyed a long and successful career: "I think that a great many people are not content to [do their best] . . . just to do their best and let success follow or not. If you are really trying to give your best; if you are sure that you have brought yourself up to the best that is in you, then you need have no fear of the results."[369]

Charlotte Lund is buried in Tappan Cemetery, Tappan, New York (figure 1.35).

Figure 1.35. Madame Charlotte Lund is buried in Tappan Cemetery, Tappan, New York. Courtesy Robert McCue, Findagrave.com.

Lida Scovil Penfield

Born into wealth and social connections, Lida Scovil Penfield used her education and talent to influence generations of students at the Oswego Normal School. Her legacy of teaching, writing, and serving the community at large is felt to this day.

Lida Scovil Penfield was born on January 28, 1873, to Joel Benedict Penfield (January 4, 1810–July 7, 1873) and his second wife, Cynthia Adelaide Taft (March 18, 1843, February 15, 1929). Joel operated the Washington Mills in Oswego City with John E. Lyon and Samuel Johnson under the name Penfield, Lyon & Co. until ill health forced him to retire. The family was returning from a trip that was intended to help him recover his strength but instead proved fatal. He died in a railroad car at Harrisburg, Pennsylvania, after suffering a stroke.[370]

Later that year Cynthia married Newton Wright Nutting (October 22, 1840–October 15, 1889). Nutting was a lawyer, county judge, and member of the House of Representatives. He died after suffering for almost a year with cancer of the jaw.[371] Her mother did not remarry. She died at her home in Oswego of pneumonia in February 1929.[372]

Lida, a graduate of Oswego High School, entered Boston University and earned a bachelor of arts degree in 1894. She was very active while in college. Among others, she was a member of Phi Chapter, Kappa Kappa Gamma sorority. In her senior year she served as class president.

The seniors of Boston university held their "class day" this week. The president of the class is a young lady, Miss Lida S. Penfield of Oswego, N. Y., who is well known in this city [Auburn, New York] where she has visited as the guest of Mrs. Jennie M. Pearson of Owasco street. The Boston Herald says of her: "She was the choice of the students and the graceful and easy way in which she carried out her part of the programme convinced them that they had made a very proper selection. Miss Penfield has devoted much of her time to the many societies of the university and has figured prominently in the recent private theatricals given by the Philomathians.[373]

After graduation Lida embarked on a lengthy tour of Europe, leaving in June and returning on October 27, 1894.[374]

Penfield returned to Boston University and in 1896 was awarded a master of arts degree.[375] She subsequently obtained a teaching position in Miss Hersey's School for Girls at Beacon Hall, near Boston, Massachusetts.[376] She next taught in the Ogontz School for Girls in Philadelphia.[377] From 1905 to 1909 she worked as the general secretary of the Cleveland, Ohio, YWCA.[378]

Lida left Cleveland for a position with the YWCA in Scranton, Pennsylvania, in September 1910: "Miss Penfield comes to this city from Cleveland, Ohio, where for the past three years she was general secretary of the association in that city. Her home is in Oswego, N.Y."[379] While she was there, she helped launch an athletic association for high school girls who had no gymnasium at their home school.[380] The following excerpt is illustrative of her endeavors in Scranton: "Miss Penfield, the general secretary, gave her report. This consisted chiefly of points regarding new work taken up this year or new developments of work. Among these were mentioned the scholarships offered in the Domestic Arts and Domestic Science departments by some of the members."[381]

Penfield resigned her position effective April 1, 1914: "It is understood that Miss Lida S. Penfield, who has been the general secretary of the Young Women's Christian association for several years, will resign the position on April 1st."[382] On September 1, 1914, Lida was appointed librarian and assistant in the English Department at the Oswego Normal School at a salary of eleven hundred dollars (figure 1.36). Thus began a teaching career that was to span over a quarter of a century.[383]

Lida Penfield threw herself enthusiastically into campus life. In addition to her professional duties, she was the sorority "mother" for Epsilon Chapter, Ago Sorority. She was the first advisor of Sigma Rho Pi, the women's honorary society at the Normal School, when it was organized in 1936, holding the position until shortly before her retirement in 1940.[384] She was a frequent speaker at local teachers' conventions. In 1916, for example, she lectured at a convention held for Jefferson County teachers on English in the lower and higher grades.[385] The following year her topic was oral English.[386]

One of her contributions to campus life was the creation of the Torchlight Ceremony. Observed during Graduation Week at SUNY Oswego, the torch of learning is passed from the alumni to the undergraduates. According to Dorothy Rogers, the idea for the ceremony originated with Professor Isabel Hart upon the seventy-fifth anniversary of the founding of the Normal School, but it was Lida Penfield who composed the *Message of the Torch*: "This torch is the symbol of the illumination of learning lighted for us at the

Figure 1.36. Lida Scovil Penfield was beloved by students and peers at Oswego Normal School. SUNY Oswego Archives and Special Collections.

fair shrine of truth. We, the alumni of this State Normal School, dedicate its bright burning to our memories of the past and to our hopes for the future. As we hold it in hand, we think of the light our school gave us. As we pass it, we think of the light that our school, through us and through others, still gives to youth. May its glory never be dimmed."[387]

She became an expert on local history. As a direct descendant of Captain Peter Penfield, Jr. (September 13, 1743–January 12, 1812), a Revolutionary War soldier from Connecticut, and his wife, Hannah Lewis (October 18, 1744–September 15, 1839), she qualified for membership in the Daughters of the American Revolution. In 1935 she was the regent of Fort Oswego Chapter.[388]

Her love of local history led to the composition of a series of stories, written for Normal School children, titled *Stories of Old Oswego*. These delightful tales, composed with age-appropriate language, chronicled the history of the settlement of Oswego, including the arrival of Father LeMoyne with the Onondagas, the area's participation in the French and Indian War, the evacuation of Fort Ontario, and prominent early settlers such as Matthew McNair, Rankin McMullin, and Alvin Bronson. One story focused on the important starch industry founded by the Kingsford family. The last story, lovingly told, concerned Edward Austin Sheldon and how he created his "ragged school" for orphaned and neglected children that led to the establishment of the free public schools in Oswego City.[389] Lida knew Sheldon personally, having been a student in one of the first kindergarten classes at the Oswego Normal School.[390] Her regard for the man is manifest in her children's tale.

With the resurgence of interest in the Oswego Historical Society in the early 1920s, Penfield became one of its most active members and supporters. Together with Harriet Stevens and others, Lida integrated the society, which until the early 1920s had been open to men only. In 1942 the society dedicated its annual publication to her. The dedicatory article outlined her long and faithful service to the history of Oswego in particular and of New York State in general:

> A member of the "Committee of Thirty" named in April, 1924, to bring about the reorganization of the Oswego Historical Society upon a more secure basis, Miss Penfield has since continued vigilant in the interests of this Society. In 1925 she served as a member of the Committee of Three which arranged for the presentation of the memorable pageant, sponsored by this Society, to mark the 200th anniversary of continuous activity by white men at Oswego. Miss Penfield directed the rehearsals for the pageant, witnessed by more than 20,000 people, on the Fort Ontario Parade Ground on July 5. . . . Through the years, Dr. Penfield has contributed many noteworthy papers to the programs of this Society, including a series upon "Writers of Oswego County" now in progress. In 1942 both Dr. Penfield and our Society were honored through her appointment by Dr. Arthur Pound, New York State Historian, to represent the State of New York upon an Interstate Committee which contemplates a series of state celebrations opening in 1945 to mark the 150th anniversary of the surrender to United States authority of the border forts (of which Fort Ontario at Oswego, was one) held by Great Britain for thirteen years after the close of the American Revolution. In recognition of Dr. Penfield's long and unselfish service rendered to this society and her distinguished contributions to its work, Oswego Historical Society, through formal action by its Board of Managers, appreciatively dedicates this volume to her.[391]

As stated in the dedication, Penfield presented many historical articles for the society. The volume dedicated to her contained her study "Morgan Robertson and His Sea Stories."[392] On March 16, 1943, she delivered "Ned Lee, His Life and Times."[393] She authored "Charlotte Blair Parker, Author, Actress, Playwright," read before the society on April 17, 1945.[394] In fact, her association with the Oswego Historical Society continued until 1948, when she resigned from the board of managers on account of ill health.[395]

Many organizations exploited Lida's expertise in local history. The Scriba Men's Club, for example, was the setting for a speech on the papers and possessions of the Scriba family: "Her knowledge of the family history, therefore, is of the most unimpeachable kind. This is the first time that Miss Penfield has delivered this talk on the Scriba family and it promises to be most interesting."[396] Demonstrating an interest in and a knowledge of world affairs, Penfield presented "Conditions in China" for the Woman's Society of the Presbyterian Church in Oswego.[397] At a conference of regional historians, Penfield delivered a speech titled "Willard Straight by One Who Knew Him."[398]

One of Lida Penfield's favorite organizations was the College Women's Club, founded in 1916, and for which she served as the first president.[399] She was reelected president for the ensuing year. In 1918 she represented the club at a conference in Ithaca, New York, at which time the group formally joined with the American Association of University Women.[400] Lida was elected the new organization's first president. In 1942 she was elected third vice president of the New York State Division of the American Association of University Women.[401]

Another favorite organization was Winter Club, a literary society that met only in the months of January through March and whose active membership was limited to twenty-four at any given time. In 1946 Lida served as secretary of the organization.[402]

Other interests included the Woman's City Club and its Supper Club. She actively supported the Presbyterian Church as a member of the Missionary Society and the Ladies' Society. During the world wars Lida volunteered for the Red Cross and the United Service Organizations.[403] She was a member of Pine Twig, one of the volunteer organizations associated with Oswego Hospital.[404]

Lida Penfield was a lifelong student. She attended summer sessions at various institutions.[405] She enrolled in the Normal School and graduated in 1919. In 1932 she earned her doctorate in English literature from Boston University. Her dissertation was titled *Henry James and the Art of the*

Critic.[406] In 1932 she replaced Carrie V. Sinnamon as head of the English Department, retaining that office until her retirement in 1940.[407] The regard students had for her was demonstrated when they dedicated the *Ontarian,* the college yearbook, to her in 1940.[408]

Retirement from the college did not mean that Dr. Penfield was forgotten. In 1961 a new library was named for her.[409] Seven years later a newer library was also named in her honor (figure 1.37).[410]

Once described as "a genteel, loving cultured teacher of English," Lida was revered by students and admired by peers.[411] According to Charles Wells, her successor as chair of the English Department, "she set a tone of culture that no one else can ever beat."[412]

Lida Penfield died in Oswego City on July 4, 1956, which seems an appropriate date, given her interest in and love of history. An extensive obituary described her as "one of the most popular and beloved members of the college faculty for a quarter of a century." and reviewed her career and community involvement.[413] The obituary, however, does not convey the love and respect that students had for her. Perhaps, therefore, it is best to let them provide Lida's eulogy:

Figure 1.37. Penfield Library on the SUNY Oswego Campus is the second to bear Lida's name. SUNY Oswego Archives and Special Collections.

Full realization of impending loss was brought to the students of Oswego Normal with the official announcement of the resignation of Dr. Penfield. Those of us who have had Dr. Penfield as an instructor vividly realize the worth and offering of this truly fine teacher. She leaves us with a desire to attain her standards and results of teaching. She will always serve as a model and inspiration to all of us. If we can attain even to a degree that rare combination of intelligence, personal charm and wit of Dr. Penfield, we will have reached that desired goal, a teacher who truly serves. . . . We have much to appreciate as those who have studied under Dr. Penfield realize. She brought more to her classes than the presentation of literature that was vital because of her personal charm and rich experiences, but also a presentation that gave us an insight into a life and manner of living and speaking that was truly inspiring. . . . We humbly, proudly and sadly bid farewell to Dr. Penfield as our instructor, but we will always retain her as our friend and guide.[414]

Dr. Lida Scovil Penfield was interred in the Penfield family plot in Riverside Cemetery, Scriba, New York, after a long and fulfilling career as a professor of English literature and local historian (figure 1.38).

Figure 1.38. Lida Scovil Penfield, PhD, lies with members of her family in Riverside Cemetery, Scriba, New York. Author's Collection.

Una Clayton

Actress, singer, composer, playwright, and activist Una Clayton used her varied talents to entertain thousands of theatergoers. She also found ways though her acting and writing to raise awareness of important social and moral issues.

Born in the tiny hamlet of Kasoag, New York, Una's birth name was Fanny Pearl Keyes. She was born on April 9, 1875, to Van Rensselaer Keyes (January 13, 1839–May 30, 1902) and Julia Davey (September 6, 1845–March 31, 1904). In 1875 she, her parents, and an older sibling, Mabel (November 2, 1867–February 2, 1914), lived in Williamstown. She also had a younger sibling, Raymond Llewellyn (September 29, 1884–November 26, 1975).

The family moved to Utica when Fanny was a child, and it was there that she developed her interest in acting:

> Probably no one who witnessed the acting of Una Clayton at the Shubert this week recognized the actress as Fanny Keyes, who used to live in this city and attend the Mary Street School. It is a fact, however, that Miss Clayton too lived here for a number of years and even when a little girl she had a great longing to be an actress. The Keyes family came to Utica when Fanny was eight years of age and in old Trinity Church on Broad street was confirmed. She displayed talent as a singer while a little girl and often sang at church fairs.[415]

Before that dream could come true, however, Fanny made a decision that altered the course of her life. On November 29, 1890, she married John George Halsey (January 1, 1872–April 27, 1944) in Utica. She was fifteen years old. Less than two years later she gave birth to her only child, John Glendon (February 28, 1892–April 16, 1968).

What prompted Fanny to abandon her husband and son is unknown, but with a new name, Una Clayton, she began a career stretching from 1893 to 1956. While it has been impossible to trace her exact movements during the 1890s, some facts are known. In 1897 she was touring with Kathleen Rober's Theatrical Company. In 1898 she appeared as Mercedes and Fanchon in a production of *Monte Cristo* staged by the Spear Comedy Company in Portland, Oregon. A reviewer remarked that her portrayal of Fanchon was "most successfully and well supported."[416] In 1899 Una was with the Clair Patee and Russell Comedy Company.

By 1900 Una had organized her own touring group, said to be "the largest of its kind," with twenty-five performers, the Ladies' Symphony Orchestra of Boston, and eight vaudeville acts "interspersed during the action of the play, making a continuous performance."[417] When Una's father became gravely ill in 1902 she cancelled her touring schedule and returned home to nurse him during his final days. In a letter sent to his brother-in-law, Edward Brooks French, Van R. Keyes refers with gratitude to Una's selflessness:

> I have been some better so I begin to feel hopeful. Dr. thinks I am better—my nurse thinks so. Aforesaid nurse is no less a personage than Una Clayton—made all haste to come home and nurse her [dear old] father. She worked the Rail Road Oficials [*sic*] for Passes until she reached here! And yet she could have had her choice of the management of two summer resorts as they had last summer and they have the best of prospects for next season. So she is hopeful and happy. Frank is working for his father at the [illegible] Business in Buffalo. They closed the show and paid up every member of the company. They do not owe a dollar, have about two thousand dollars' worth of wardrobe, about the same of scenery, and as she expresses it, "thousands of dollars of experience and reputation."[418]

Una's mother, Julia Davey, met with an unfortunate end. Mrs. Keyes was an alcoholic and, in desperation because she could not obtain any other alcoholic beverage, drank a bottle of wood alcohol that was supposed to be used for a magic lantern. Despite receiving medical attention, she succumbed to alcohol poisoning.[419]

The man named Frank mentioned in Mr. Keyes's letter was Francis Lee Morey (July 1868–December 14, 1951). For many years he was an actor in Una's company, usually her leading man, as well as the troupe's booking agent. He was also Una's husband. According to a marriage license procured in Northumberland County, Pennsylvania, Franklin L. Morey and Fanny Halsey were married on January 24, 1899. The document is very interesting. It reveals that the groom's father was Ira E. Morey, and the bride's father, Vanrensselaer Keyes Halsey. Fanny and Frank both claimed that this was their first marriage. He was a traveling salesman and she had no occupation.[420] Obviously Fanny lied about her name and her marital status. John George Halsey finally obtained a divorce from her but not until

March 1910.[421] So far as can be ascertained, he never remarried. He died in Los Angeles, California.[422]

While it seems somewhat bizarre, Una's bigamous marriage to Morey apparently was condoned or simply overlooked. For example, shortly after Keyes's death, the couple performed at a local auditorium: "Francis Morey and wife, alias Miss Una Clayton, played to a large house at Mattison Hall Monday evening, June 23."[423]

Una's talent was evident from the start. Review after review spoke of her acting ability in glowing terms:

> Una Clayton, that clever little soubrette, will open a three nights' engagement at the Grand Thursday night, at popular prices—10, 20, and 30 cents. Miss Clayton is considered one of the most versatile actresses on the stage. Her range of characters includes everything from such emotional roles as Ilda Barosky in Darkest Russia to Jack, a street singer, in the Little Pauper. Besides being a capable actress, Miss Clayton is considered one of the leading specialty artists now before the public, and her singing and dancing have been the cause of much favorable comment.[424]

She starred in a production of *Nell Gwynne* in 1902, about which a reviewer wrote, "The character of Mistress Nell best suits Miss Clayton and she was dainty, capricious, charming and daring, just as Nell should be."[425]

Her reputation as an actress increased with each passing year (figure 1.39). The review for her playlet, *His Local Color*, was typical:

> There is no expression that conveys so much to an artist as "local color"—in painting a picture where character is involved, the artist always looks for local color, either by visiting a certain neighborhood or by securing a model that is the embodiment of the character desired. Una Clayton has named her new vaudeville offering "His Local Color." The story told is of a poor little East Side waif, a pickpocket—she has stolen a pocketbook from the sweetheart of Harold Sherman, an artist: an old photograph of a sweet-faced old lady with the word "Mother" on it, awakens her better nature, and getting the address of the artist by a card in the purse, comes to return it; he takes her for a thief and is going to turn her over to the Police. She tells him that in this case she is not a thief, but is returning the "leather." Sherman is drawn to the little waif by reason of her being the exact

type he has been trying to paint with the use of a "lay figure," without success and he at once determines to employ the girl as his "local color," though he has promised his sweetheart, Jean LaRouch, that he will never employ a live model. In a spirit of mischief Tina dons a dress that belongs to the lay figure, "Bettina"—Jean takes her for a French model and her jealousy is aroused; Sherman, in trying to fix matters, says that it is a mechanical figure and gets Tina, the waif, to impersonate the dummy. This scene is said to be the funniest on the stage today. There is the strongest of heart interest throughout the action of the playlet, and Miss Clayton has an opportunity of displaying her wonderful dramatic ability, playing on the feelings of her audience at will; tears follow laughter and laughter follows tears. While comedy predominates, there is enough of the dramatic to give spice to the comedy. Miss Clayton is peculiarly adapted to the part of Tina, being young in face and figure, and blessed with the power of wonderful magnetism—and the ability to play both comedy and the strong dramatic incidents of the act.[426]

Figure 1.39. Una Clayton enjoyed an excellent reputation as a vaudeville actress. Courtesy Shawn P. Doyle and the Half-Shire Historical Society.

Una once spoke of her preferences when writing plays:

Why, that I am such a frequent producer of vaudeville plays do I not try something classical, scientific or historical, I am often asked. It's because there is more actual drama behind the soda water fountain, at the dry goods counter, and in the pawnshop, than about all the neurotic queens history ever produced. The characters I create and my acting of them are for real people and not for college professors with musty dogma in their hearts, and drama faddists who bring their encyclopedias with their theater tickets. Be consistent, yes; an intellectual icebox, never. Even long plays which have the biggest successes are those which are about those little human characters which one meets wherever you turn any and every day. . . . You will find that when you write the thoughts and emotions of real, everyday people, you will have the biggest audiences, because such are made up of them and they are vastly in the majority.[427]

Over the years Una was variously described as anything from "quaint" to "a rare picture of beauty."[428] Of her starring role in Bartley Campbell's *White Slave* she was said to have "a very easy, graceful possession, that never fails to win the admiration of the audience and her clever work last evening won her many new friends" (figure 1.40).[429]

Her acting versatility was put to the test in *The Little Detective*, in which she donned five different costumes: "The remarkable good business of the Una Clayton Company at the Academy of Music continues and the excellent performance of 'The Little Detective,' given by Miss Clayton and her clever supporting company last night is a guarantee of a good house tonight. Miss Clayton in the protean part of Della Ridtsdorf showed her great versatility—assuming no less than five distinct disguises, one being from a swell young man in dress suit and overcoat to a ragged Irish boy in less than two minutes."[430]

As late as 1924 Una was receiving positive reviews for her theatrical performances: "Another colorful figure is pretty Una Clayton, star of 'Keep Smilin,'" a comedy of the first water. Miss Clayton is a comedienne of unusual talent. She has a way about her that is peculiarly her own, a manner that instantaneously endears her to her audience."[431]

Yet Una was more than an actress. Known as the Mary Roberts Rinehart of vaudeville sketch writers, she wrote many of the pieces in which she

Figure 1.40. Una Clayton was a strikingly beautiful woman, a fact frequently mentioned in reviews. American Vaudeville Archive.

UNA CLAYTON.

appeared, notably *The Little Detective, A Little Child Shall Lead Them,* and *Keep Smilin.'* In 1911 she was reputed to have written nearly forty playlets during the previous five years, and at that time twenty-six of them were in production.[432] By 1919, that figure had risen to sixty-five produced shows. In 1942 the number was reportedly 150 separate acts.[433]

In addition to writing playlets and vaudeville sketches for herself, Una composed material for others to use in their productions:

> For three seasons she headed her own organization in Montreal, and it was while there that she first took up literary work. Lew Dockstader had been seeking a comic song for his minstrel show but was unable to get just what he wanted. Miss Clayton hearing of the comedian's predicament wrote a song and submitted it to Dockstader. It was accepted and it proved one of the most popular songs the famous minstrel ever had. Since then Miss Clayton has written at least twenty songs, but has never had one published. All her songs are purchased outright by professionals

for their exclusive use. Shortly after taking up song writing Miss Clayton was commissioned to supply the book and lyrics for a musical burlesque to be produced in vaudeville. Her later work includes "A Corner in Hair," "Settled out of Court," "Miss O'Leary, Detective," "Handcuffed," "Wanted, a Kiss," and "His Local Color."[434]

The grit, determination, and courage Una displayed in her quest for theatrical success was reflected in other ways as well. One day while she and Morey were attempting to reach a train station in Montreal they hired a sleigh to take them there. Suddenly the driver collapsed and would have fallen out had not Morey grabbed him. In the process the horse became frightened and ran away. While Morey struggled to keep the driver in the sleigh, Una reached for the reins and succeeded in stopping the terrified horse: "In the meantime Miss Clayton had cleared the dashboard and was on one of the thills, and in that way succeeded in bringing the horse to a stop. The driver was having an epileptic fit and needed aid at once; so, with Mr. Morey trying to hold him in the sleigh, Miss Clayton drove the horse a mile through the blinding blizzard to the nearest house where she had the man cared for. Then they dashed on to the depot, where they found the train waiting and made the rest of the journey in comparative comfort."[435]

On another occasion Una saw a crowd gathered on a sidewalk. As she approached she realized the crowd was watching a dog fight. Rather than stand idly by, as were others, Una took action: " 'I just couldn't bear to see those poor dogs fighting so madly and so I interceded.' Thus spoke that graceful little actress Una Clayton as she disappeared into the stage entrance to Keith's theatre after having caused the separation of two bull dogs who were chewing each other's heads in the presence of many people on Lisbon street yesterday afternoon. 'Of course,' continued pretty, petit [*sic*] Una, 'it was not a very pleasant thing for a woman to do, but none of the gentlemen who lined the sidewalks on either side of the street, showed any inclination to stop the dogs from tearing each other into shreds, so I felt it my duty to interfere. After I had broken my umbrella over the dogs, two gentlemen volunteered and pulled the enraged animals apart.' "[436]

She also had no qualms about dealing with unruly theatergoers: " 'If this show is so amusing that you cannot restrain your amusement, please go to the box office and get your money back,' said Miss Una Clayton to a number of people in the audience at Straub's last night. The people to whom she spoke had been disturbing the action of the play and Miss

Clayton promptly called them down and then, as if nothing out of the ordinary had happened, resumed speaking her lines. The call down had the desired effect."[437]

One of Una's most prominent crusades dealt with the dairy industry. Angered by underhanded milk distributors who were selling "impure" milk to poor women for their babies, Una wrote and starred in *Milk,* a one-act play designed to call attention to the problem: "Miss Clayton, who wrote the sketch, appeared in the role of a little mother of the slums who aids a newspaper man to expose the manner in which a big milk dealer is selling impure milk for the use of babies."[438] Una's effort to expose the milk industry's negligence "has resulted in the proper grading of milk so that the quality of the milk may be known to the mothers, which grading is now in operation in Buffalo through the action of the local health department . . . 'Milk' is described as a playlet presenting Miss Clayton as 'Dooley,' the little East Side 'mudder,' who tackles the Milk Trust and compels its head to furnish milk fit for babies and safe for them also."[439]

While Frank Morey continued to perform with Una for many years, he eventually found other interests, such as the Vaudeville Comedy Club in New York City. Replacing him was a young man named Herbert Lauris Griffin. Born in New York City to John William Griffin (September 23, 1860–March 4, 1934) and Hannah Engelsheim (June 1862–May 14, 1946) on April 6, 1887, Herbert was a star high school athlete in New Jersey.[440]

Griffin was Una's leading man in *Milk,* and their professional relationship grew into something stronger. On February 19, 1915, the couple married at the Press Club in Chicago.[441] Just as with other circumstances related to Una, however, this marriage had something mysterious about it, evidenced by the fact that on May 29, 1917, she married Griffin for a second time, again in Cook County, Illinois.[442]

As Una herself admitted, the advent of the motion picture spelled doom for vaudeville, although she and Herbert continued to entertain in New Jersey during the early 1920s.[443] By 1928 they were living in Wanaque, Passaic, New Jersey, and he was working as an inspector for the local waterworks commission, a position formerly held by his father. When the 1930 census was taken, Una claimed to be an "authoress," but in 1940 she listed no occupation at all.

She was not idle by any means. She joined Little Falls Chapter No. 224 Order of the Eastern Star.[444] Una's name was often mentioned in local newspapers as assisting with chapter affairs, including the celebration of the group's fourth anniversary.[445] She also was involved with the Wanaque

Woman's Club, and in 1943 her play *Our Servant Problem* was staged to raise money for Christmas presents.[446] She attended the Christian Science Church in Wanaque.

Herbert L. Griffin suffered a fatal heart attack while at work on November 17, 1949, and was buried with his parents in Arlington Memorial Park in Kearney, New Jersey.[447]

Una was enumerated in Wanaque in 1950 but, if her obituary is correct, she moved to Cooperstown, New York, in 1963. Her brother, Raymond, was living in the area and she probably wanted to be near him in her last years. She died "following a long illness" on April 3, 1968, only six days away from her ninety-third birthday. Her body was cremated.[448]

Una Clayton Griffin's ashes were buried in Fly Creek Valley Cemetery. Her brother, Raymond, and his third wife, Marion L. Becker, are also buried there. Una's son, John Glendon Halsey, died in the New Jersey State Hospital, Parsippany, New Jersey on April 18, 1968, two weeks after his mother died. According to his death certificate, his body was cremated at Waterville, New York Crematory. What happened to his ashes is unknown.

The Sisters Taylor: Isabel, Grace, Harriette, and Jane

Each of these daughters of Oswego County carved out for herself a career rivaling that of any contemporary male. They are especially noteworthy on account of their participation in the struggle for women's suffrage.

Hiram "Harry" Taylor (1828–August 11, 1898) and Adelia "Delia" Cezarine Fish (June 4, 1834–March 29, 1916) were married in Williamstown, New York, on July 16, 1857.[449] A year later their only son, Willard Hiram (1858–February 2, 1866), was born.[450] Following him came five daughters, four of whom are the focus of this biography: Isabel (May 20, 1862–March 20, 1935); Grace Taft (October 9, 1866–February 6, 1949); Helen Fish (1869–July 29, 1924); Harriette Newton (February 1870–December 12, 1931); and Jane Bliss (December 1, 1878–October 11, 1955). With the exception of Jane all were born in Williamstown (figure 1.41).[451]

On their mother's side of the family, the Taylor girls could trace their lineage to two Revolutionary War veterans, Moses Fish (1759–1836), born in Groton, Connecticut, and Stephen Taft (1710–1803), born in Uxbridge, Massachusetts. They were distant cousins of President William Howard Taft (figure 1.42).

From extant letters it appears that Hiram and Delia were a loving, happy couple. Delia disliked the fact that Hiram, a traveling jewelry and

Figure 1.41. The Taylor family included five very talented daughters. Courtesy Sarah Pullar Gagne.

Figure 1.42. Adelia Cezarine Fish Taylor was committed to the cause of women's suffrage and encouraged her daughters to become involved. Courtesy Sarah Pullar Gagne.

notions peddler, was absent from home so frequently.[452] In 1878, shortly before Jane was born, the family moved to Oswego City, where Hiram opened a store in Room 50 of the Doolittle House, selling watches, rings, and other luxury items.

Delia, once referred to as the "dean of the suffragists" in Oswego City, was evidently a very accomplished woman who had high hopes for her daughters.[453] All received excellent educations and achieved success in their chosen careers.

Isabel Taylor's life between finishing high school and graduating from medical school is, as Gagne points out, shrouded in mystery. Why she decided to become a doctor is unknown, given the prevalent prejudice against female practitioners. Nevertheless in 1889 she graduated with a degree in general medicine from the Women's Medical College of Northwestern University in Chicago, Illinois. She next held an internship at Rush Hospital, also in Chicago, and subsequently opened a practice there.[454]

On May 21, 1894, Isabel, who later spelled her name Isabelle, married Newton Macmillan (1860–December 7, 1920). Allegedly to save the family the expense of a wedding, the couple eloped to Kenosha, Wisconsin.[455] At the time Macmillan was employed by the *Chicago Times and Express*.

Hiram Taylor's health was deteriorating rapidly in 1895. Reportedly he was suffering from heart disease which caused his death on August 11, 1898.[456] Isabel returned to Oswego to help her mother care for him. Newton, who was working in New York City at the time, joined her later and was hired as an editor for the *Oswego Daily Times* in January 1898.[457] The couple remained in Oswego until 1904, when Newton was offered an editorial position with the *New York Herald* in New York City. He retired in 1910 due to alleged health-related issues and died on December 7, 1920.[458]

Isabel's public life in Chicago was extensive, as shown by this article: "Dr. Taylor graduated with honor from the Woman's Medical College of Chicago four years ago and when that institution was merged into the Northwestern university, she received an appointment in its faculty to the chair of Dermatology. She has identified herself with charitable and reform work. She is the physician at the Erring Woman's Home and the Waif's Mission, and is also engaged in many other charitable works."[459]

In Oswego Isabel found more outlets for her ambition. According to a letter Delia wrote, "Isabelle has a busy time, is getting into good practice, and is bright and almost herself again."[460] She became friends with local female doctors, such as Elvira Rainier, and served on the school inspection team organized by her and other members of the Woman's Outlook Club in 1898.[461] In 1903 she delivered a talk to the group on American Portrait Painters.[462] She took an active role in the suffrage movement in Oswego County along with her mother and sisters.[463] On June 17, 1904, Fort Oswego Chapter of the Daughters of the American Revolution (DAR) was constituted, and Delia, Isabel, Grace, and Jane were among the twenty-four charter members.[464]

After Isabel and Newton moved to New York City, she became affiliated with the New York City Infirmary for Women and Children, serving as the head of its gynecological clinic. She was a member of the American Medical Association, New York Academy of Medicine, and Medical Society of New York County. At one time she was the secretary of the Women's Medical Association. She also served on many of the county society's public health education committees.[465] She was a member of the New York City Federation of Women's Clubs.[466]

Isabel suffered a heart attack on March 25, 1935, and died in New York Hospital the following day. Her body was cremated "as the Doctor believed in this method of disposition, and her sisters now residing in New York expect to bring the ashes to Oswego in the late spring or early summer for interment in the family plot in Riverside cemetery. Cremation took place at Fresh Pond Crematory, Middle Village, L. I."[467]

Gagne recalls that her father was very fond of Aunt Isabel, who was "someone who understood everyone's problems, and who would listen. He thought a great deal of her."[468] His recollections of Aunt Grace were different: "My father remembered Grace as quiet and somewhat distant, a person he didn't know well."[469] His perceptions of her accurately reflect the difficulties encountered when attempting to research her life and career for this book (figure 1.43).

Grace Taft Taylor was named for her maternal grandmother, Mercy Taft Fish (1794–1878). Born on October 9, 1866, she was considered a replacement for Willie, who had died in February. She attended the public schools in Oswego City and graduated from Oswego High School in January 1883. She was one of the speakers at the ceremony, choosing for her topic "The Progressive Woman of Today":

> The essayist began by referring to the time when women had no legal rights, when they were sold or exchanged in the matrimonial market. Time, she said, has, and is changing the condition of women. Intellect reigns, and knows no sex. Agriculture for man through labor saving machinery has become comparatively easy.

Figure 1.43. Grace Taylor was a public school teacher for fifty years. Courtesy Sarah Pullar Gagne.

So with woman; machinery takes the place of hand labor and the women are turning their attention in other directions. They are now found in the universities preparing to become doctors, editors, professors, and in these positions they have proven themselves almost if not equal to the men. Another decade, said the young lady, will see her their political equals. And she will be none the less womanly. Is Queen Victoria any less a woman, she asked, because she wields a political scepter over Great Britain? Was Florence Nightingale any less a woman because of her donning the garb of a nurse and going to the relief of the soldiers on the battle field? . . . This matter of women's progress, she continued, is being earnestly carried forward in England, France, Italy and Germany. Women will become victorious in the future and fitted for the stormy days ahead.[470]

At the age of seventeen, Grace was already exhibiting her belief that women should be allowed to vote. It was a position she would defend until the Nineteenth Amendment became law.

Grace continued her education at Oswego Normal School, graduating in the elementary program in June 1885.[471] She was a member of the Adelphi Society, which once presented a program of speeches and readings dealing with Spain. Grace's topic was Queen Isabella. Her sister Harriette, also a member of this club, read a selection from Cervantes's *Don Quixote*.[472]

The earliest confirmed date of Grace's employment in the public schools was February 1888, when she was hired to fill a vacancy in Primary School No. 7.[473] She later taught at Senior School No. 6. That Grace was attached to her students is shown by the fact that she annually held a reception for graduates. And while her nephew Robert Pullar, Jr. might have perceived her as quiet and distant, she could be provoked to anger, as evidenced by the case of Verna Murdoch, a student at School No. 6 whom Grace allegedly slapped across the face. William Murdoch, the girl's father, complained to the board of education that Grace had violated state law and local rules prohibiting corporal punishment. After a hearing at which many witnesses testified, the commissioners suspended her for thirty days.[474]

The writing ability Grace demonstrated with her high school graduation essay can also be seen in a speech she delivered to the Oswego Teachers' Association. Inspired perhaps by the fact that her sister Isabel was practicing medicine in Chicago during the Columbian Exposition, Grace titled her speech "The Columbian Exposition in Its Relation to Education." The excerpt given here represents only a fraction of the text:

> The erection of this dream city, appearing as a wondrous vision to charm us for a moment, as it were, and then to vanish forever, is a proof of the quick adaptation of the thought to the action, the word to the deed that characterizes the genius of the American nation, a genius which knows no limit, a genius teeming with promptitude and restless with the desire to utilize the best gifts of the Creator to sculpture the precious material of His bounty into a pure and harmonious monument. "The Columbian exposition," says an enthusiastic writer, "is the concentrated expression of the glory of the earth." Such words fitly express the thoughts of one, who, for the first time approaches the White City, sailing to it over the sparkling waters of Lake Michigan. An ideal vision, moonlight and music and marvel! That is what lingers in the memory after the evening on the lagoon, when electric launch and gondola glided over its waters, side-illumined by thousands of incandescent lights and the white beams of the arc lights shed their pure and softening influence over all.[475]

Grace had many interests, foremost of which was her dedication to the suffrage movement. She was heavily involved in the formation and activities of the Oswego County Political Equality Club. In 1894, when suffragists were celebrating the fiftieth anniversary of the Seneca Falls Convention, Grace was the organization's corresponding secretary.[476]

Her membership in Fort Oswego Chapter DAR provided both social and intellectual stimulation. As the chapter's longtime secretary, she took a leading role in the project to place a marker on the site of Old Fort George and to develop Montcalm Park. In 1917 she was elected the chapter's registrar.

Chautauqua programs offered more intellectual opportunities. In 1917, for example, Grace was secretary-treasurer of the committee established to plan a week's worth of events in August.[477]

Grace's awareness of civic responsibility was evident in other ways. She was a member of the Woman's Auxiliary of the Society for the Prevention of Cruelty to Children, serving as treasurer numerous times.[478] She belonged to the Humane Society in Oswego City and served on its board of directors.[479] Like her sister Isabel, she was a member of the Woman's Outlook Club whose goal was to improve conditions in Oswego City.[480]

An active member of the Oswego High School Alumni Association, she attended reunions faithfully. She was also involved in the Normal School's Alumni Association. In 1894, for example, she was one of the presenters of the necrology report at the annual reunion.[481]

Grace's life changed dramatically in 1911, when she petitioned the board of education for a leave of absence. Originally granted for one year, it was extended into two. Her reason for the request was that she wished to teach "manual training" in a private school located in New York City. To prepare for this new job, she reportedly had taken a special course at Columbia University's summer school.[482] No other information about this move has been located. Gagne reports that Grace received a bachelor's degree from Columbia University's Teacher's College in 1913. Is it possible that she had simply concocted the story about teaching "manual training" to hide her real purpose for requesting a leave of absence?[483]

When Grace returned to Oswego two years later, she requested to be reinstated in School No. 6. The board instead assigned her to School No. 7, where she remained until ending her career in Oswego.[484]

In January 1918 Grace resigned her position to become the principal of a school in Cold Spring Harbor, New York.[485]

That she actually took the position is borne out by the fact that several months later an article about her "war garden" appeared in the local newspaper. The article revealed that the photogravure section of the *New York Sunday Times* on May 26 had featured a picture of her standing in the garden: "Many Oswego friends will be interested in knowing that the principal of the school, who is shown in the center of the picture, is Miss Grace Taylor, formerly of this city, and for several years a teacher in the public schools of this city. Miss Taylor has taken great pains to develop the spirit of patriotism among the students in her school. She feels this practical work in the war gardens gives children an understanding of food productions and conservation as urged by President Wilson at this time."[486]

By 1920 Grace was living and working in Saranac Lake, Franklin County, where she remained until she retired in 1932.[487] In 1940 she and Jane were living in New York City with Isabel, and both claimed they had resided at the same address on April 1, 1935.

Grace died on February 6, 1949, in New York City. Her death was widely reported, and special attention was paid to her participation in the campaign to win female suffrage.

> Miss Grace Taft Taylor, 82, a leader in the drive for woman suffrage in New York State, died here [New York City] yesterday. Miss Taylor took part in the organization of the first Political and Equality Club [*sic*] in Oswego, N. Y. Miss Taylor was suffrage editor of the women's special edition of the Oswego Daily Times when William B. Alexander was the editor and circulated a petition calling on the New York State Constitutional Convention to give women the vote. She retired in 1932 after teaching in public and private schools in New York State for 50 years.[488]

Her body was cremated at Fresh Pond Crematory, Middle Village, Long Island, and the ashes transported to Oswego for burial in the family plot in Riverside Cemetery.

If Isabel was understanding and Grace was distant, Harriet Newton Taylor was driven. Born in Williamstown on January 4, 1870, she spent her girlhood in the home at 30 East Oneida Street. She attended the public schools and graduated from Oswego High School on January 28, 1886. Her graduation essay was well-received: "Then came Hattie Taylor's essay 'How the Leaves Unfold,' which was indeed perfect, her enunciation being clear and self possession complete, making it one of the best parts of the evening."[489] She graduated from Oswego Normal School in the Elementary Program in June 1888.[490]

Harriette began her teaching career in Chicago's elementary schools in 1889, reportedly spending four years in Hegewisch Elementary School and twelve in Forestville School.[491] By 1895 she had obtained a principal's certificate and was eligible for such a position.[492] In 1905 the board of education put her in charge of Joseph Warren Elementary School. People were surprised by her selection because earlier that year she had been elected president of the Chicago Teachers' Federation and as such was ineligible to be a school administrator. Harriette decided to resign her office rather than turn down an opportunity for professional advancement.[493] She was successively transferred to West Pullman School, Scanlon School, and finally Gompers School.

In 1923 Scanlon School was involved in an experiment known as the platoon system. Harriette made significant changes in scheduling and room usage, instituting a new policy that made use of the entire physical plant. Before this experiment began, students were on half-day schedules, something Harriette deemed irresponsible and dangerous to their welfare. Scanlon School housed 1,935 students with fifty-three teachers. The building, which contained only thirty-six classrooms, had to accommodate forty-two classes. After she reorganized the scheduling pattern, half-day sessions were no longer necessary and every room in the building was used to its utmost.[494]

Harriette also instituted policies geared toward improving her students' physical health. She brought in doctors who gave physical examinations and performed dental work. Surgeons carried out tonsillectomies gratis. When the students were examined, it was discovered that 346 girls and 184 boys had goiters in one stage or another. These children were treated with iodine, and others received preventive medicine. Eighty-five heart-related cases were discovered. Harriette made low-cost toothbrushes available to the students and even sent home recipes for summer diets.

Her attempts to assist her pupils helped to bring the school and the community closer together. She summarized her efforts thus: "We have begun a superb piece of work which we hope will be continued for the health-happiness of the child everywhere."[495]

In an effort to encourage children not only to read but to read good literature, Harriette and Margaret Free authored a series of six primers known as "reading-literature readers." Each volume used language geared to the intellectual development of the reader. For example, *The Primer* (1910) focused on simple stories such as the Little Red Hen and Chicken Little. The *Second Reader* (1912) included retellings of *Aesop's Fables,* Mother Goose poems, and James Barrie's *Peter Pan.* The language in the *Sixth Reader* (1914) was quite sophisticated, and the material included Jason and the Golden

Fleece, Odysseus's wanderings, and poems by Henry Wadsworth Longfellow, James Greenleaf Whittier, Alfred Lord Tennyson, and Lewis Carroll.[496]

Harriette was a frequent speaker at education conferences. In January 1900 she addressed the Illinois Teachers' Association on students' "construction work," what might today be called shop projects. In doing so she repeated Edward Austin Sheldon's philosophy that children learn by doing. Some of the "poorest" efforts might actually be those students' best and for that reason should be praised. As for the teacher's role, she wrote, "And since the highest and only motive of the teacher should be to help the child to the highest development of himself, that teacher should be herself high-minded, self-controlled, loving and lovable. She should make herself the most cultured woman possible. Culture is head education plus heart education."[497]

Early on Harriette involved herself in Illinois' struggle for female suffrage, becoming associated with the Chicago Political Equality League. An eloquent speaker, she was unafraid to voice her opposition to male-dominated governments and exhorted women to become involved in politics: "The sorry work of one-sided, man-ruled governments appeals to the country for women to make things perfect," she stated at a meeting of the Chicago Political Equality Club in April 1910. In a speech dubbed "Woman Suffrage and the White Slave," she proceeded to lay out eleven rules "for the cures of existing evils." She argued for establishing one standard for men and women; rearing children carefully; and making legislation effective and enforcement rigid. She urged her listeners to "live quietly, think rightly, love truly, and remember that woman's vote tends to all these ideals."[498]

Harriette went so far as to attack that all-male bastion of the American judicial system, the US Supreme Court, referring to the justices as "nine elderly gentlemen of antiquated ideas": "I would have the Supreme Courts of the Nation abolished as being courts of law, and not of justice," she said, continuing, "I believe that there should be no Supreme Court of Illinois, or of the United States. They are courts of law not justice. . . . As it is, under our present machinery, it is almost impossible to carry a law through the legislature, through Congress and then secure its constitutionality from the Supreme Court. It is a miracle when that happens." The reporter covering her speech added: "The old crowd could stand it no longer. This was revolutionary! If her plans were carried out none of the moss-covered judges that now decorate the bench of the country could be sure of his job." According to the reporter an assistant city attorney named Roman G. Lewis, who was seated in the audience, jumped to his feet, declaring that Harriette's ideas were incorrect and challenging her to prove by one example that the Supreme Court was more concerned with law than justice. He was squelched when attorney Mary E. Miller rose and responded, "Well, there's the Dred Scott decision in the U. S. Supreme Court . . . and also the case of Ritchie vs. the People in the Illinois Supreme Court. The former declared a human being was property the same as cattle, and the latter declared a woman could not practice law because of an ancient English precedent."[499]

In 1913 Harriette was elected Equality Club president.[500] She advocated public speaking classes for women so they would appear more confident and more knowledgeable when called upon to address large gatherings. According to Harriette, "[O]ratory consisted in knowing what to say, saying it, and then 'sitting down' . . . the men don't know when to quit."[501] She urged women to avoid being identified with a political party, arguing that their most effective means of promoting change was to remain neutral. Their focus should be on legislation and reforms primarily affecting women and children. Years of protests, speeches, and education finally paid off when in 1913 the Illinois State Legislature granted women the right to vote.

A highlight of Harriette's first term as president was the visit to Chicago of the British suffragist Emily Pankhurst, who was scheduled to speak at Auditorium Theatre. Harriette was one of the women who met Mrs. Pankhurst at the train station (figure 1.44). There was controversy as to

Figure 1.44. Harriette Taylor Treadwell was one of the official greeters when suffragist Emily Pankhurst visited Chicago. *Chicago Tribune.*

who should have the honor of introducing the English suffragist when she spoke that evening and finally it was agreed that Harriette should introduce Mr. Barratt O'Hara, the lieutenant governor, who then would introduce Mrs. Pankhurst.[502]

Harriette's advocacy for female participation in government did not end with the passage of the Suffrage Bill in Illinois. She and others held women's legislative congresses in which the participants developed bills and discussed them in open forum. She addressed the delegates at a Congress for Illinois Women, saying she expected many of them to "sit in the legislature of Illinois and help the men determine the laws that are best for both men and women." She said female participation would help improve things in Illinois "using good old common sense and justice." According to Harriette, "The men have made a terrible mess of things."[503]

Yet even Harriette could be accused of party politics and "bossism." During her second term as president of the Women's Equality Club she aroused the ire of fellow club members by using "high-handed" tactics to appoint seventy-two delegates to the upcoming Illinois Equal Suffrage Convention. She was accused of "playing partisan politics in the interests of Mrs. Grace Wilbur Trout, candidate for re-election as president of the state association."[504]

In 1920 the Illinois Equal Suffrage Association was disbanded and a new group, the Illinois League of Women Voters, was born. Harriette was one of the celebrants at a farewell banquet held in the Congress Hotel in Chicago. Given the honor of prophesying what the United States might become since women had finally gained the right to vote with the passage of the Nineteenth Amendment, Harriette said that her dream for the future "included children in school until 18 years old, pensions for mothers, elimination of contagious diseases, and a minimum wage."[505]

Harriette's private life was focused on Charles Humphrey Treadwell, Jr., her husband, and Charles, her adopted son. Charles Treadwell, Jr., her future husband, graduated from Syracuse University in June 1895 with a bachelor of science degree. He and Harriette were married on July 3, 1897, in Oswego.[506] After the couple spent their honeymoon in Grand View Park, Thousand Islands, New York, Treadwell's parents hosted a large reception for them at their home. Some three hundred guests attended.[507] Treadwell was still under contract as a mathematics instructor with Syracuse University, and conventional wisdom would suggest that Harriette resign from her position and remain with him. That did not occur: "She was married in 1897 to Dr. Charles Treadwell, but did not give up her professional work."[508] After finishing his contract at Syracuse University, Treadwell moved to Chicago and found work teaching science and electricity at John Marshall High School. In 1905 he received a degree from Harvey Medical School but did not practice full time. According to an obituary, he used his medical training to treat the poor "accepting no remuneration for his services."[509] A year before his death from diabetes he transferred to Hyde Park School.

Harriette and Charles had no children, but on April 18, 1908, they adopted five-year-old Charles Smith. The boy had had a rough start in life. His mother died when he was born and his father abandoned him. He had spent much of his short life in the Chicago Orphanage.[510]

Harriette remained active for many years after her husband's death. She had finally obtained her bachelor's degree in 1907. She was prominent in the Chicago Woman's Club. In 1920 she traveled to Europe for a lengthy vacation. She served as president of the Chicago League of Women Voters and as president of the Illinois Woman's Legislative Congress.[511] Shortly before her death she was named the principal of Gompers School.

In December 1931 Harriette and her son Charles drove to Indiana to visit relatives. On the way home she suffered a massive heart attack near Hammond, Indiana. By the time medical assistance became available, she was dead.[512] According to her wishes, friends were invited to say nice things about her at the funeral but they were forbidden to shed tears.[513] Her body was cremated and transported to Oswego (figure 1.45).

In the weeks following her death, associates found ways to pay tribute to Harriette's life and career. The Chicago Woman's Club held a memorial service at Abraham Lincoln Center.[514] Friends and colleagues gathered to mourn their loss a week later, but again, no tears were permitted.[515] Two years later students at Gompers School purchased a tree and memorial hedge for their "widely known and loved" principal.[516]

The youngest child in the Taylor household was Jane Bliss, born on December 1, 1878, shortly after the family had moved to Oswego City. She attended the public schools, graduating in June 1896.[517] Jane was an actress and as part of the graduation exercises she played Sybil Amberly in the class production of *My Lord in Livery* (figure 1.46).

Long before this date, however, Jane was involved with theatrics. In 1891 she was a member of a group performing a benefit for the Stebbins Kindergarten. She read "The Marriage of the Flowers."[518] She played Constance Warburton in *Won at Last* at the Richardson Theatre in Oswego on August 23, 1895.[519]

Figure 1.45. Harriette and Charles Treadwell are buried in the Treadwell family plot in Riverside Cemetery, Scriba, New York. Author's collection.

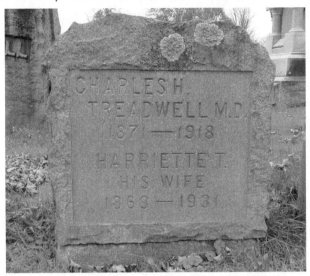

Figure 1.46. Jane Bliss Taylor was associated with amateur theatrics during her teen years in Oswego. Oswego County Historical Society.

After spending a winter studying the theater in Chicago in 1897, Jane returned to Oswego to play Mrs. Featherstone in Sidney Grundy's *The Snow Ball* at the Richardson Theatre for the benefit of the Women's Auxiliary of the Humane Society. Her development as an actress was lauded in a flowery review:

> Those who failed to see Miss Taylor in the former occasion may be surprised to find how startling has been the fulfillment of the poise of beauty and talent held out by her earlier public appearances even so lately as a year ago. At her earliest appearances in public Miss Taylor's work displayed the witchery of talent joined to youthful beauty. Both have ripened under a year of careful training. Those who were present on the occasion of her latest appearance at Richardson's a few weeks ago found a young woman of tall and graceful figure, a face at once striking and beautiful, finely poised, and under complete control, yet still charmingly touched by the naivete of youth. But Miss Taylor is one of those fortunate young women whose personal beauty and gracefulness of figure invest everything she does with interest and make even her presence on the stage seem like a personal favor to the audience.[520]

The writer hinted that Jane might turn professional, then added, "But it is understood that Miss Taylor has not yet concluded to enter upon a professional career, but will, for the present at least, exercise her gifts only before home audiences."

Even after she became a professional actress, Jane continued to do benefits in Oswego. She volunteered to perform at the Richardson in September 1900 to assist the victims of the destructive Galveston hurricane.[521] In August 1902 she directed and took a leading role in *Hummingtop's Dilemma* at the Richardson to benefit the Home for the Homeless: "A number of people prominent in Oswego society are in the cast, as is Miss Jane Taylor, who is well known in theatrical circles, having been with 'Arizona' and other professional companies."[522] The following year she returned to direct *Kettle of Fish* at the Richardson, again to benefit the Home for the Homeless: "Miss Jane Taylor, who managed and directed the staging of the piece and drilled the choruses in the curtain raiser, deserves the highest praise, for to her much of the credit of the great success is due."[523]

Jane made her professional debut at the Metropolitan Theatre in New York City in June 1898 in *East Lynne*: "Miss Taylor was cast in the important role of Barbara Hare and, to judge from the comments of the New York press, made an instant success. Her intelligence, charming stage presence and personal beauty were remarked in New York as they have often been here, insomuch that the young amateur fairly divided the honors with the seasoned star."[524]

Jane later appeared as Estrella in *Arizona* in 1900 and was described as a "nut-brown beauty, tall, slender and graceful."[525] She performed in that play at the Richardson Theatre later in the year: "Oswego theatre goers will be pleased to learn that Jane Taylor, the well-known actress, will appear here in *Arizona*. Miss Taylor is a resident of this city and it is expected that an immense crowd will be present."[526] She returned to the Richardson in *Hoch the Consul* in 1902.[527]

From letters written by family members it is evident that mother and sisters were both proud and worried about Jane's choice of career. Delia wrote to Isabel and Grace, "If Jane represents a duchess, I hope she will act every whit the character of a royal good one. Every friend and neighbor have high hopes of her success in the line she has taken up."[528] Helen had mixed feelings: "I noted well what you wrote me about Jane. . . . I do hope Jane will not return to the stage. If Jane can be persuaded to leave the stage it would be well. It's a dog's existence, at the mercy of unscrupulous men, and I fear she will never rank first class. I'm awfully sorry I ever helped her on, but it seemed 'the leading of providence'—will pray she may come safely out of it."[529] The letters mention places Jane performed: Utica, Pawtucket, Worcester, Chicago, Binghamton, and San Francisco.[530]

Like Lottie Blair Parker, however, Jane was well aware of the fate of aging actresses and determined to find another occupation. In 1907, with the assistance of Helen, she took a teaching position at an unnamed school. In 1910 she was listed as a teacher in District 10 of Putnam County.[531] She subsequently taught at the Kelwin School in New York City, Friend's School in Brooklyn, and the Short Hills High School in New Jersey.[532]

Obviously dissatisfied with teaching at the high school level, Jane enrolled in the School of Education at Columbia Teachers College in 1916, graduating with a bachelor of science degree in 1920. In 1922 she became a faculty member in the English Department of Vassar College.[533]

While employed there, she became one of twenty-five charter members of the Academy of Speech Correction.[534] She ended her tenure at Vassar in June 1926 and took a position at Hunter College in New York City as an instructor of English.

Perhaps on account of her theater training, Jane became interested in speech education. In 1936 she was elected president the New York League for Speech Improvement.[535] In 1940 she participated in the Eastern Public Speaking Conference, organizing a section on speech correction.[536] She made news in 1940, when, as chair of the English Department's committee on recording, she introduced the use of the tape recorder into the classroom so students could hear their own voices.[537] From 1937 to 1946 Jane was the chair of Hunter College's Speech Correction Clinic.[538]

Like her sisters Isabel and Grace, Jane was a member of the DAR. She and Grace operated a small travel agency, acting as tour guides for groups of students.[539] Their nephew, Robert Pullar, Jr. sometimes accompanied them.[540]

Jane was the last Taylor sister. In 1935 she and Isabel were living together at 251 West 97th Street. After Isabel's death, Grace moved into the apartment and the two sisters lived together until Grace's death in 1949. Jane occupied the apartment until her death from cancer on October 11, 1955. So far as can be ascertained, no obituaries were published. Gagne, who did not meet her Aunt Jane until after Grace died, described her as an elderly woman: "Jane was a woman of medium height, and stout, perhaps 200 pounds when I knew her. Her long hair was parted down the middle and drawn tightly back into a low bun, sometimes with a net covering it all. Often she brought a gift of intriguing old jewelry from her apartment: a necklace of blue-patterned art deco glass beads, some lavalieres, a turquoise necklace from Cairo, a ring for my mother."[541] Her reminiscences of Jane include Christmas parties, a trip to see Barnum and Bailey's Circus at Madison Square Garden, and gifts of sheer nylon blouses. Near the end of Jane's life, Gagne spent a night with her since her aunt feared being alone. She remembered looking at the "ancient portraits" hanging on the wall but did not think to ask who they were. According to Gagne, fifty portraits remained on the wall after the apartment was cleaned out following Jane's death.[542]

In the upper portion of Riverside Cemetery can be found the Taylor family plot. A large monument lists many names. All are buried there except Harriette (figure 1.47).

Figure 1.47. The Taylor family plot is located in the upper portion of Riverside Cemetery, Scriba, New York. A large monument lists many names. All are buried there except Harriette. Author's collection.

Those Mott Women: Ruth, Alice, Dorothy, and Bailey

Mention the Mott name to almost anyone familiar with Oswego City history, and Thomas Smith Mott, John Thomas Mott, Elliott Bostick Mott, Elliot Wheeler Mott, and Luther Wight Mott will quickly be identified. Not so swiftly named will be Ruth Woolsey Johnson Mott, Alice Wright Mott Tifft, Dorothy Mott, and Bailey Elizabeth Mott, even though each of these remarkable women contributed to and left a definite mark upon life in Oswego City.

It was one of *the* social events of the season. Ruth Woolsey Johnson was marrying Luther Wright Mott, scion of the well-known and wealthy shipping and banking family. So important was this union that even the *New York Times* announced the occasion (figure 1.48).[543]

Figure 1.48. Ruth Woolsey Johnson's marriage to Luther Wright Mott was considered important enough to be reported in the *New York Times*. Courtesy Nancy Mott Frank.

Ruth (February 8, 1881–January 16, 1971) was the daughter of Edgar Dole Johnson (January 8, 1847–July 24, 1918) and Isabella Graham Cole Johnson (October 19, 1848–May 14, 1930). Johnson was a successful merchant in Oswego, one of the partners of Penfield, Lyon, and Company, who operated the Washington Grain Elevator. He was also a longtime bank trustee.[544]

Luther (November 30, 1874–July 10, 1923) was the son of John Thomas Mott (October 11, 1848–February 22, 1936) and Alice Jane Wright (June 1, 1847–July 1, 1921). Mott was the president of the First National Bank as well as a prominent political figure.[545]

Luther Mott graduated from Harvard, and Ruth attended Vassar. The wedding of these two young people on December 10, 1902, was the beginning of a partnership lasting over twenty years.

Like his father and grandfather before him, Luther worked in the bank, but he was also very interested in local politics. In 1910 he was elected to the US House of Representatives. His popularity was evident in the fact that he was reelected to a seventh term (figure 1.49).

Ruth played the part of a dutiful wife, hosting parties and supporting her husband's legislative career. In time she gave birth to Luther Wright, Jr. (September 7, 1903–October 9, 1970), Alice (August 10, 1905–February 15, 1985), and Dorothy (April 28, 1909–November 24, 2000).

Yet not all her energies were directed toward her husband's career. In 1904 she was the prime organizer of Fort Oswego Chapter Daughters of the American Revolution in Oswego and its first regent. Upon the group's fiftieth anniversary, Ruth gave a long speech detailing how the club was formed and her role in it:

> Sometime before Fort Oswego Chapter Daughters of the American Revolution was formed in 1904, efforts had been made to organize without success. Patriotic women in Syracuse, Pulaski and Mexico had already founded their chapters and there was an increasing interest in forming a chapter in Oswego. My mother-in-law, Mrs. John T. Mott, belonged to Knickerbocker Chapter

Figure 1.49. Luther Wright Mott was elected to the House of Representatives seven times. Library of Congress.

in New York City and both Mrs. Hasbrouck the Regent and Mrs. Donald McLean, a member and the President General of the Daughters of the American Revolution, had urged her to organize a chapter in Oswego because of its historical importance. Mrs. Mott could not be persuaded to accept the responsibility and so the mantle fell on my young shoulders. On June 22, 1904 a meeting was held at my home with 24 women present whose applications for membership had previously been filed, and the chapter was officially organized. Officers were elected, committees were formed and the name "Fort Oswego Chapter" was selected.[546]

One of Ruth's greatest civic contributions was her unflagging support of women's suffrage. In 1913 she was instrumental in forming the Oswego County Suffrage Assembly of which she was elected president.[547] She traveled all over the county to hold meetings for both women and men in an effort to garner support for votes for women.[548] She marched in the infamous Suffragists' Parade on March 3, 1913, in Washington, DC. This event, which had been planned for a year, took place the day before Woodrow Wilson's inauguration. Women of all states and from all social strata took part, only to be met with derision and violence from male onlookers, while the police made few attempts to keep the marchers safe. So angry were ordinary citizens that the suffrage movement gained popularity even among men heretofore either antisuffrage or undecided.[549]

In January 1914 Carrie Chapman Catt appointed Ruth to head the congressional movement in the 32nd District.[550] The following year she was a delegate to the first joint meeting of the suffrage organizations of Onondaga and Oswego Counties and a member of the welcoming party for Catt, the featured speaker.[551] She represented the 32nd District again in 1916 when the various suffrage groups met for an all-day Suffrage Congressional Conference in New York City.[552]

An attempt to pass a state amendment for female suffrage was made in 1915, and Ruth did her utmost to ensure that it would succeed. She outlined her position in an open letter sent to several local newspapers:

> I feel very confident regarding the result of the vote on Amendment No. 1 extending the right to vote to women. The voters of this district have been very enthusiastic in their reception of the women speakers and workers who have tried to bring the

amendment to their attention. Save in the city of Watertown and the village of Cazenovia there seems to be but little organization work opposed to it. But it is necessary that every one in favor of votes for women should remember to vote and work on election day for the passage of the amendment. There are so many propositions to be voted upon that this most important one should not be lost sight of. It is not a party question. . . . The women are merely asking for Justice. I cannot believe that our sturdy Northern New Yorkers wish to deny it to them. For the sake of mothers and daughters, I urge every voter to vote for the woman suffrage amendment—Amendment No. 1 on the ballot, on Election day.[553]

She bought a car dubbed "the Franchise Franklin" and drove throughout Oswego County to speak with local leaders and private citizens about the suffrage amendment.[554] Despite the women's best efforts, however, the measure was defeated 57.49 to 42.51 percent.

The entry of the United States into World War I in on April 6, 1917, temporarily slowed the suffrage campaign. Nevertheless, Ruth encouraged women to become involved in the war effort to demonstrate their patriotism (figure 1.50). Her statement was deemed "a model for patriotic women everywhere and demonstrates that Oswego county has women who have the war spirit of the Revolutionary and Civil War days."

Fifty percent of the work of this war must be done by women. This not merely opinion, but it has been expressed by Secretary Lane and others. Our own Northern New York district is setting such a good example in the way that the men are taking hold of the situation and trying to find the places in which each may best serve the country that I want to have our women do their share and realize what an important part they have to play when the country is in need and stress. It is an old idea that women do not perform military service and now is heard only as a campaign argument, and a discredited one at that, by the anti-suffragists. . . . The women want to help the country in the war, but many of them don't know how. Well, everyone has an opportunity, great or small. The women in official life in Washington or many of them are trying to set an example. We have many of us signed a pledge to use the utmost economy in expenditures for dress and food during the war. When we entertain we are going to do so as simply as possible. We are going to do without meat in our homes for at least one day a week. We are never going to have more than three courses at a meal, no matter how important the affair may be supposed to be. We are not going to use expensive food of any sort. . . . The Red Cross work is a splendid chance for women to have a share of war work. . . . Let the women see that every bit of fertile soil they can use produces food. . . . I am glad to hear that the women [at] home are taking hold of the situation and trying to do their share. Let us work together to the end that we may be as proud of our women as we are of our men who will make such a fine record in the war. And every woman who can must remember that very soon there will be an opportunity for her to help with her purse by taking at least one of the war bonds to be issued. Instead of extravagant dresses and food and entertainments let us all buy bonds if we can and help pay the men on the firing line.[555]

Later in the year Ruth issued another statement lauding the efforts of women across the state:

Figure 1.50. This poster reinforced Ruth Mott's belief that women should become active in the war effort in order to secure male support for women's suffrage. New York State Library.

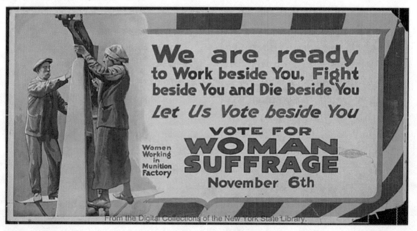

War came early in 1917, just as we were about to open our Statewide campaign and the first thing done by the State Suffrage party was to offer our entire organization to the Governor for whatever service he might see fit in our war against Germany. Since then the women of our party have carried on many big undertakings for the government. Nassau and Westchester county suffragists had entire charge of the census-taking in their counties. In New York city over 11,000 women worked in 400 registration bureaus. In every county the suffragists helped in the census work.[556]

The year 1917 was significant for the movement because the suffrage amendment was again on the ballot in New York State. It was hoped that the willingness of millions of women to volunteer for service would effect a positive reaction from male voters. President Woodrow Wilson added his support. In October he invited several women, including Ruth Mott, to the White House to give them a written endorsement: "Mrs. Luther W. Mott was one of the Woman Suffrage delegation who called upon President Wilson yesterday and to whom he gave his message to be delivered by them to the voters of the State of New York urging them to vote for Woman Suffrage."[557] On November 7, 1917, the amendment finally passed, and New York State became the first eastern state to grant women full voting rights.

Ruth's political career did not end with the passage of the equal suffrage amendment. She was one of five women appointed by the New York State Republican Party in 1918 to organize the reelection campaign of Governor Whitman. The announcement lauded her activism: "Mrs. Luther W. Mott, wife of Representative Mott, has been for several years county suffrage leader in Oswego. She has been active in every division of war work, and has been prominent in every Liberty loan campaign. Mrs. Mott is the treasurer of the Woman's Congressional club, Washington, and is a former regent of the Daughters of the American Revolution."[558]

Ruth used her influence in the female Republican ranks to support Assembly Speaker Thaddeus Sweet in his reelection bid. It was alleged that she had spoken to "hundreds of women" about his candidacy: "She urges every woman in the city and county, who wants to see the interest of the women advanced in the city and county to work and vote for [Sweet and Mr. McGraw] and their associates on the Republican ticket."[559]

When George A. Glynn, chair of the New York State Republican Committee, named her to the Executive Committee for the 1920 election campaign, she and the other women appointees bluntly stated they would not support Senator Wadsworth's candidacy for reelection on account of his antisuffrage stance.[560]

In addition to her political efforts, Ruth used her time in Washington, DC, to advance good causes, among them the Young Women's Christian Association (YWCA). In 1922, for example, she headed a team that led in pledges for a goal of over twenty-five thousand dollars.[561] At one time she was a member of the YWCA Board of Directors in Washington.[562] She was honored in 1921 by being selected a member of the YWCA World Service Council.[563]

As a congressman's wife, Ruth Mott was expected to entertain. The newspapers frequently reported that she had hosted luncheons and receptions for wives of cabinet members, congressmen, and even the vice president's wife.[564] Such events were naturally expensive, but since the Mott family was reputed to be extremely rich, no one had any idea that Luther and Ruth were living beyond their means.

The salary of a member of the House of Representatives was $7,500 per year.[565] An interesting article reinforced the fiction that Luther and Ruth were wealthy people, describing him as a "millionaire banker and former president of the New York Bankers' Association."[566] Maintaining residences in Oswego City and in Washington, DC, must have put a serious drain on the family finances. Their son, Luther Jr., was attending St. Mark's private school in Southboro, Massachusetts. At the time of his father's death, he was at sea on his way to South America.

Luther Mott's congressional career ended abruptly when he died in Oswego on July 10, 1923. He had been ill for a week with something obliquely described as "intestinal troubles." His unexpected demise resulted in many glowing obituaries and resolutions of respect.[567] After his funeral he was buried in the family plot in Riverside Cemetery, Scriba, New York (figure 1.51.).

As upsetting as Mott's death was for his survivors, even more so was the revelation that he had died intestate leaving an estate valued at only five thousand dollars.

> That the late Congressman Luther W. Mott died a poor man was revealed in Surrogate's Court [in Oswego] when letters of administration were issued on his estate to his wife, Ruth W. Mott. The petition gives the value of his estate as $5,000 real and personal of uncertain value. Persons in a position to know

Figure 1.51. Luther Wright Mott is buried in the family plot in Riverside Cemetery, Scriba, New York. Author's collection.

state that Congressman Mott's salary from the government and as cashier of the First National Bank, which is largely owned by his father, Col. John T. Mott, was spent in entertaining which he did in New York and Washington on a large scale. His last social function in Washington was Mrs. Mott's elaborate dinner to Mrs. Calvin Coolidge, then the wife of the vice president.[568]

Ruth quickly emptied the Washington apartment and moved into the family home at 73 West Schuyler Street in Oswego. She applied for letters of administration on Mott's meager estate and probably wondered how she was going to support herself and three children.[569] According to granddaughter Nancy Mott Frank, Ruth was forced to sell most of their stocks. Only retained were the Eastman Kodak holdings.[570]

Almost immediately Ruth's female friends began to agitate to have her named Luther's successor in Congress: "Club women and others in Oswego, N. Y., have started a movement to place Mrs. Ruth W. Mott . . . in nomination for election to the house of representatives."[571] Despite the women's enthusiasm, the Republican "powers that be" had other ideas. It was not so long ago that women could not even vote, and the "good old boy" system was not about to permit this woman, or any woman, to challenge their authority. An editorial published in a downstate newspaper gave voice to the backlash to Ruth's proposed candidacy:

> When a man dies and leaves a widow, or children, unprovided for it becomes the duty of the fellowship of man, as expressed in almost any fraternal order, to lend a helping hand. . . . To those who are privileged to participate in it comes an understanding of the joy of giving, an appreciation of the satisfaction that imparted by the knowledge that even to a small way we have helped to lift another's burdens. That is a fine thing, is it not? But the principle should not be subverted to unworthy uses. It is getting to be more or less the practice of political parties to name as successors of men who died in office some feminine member of their families. In the Congress of the United States women have encumbered offices from which the Grim Reaper for some reason removed their husbands. In the 32nd Congressional District of this State it is now proposed to fill the place made vacant by the death of Representative Luther W. Mott by naming his wife, Mrs. Ruth W. Mott, to fill out the unexpired term. Political sentimentality thinks that it is a fine and lofty compliment to a dead Congressman to throw the mantle of his office over the sorrowing form of his widow. The question of her competency is not considered. Possibly as a Member of Congress she would make a fine fourth at bridge. These discursions are not intended as a reflection upon the lady mentioned, but as a criticism of a nonsensical practice.[572]

In the following weeks it became apparent that former New York State assembly speaker Thaddeus C. Sweet was the party's favored candidate.[573]

At about the same time the news broke that the position of postmaster in Oswego City would become vacant in early 1924. The party leaders, especially Sweet, were willing to offer this office to Ruth as a way to recompense her for not supporting her candidacy and to pay some measure of homage to the memory of her late husband.[574] Ruth accepted the job, was approved by the civil service, appointed by the president, and confirmed by the US Senate.[575]

She became, thereby, the first woman to hold the office of postmaster in Oswego City.[576] As if to mend fences and soothe bruised egos, local politicians paid Ruth a visit on her first day as postmaster: "She wanted to state that the Oswego Post Office would be administered as efficiently and carefully as her best effort would produce" and the "watchword would be service at all times."[577] When she left the position in 1936, she had been reappointed twice.[578]

Ruth was fifty-five when she retired from the post office, not elderly but not young either. She applied for and obtained a position as a dormitory director at Goucher College in Baltimore, Maryland, in 1938, remaining there until 1949, when she retired and returned to Oswego for good, making her home with her daughter, Dorothy.

When Ruth Woolsey Johnson Mott died on January 16, 1971, obituaries paid tribute to her many and varied associations and accomplishments. In addition to her membership and leadership in the DAR and her extensive work for equal suffrage and subsequent activity in the New York State Republican Party, she was a member of the board of trustees for Oswego Hospital; member of the Board of Welfare, City of Oswego; member of the Board of Directors, Oswego County Humane Society; and member of the Oswego County Historical Society. She also belonged to the Oswego Country Club (figure 1.52).[579]

Alice Wright Mott, named for her paternal grandmother, was born on August 10, 1905, the second child and first daughter. Luther was then cashier in his father's bank, and Ruth was involved with the DAR. By the time she was six years old the family was living in Washington, DC. For the next twelve years Alice enjoyed the life of a congressman's child, attending the private Madeira School and socializing with other legislators' children (figure 1.53). Her situation changed dramatically with the death of her father in July 1923, when her widowed mother moved the family back to Oswego and tried to build a new life.

Alice entered Antioch College in Yellow Springs, Ohio, that same year. In 1927 she enrolled in the University of Pittsburg, studying department store administration. She completed that program in June 1928 and then obtained her AB degree from Antioch on June 23, 1928. After graduation she accepted a position at Mechanical Institute in Rochester, New York.[580]

Figure 1.52. Ruth Johnson Mott is buried beside her husband in Riverside Cemetery. Author's collection.

Figure 1.53. Alice Wright Mott spent much of her girlhood in Washington, DC. Courtesy Nancy Mott Frank.

She subsequently lived and worked in retail personnel in Dayton and Cincinnati, Ohio.[581] In 1937–1938 she and a cousin, Carol Emerick, took a four-month trip to Europe, where they reportedly saw the Duke and Duchess of Windsor in Paris and had an audience with the pope.[582] By 1940 Alice had moved back to Oswego and was working as an investigator for the city's Welfare Department.

She occupied that position when the United States entered World War II in December 1941. In January 1942 she was hired by the local Red Cross to be the chapter's executive secretary. Alice had had experience with the Red Cross earlier, working in 1919 in the hospital supply room for the local chapter. She was, therefore, knowledgeable about the organization's aims and goals.[583]

After four weeks of administrative training in Washington, DC, Alice officially took charge on February 23, 1942.[584] For the next year she arranged training classes and organized volunteers in advancement of the war effort, cooperating with county Red Cross chapters. She urged citizens to stockpile basic foodstuffs in case of enemy bombings:

> Aware at last that this business of bombs falling on American cities is more than just a vague possibility, Mr. and Mrs. America are beginning to make plans for home living during emergencies. Paramount in their minds is the food question and how the family can eat if public utilities are shut off and the grocer decides to stay home for a few days. "War pantries" seem to provide the best solution to this potential problem and in stocking up foods, nutritionists advise that strict attention to be paid to the kind that will supply the energy necessary to keep spirits from flagging.[585]

Alice suggested several items for the pantry, including cans of unsweetened milk, canned meat, cheese, and peanut butter.

In the midst of the war effort, Alice got married. Edwin Charles Tifft (June 12, 1904–October 30, 1971) was, like Alice, an investigator for Oswego's Welfare Department and involved with the Red Cross at the beginning of the war. The couple married on May 10, 1942, and at some point thereafter, probably early 1944, Tifft left for overseas duty. He did not return until late 1945: "Edwin C. Tifft, a field director with the American Red Cross during the war, who was stationed for some time in Hawaii and later with the 319th bomber group on Okinawa, has been released from duty and arrived home Wednesday night. He was with the Red Cross for four years."[586] Alice left the Red Cross in March 1943, returning to the city's Public Welfare Department as an investigator. Why she decided to change jobs is unknown but the motivation may have been financial. She had been a paid worker for the Red Cross, although the salary probably could not equal what the city offered. It was not because she performed poorly: "[A]s executive secretary of the Oswego chapter she has been instrumental in organizing the various corps of volunteer workers and bringing the chapter to a full wartime basis."[587]

On September 30, 1944, Alice gave birth to her only child, Edwin Charles, Jr.[588] The arrival of her son, the end of the war, and her husband's return did not mean the end of her community participation (figure 1.54). She was a member of the Women's College Club, which later became the Oswego Branch of the American Association of University Women.[589] She enjoyed playing bridge and was good enough to participate in tournaments.[590] She was an active member of the Woman's City Club.[591] She was a longtime member of the Business and Professional Women's Club. She enjoyed golfing and bowling.[592]

Figure 1.54. Alice and Edwin Charles Tifft were the parents of a son, Edwin Jr. Courtesy Nancy Mott Frank.

Alice participated in the efforts of the local Community Chest.[593] She and Dorothy P. Wells cochaired the residential section of the campaign in 1950. She was appointed to the Community Chest's budget committee in 1951.[594] She also was involved with the Sugar Cane Twig Auxiliary at Oswego Hospital. She served as an officer of the board of managers for the Oswego Children's Home.[595]

Edwin Tifft died on October 30, 1971.[596] Alice lived with her sister Dorothy for the next fourteen years, dying "after a short illness" on February 15, 1985.[597] The couple is buried in Riverside Cemetery, Scriba, New York.

Luther and Ruth's youngest child, Dorothy, was born on April 28, 1909, in Oswego City. The first fourteen years of her life were spent primarily in Washington, DC (figure 1.55). She enrolled in Oswego High School when the family moved back to the city, graduating in June 1927. In the autumn of that year she entered the University of Rochester and was elected president of the girls' section of the freshman class.[598] She spent two years in Rochester and then transferred to Antioch College in Ohio, where she majored in physical education. She obtained a teaching position at Antioch

Figure 1.55. Dorothy Mott was Ruth and Luther's youngest child. Courtesy Nancy Mott Frank.

after graduating in 1933. Two years later she resigned that position and took a job tutoring two daughters of a New York City banker who was going to spend the winter in Budapest, Hungary.[599]

After returning to the United States, Dorothy obtained a teaching position at Goucher College, Baltimore, Maryland. Two years later she took a job at Wheaton College, Newton, Massachusetts, and was there when war was declared in 1941. In 1943 she decided her country needed her, obtained a leave of absence, and enlisted in the Women's Marine Corps. Her initial training was done at Mount Holyoke College.[600] She rose rapidly through the ranks, as she related to a reporter: "They were short of women officers," she laughingly recalled, "so at the end of our officer's training, the three women with highest scores were immediately promoted to first lieutenant."[601] Her military career lasted four years.

> Ordered to Camp LeJeune, N.C., Lieutenant Mott commanded one of the first detachments of lady Marines to arrive at the sprawling base which is the East Coast headquarters for the Corps' amphibious forces. Crusty old salts . . . were not reluctant to tell the ladies of their displeasure at having women in the Corps. In the two and one-half years Miss Mott served at LeJeune, directing training schools for women, her command increased from 20 to 1,500 Marines. She later served the Corps in an administrative center at San Francisco, and when the war ended, left the Corps with the rank of major.[602]

Why did she enlist? Many years later she told a reporter: "I joined because I thought it would be interesting work. I had been teaching physical education. The armed forces had quite a bit of glamour associated with it. No one in my family was in the service and I thought someone should be." (figure 1.56).[603]

After being honorably discharged from the Marine Corps, Dorothy returned to Oswego, where she accepted a full-time position as dean of women at the college.[604] She held that job until 1956, when she became college's first full-time director of admissions. In 1971, when she retired, it was estimated that she had been responsible for sending out sixteen thousand admissions letters (figure 1.57).[605]

Like her mother and sister, Dorothy took a keen interest in Oswego's social and civic life. She joined Fort Oswego Chapter DAR, for which she was elected treasurer in 1990.[606] For several years she acted as chair of the Good Citizen Award Committee.[607]

Figure 1.56. Dorothy Mott enlisted in the Women's Marine Corps because she thought someone in her family should be actively involved with the war effort. Courtesy of Nancy Mott Frank.

Figure 1.57. Dorothy Mott was the first full-time director of admissions at SUNY Oswego. SUNY Oswego Archives and Special Collections.

She was a charter member of Oswego Zonta, founded on June 9, 1955.[608] She served as the group's first vice president and president in 1959–1960.[609]

Dorothy became a member of the Oswego County Historical Society, an organization her father joined on January 2, 1897, number thirty-nine on the roster. Her grandfather, John T. Mott, and her great uncle, Elliott Bostick Mott, were both charter members, joining the group as numbers sixteen and seventeen on July 10, 1896. Dorothy was very involved with the society: "She was president of the Oswego County Historical Society during 1966–1967 and has continued to serve as a Vice President. Her tenure was marked by a number of improvements to Headquarters House, including the restoration of furnishings, papering and wiring and by substantial additions to the Society's collections."[610]

Dorothy's volunteerism was wide-ranging. She worked with the Salvation Army as a member and chair of the Young People's Committee.[611] She was a member and president of Oswego Branch, American Association of University Women.[612]

Dorothy Mott made church history in 1962. She had long been active in Christ Episcopal Church, serving on the Altar Guild and Woman's Auxiliary Guild. Her election as vestrywoman made news since it was the first time in the church's 140-year history that a woman had been permitted to hold that position.[613]

Dorothy Mott's greatest challenge—and her greatest achievement—centered on her efforts to bring low-cost public housing to Oswego City. In 1952 she, Marion Mackin, and Ruth Sayers were sworn in as members of a reactivated Housing Authority. Dorothy became head of the group.[614] The goal was to construct state-approved housing for Oswego's low-income residents and in time a determination was made to build 116 units on Oswego's east side, subsequently known as Hamilton Homes. Planning and organizing such a complex was difficult and complicated, to say nothing of frustrating and potentially dangerous. Dorothy received harassing and threatening telephone calls. Local landlords, envisioning a significant loss of revenue, were adamant in their opposition to the plan. Mayor Frank L. Gould refused to sign various construction contracts in early 1953, reportedly because of "the large number of persons opposing the project." His failure to act set up a confrontation with the authority. In May 1953 he suddenly suspended Dorothy and Marion Mackin for "improper conduct in office and fraud" solely on the basis of a complaint by George D. Foot.[615]

A month later Justice William J. McCluskey dismissed the case "as absurd," holding that Gould should not have suspended the women merely on the complaint of a private citizen. He ordered Mott and Mackin reinstated.[616] Not one to surrender easily, Mayor Gould took his case to the appellate division, asking for a stay in the women's reinstatement. After hearing the case, Supreme Court justice Henry J. Kimball denied the motion, alluding to McCluskey's argument that Foot's complaint was insufficient to merit Mott and Mackin's suspension.[617] The project went forward, and in 1956 the complex of seventeen buildings containing 116 units was dedicated.[618]

Several years later the city recognized a need for senior housing, and Dorothy Mott was appointed to and served as president of the Community Development Corporation, which was the guiding force behind the construction of a high-rise building known as Simeon DeWitt Apartments.[619]

Mott retired from the Oswego Housing Authority in 1976. Mayor John FitzGibbons lauded her devotion to the cause of public housing:

> The Hamilton Homes project has received praise from all quarters since its construction, and, in fact, has served as a model public housing project for other communities. The success of this project can be directly attributed to the tireless efforts of individuals such as Dorothy Mott, who have generously contributed their time and energies to making Hamilton Homes an asset to our community. We will sorely miss Dorothy on the Authority and we wish her a very satisfying and productive retirement.[620]

After a life spanning two world wars, the Equal Suffrage struggle, the Great Depression, the American Feminist Movement, and the race to the moon, among others, Dorothy Mott died on November 24, 2000, at St. Luke's Nursing Home in Oswego (figure 1.58).[621] Her obituary reviewed her career and achievements, but the eulogy delivered at the funeral by her niece, Nancy Mott Frank, better captured the essence of the woman and is excerpted here:

> In a language which is no longer in vogue, Dorothy modeled honesty, duty, family, citizenship, equality in opportunity, moral principle, Christian ethic, proper decorum, courage in service and taking responsibility for our fellow man. I remember like yesterday my earliest memory of Aunt Dorothy. I was a small child

playing on the cold linoleum floor of our old kitchen, ignored. A single glaring light overhead shone upon my father, mother, sister, grandmother and aunt seated around our old kitchen table in deep discussion. What I didn't realize then . . . was that those were the years when Aunt Dorothy was leading efforts in Oswego to construct the first public housing. It was controversial among Oswego's landlords who felt threatened. There were seven lawsuits. There were days in court. There were nasty letters in the paper. There were threatening phone calls to our house. . . . We all know the result . . . Hamilton Homes was built. . . . Originally planned as a complex built on concrete slabs, Aunt Dorothy herself traveled and researched far and wide to find a precedent for public housing with basements as she believed everyone needed a basement in our climate. She won that battle. She stood firm in her convictions during those years. She worked hard again on Simeon DeWitt though the Oswego population had changed to welcome that construction. Dorothy joined the newly formed Women's Marine Corps to do her duty in World War II. Although she has admitted to the glamor aspect she served and retired as a Major in the Reserves. There were quite a few firsts in her life: first Vestrywomen of old Christ Church, first woman Director of Admissions at SUNY Oswego. One afternoon long ago on our patio at Pleasant Point, I asked her how it had felt blazing these trails for women so early on. I was looking for wisdom. I was looking for some wonderful deep intellectual or philosophical reflection which had inspired her. Her answer: "I don't know. I never thought about it. I just did it." . . . She liked living properly and the conventions of proper decorum. . . . She lived "loving your neighbor" in large public positions and she lived it quietly. She lived it daily in every fibre of her soul . . . without thought, without decision, without over intellectualization, without the gray or fuzziness of today. The life of Dorothy Mott was about involvement, not spectatorship. It was about passion and zest for living.[622]

Thomas Smith Mott (December 15, 1826–September 14, 1891), the founder of the Mott dynasty in Oswego City, was a shrewd businessman, banker, and philanthropist as well as a devoted family man (figure 1.59). He amassed a fortune from his many and varied commercial ventures. His

Figure 1.58. Dorothy Mott's gravestone pays tribute to her military service. Author's collection.

Figure 1.59. Thomas Smith Mott actively conducted his business affairs in Oswego City even though he was blind for the last twenty-five years of his life. Churchill's *Landmarks*.

success was all the more striking since for the last twenty-five years of his life he was totally blind. John Churchill described his reaction to the affliction: "More than thirty years prior to his death Mr. Mott's sight began to fail, and during twenty years of his active life he was practically blind. Such an affliction would have caused many to abandon all business and give way to despondency, but he was made of sterner stuff and until the last continued to carry on his business operations and to wield his influence in the political field."[623] That quality of "sterner stuff" was also to be found in Mott's great granddaughter, Bailey Elizabeth.

Born in Oswego City on March 23, 1937, Bailey was the second child of Luther Wright Mott, Jr. (September 7, 1903–October 9, 1970), and Elizabeth Bailey Young (July 1, 1905–January 31, 1991). An older brother, Luther Wright III, commonly known by his middle name, had been born December 25, 1933.

Poliomyelitis was a significant cause of childhood mortality in the early part of the twentieth century, and every summer parents worried that their children might be the next victims. In August 1942 Bailey became ill and was soon diagnosed as having contracted the disease, the first case in two years.[624] A few days later Wright also showed symptoms, and both children were taken to Oswego Hospital for treatment. Two iron lungs were sent from Syracuse with a police escort, and for several days the local newspaper reported on the children's condition.[625] Wright Mott died on August 20, 1942, and his grieving parents buried him that evening.[626]

Bailey's condition improved, and she was soon discharged from the hospital. Although she initially had to sleep in an iron lung, eventually she was able to discontinue that ordeal. One article noted, "The child has somewhat increased use of her chest muscles and Friday was able to move her head, as well as her fingers and toes."[627] For the next seven years she was treated in the Ithaca Reconstruction Home, a facility created especially to rehabilitate children suffering from polio (figure 1.60).[628]

According to younger sister, Nancy Mott Frank, Bailey, confined to a wheelchair, came home at the age of twelve: "Bailey was feeling isolated at home. It was Aunt Dorothy who drove the decision for Bailey to go to the Campus School . . . and then she drove her to and from it every day in rain or snow or whatever weather Oswego dished out."[629]

After graduating from the Campus School, Bailey enrolled in and graduated from Oswego High School. She was an excellent student and was named the first winner of Fort Oswego DAR's medal given to "a senior

Figure 1.60. Bailey Mott did not permit her disability to curtail her career or leisurely pursuits. Courtesy Nancy Mott Frank.

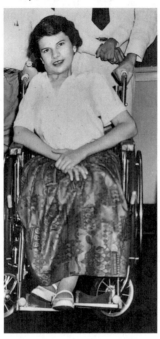

who is recommended by the History department as outstanding in American history."[630] An essay she composed titled "My High School Education" was published in the local newspaper:

> As I review my high school education, I feel a great sense of satisfaction for it brings to my mind three years of interesting and valuable experiences. Although I had long looked forward to the days when I would attend high school, I did not realize that my studies could bring me so much pleasure and satisfaction. . . . In my history classes I have gained an awareness and greater interest in the current events which are making history every day. By learning of events that have happened many years ago, I have gained a better understanding of the world's problems of today. I think that history is one of the most important courses in preparing alert citizens for the future. Another course

from which I have derived a great deal is my English course. I have learned how to appreciate good literature and have become acquainted with American authors of today and yesterday as well as the old masters of England and other lands. Besides this, in my English classes I have learned other things which will help me in my adult life, including library usage, parliamentary law, letter writing and how to find the words to express myself more adequately. . . . In summing up this evaluation of my three years at Oswego High School I can only say that I feel I owe a great debt to this school which has given me and hundreds of other young people so much. Someday I hope to be able to repay this debt by becoming a citizen of whom my school and my country can be proud.[631]

An overview of Bailey's accomplishments during her short lifetime clearly demonstrates she repaid her debt in full. After graduation she enrolled in the Woodrow Wilson School in Fisherville, Pennsylvania, where she majored in accounting.[632] She graduated from that institution and secured a position in the Dowd and Harrington Insurance Agency in Oswego (figure 1.61). At the time of her death she was the agency's manager.[633] She became involved with two professional organizations, one of which was the Oswego County Insurance Women's Association. She served as a member of the ways and means committee and as treasurer.[634] She was also associated with the Oswego City Association of Insurance Agents and served as the group's assistant secretary.[635]

Despite her disability Bailey took an active role in civic and religious organizations. She was a faithful member of Christ Episcopal Church. She belonged to Bishop Hobart Chapter of Christ Church and served as president in 1964. This group organized many fundraisers that she helped plan and execute.[636]

She involved herself with the Women's Auxiliary of Oswego Hospital and was elected treasurer numerous times.[637] Other civic activity included finishing her deceased father's term as treasurer for the Ladies' Home.

Like so many of the Motts, Bailey became a member of the Oswego County Historical Society. At the time of her death, she was in her second term as secretary. In 1975 Zonta honored her many accomplishments.[638]

In addition to theatre, photography, and reading, Bailey enjoyed traveling and visited many countries, including England, South Africa, and

Figure 1.61. Bailey Mott was an excellent student and graduated from business college after attending Oswego High School. Courtesy Nancy Mott Frank.

New Zealand. She was in Hakone, Japan, in May1976 when stricken with a fatal heart attack. She was only thirty-nine years old.[639]

Her friends and colleagues in Oswego determined to honor her memory in tangible ways. For example, the Oswego County Historical Society established an essay competition open to area high school students "proposed as a living memorial to Bailey Mott, an outstanding citizen of Oswego, who, at the time of her death, served as secretary of the Society. She won the admiration and respect of all by the positive way in which she reacted to the daily challenges of her personal and professional life."[640] The Women's Auxiliary at Oswego Hospital announced the proceeds from its annual bazaar would buy equipment in her memory. Among the items they purchased were several wheelchairs.[641]

As her sister Nancy has noted, Bailey lived in a time when the disabled had few rights and was, by her Mott grit and determination, "a wonderful example of the overcoming of a severe handicap."[642]

Bailey Elizabeth Mott was buried in Riverside Cemetery not far from the grave of her great grandfather, Thomas Smith Mott, progenitor of the Mott dynasty in Oswego City (figure 1.62).

Figure 1.62. Bailey Elizabeth Mott is buried with her parents in the family plot in Riverside Cemetery, Scriba, New York. Author's collection.

Helen Gay Purviance

Dedicating her life to the service of others, Helen Gay Purviance found her niche in the ranks of the Salvation Army. Her World War service in France garnered worldwide gratitude and probably some unwanted attention.

Helen was born on February 16, 1889, in Huntington, Indiana, the daughter of James Anson Purviance (August 19, 1859–April 23, 1928) and Ella May Palmer (October 20, 1856–June 2, 1915.) She was the fourth child in a family of five. According to an interview she gave, the family attended Bethel Evangelical Church, and she "was drawn to the Salvation Army because she felt it had the same goals as" her home church: "We were church people, and it seemed to me that the Lord worked as well through the (Salvation) Army as through the church, so I decided to dedicate my life to this service."[643]

On July 20, 1908, she finished her training at New York Corps No. 7 and received the rank of probationary lieutenant. The following year, on

July 21, 1909, she was promoted to captain. She was assigned to Paterson, New Jersey, on October 11, 1911; thence to Fulton, Oswego, New York, on July 17, 1912; and finally to Oswego City on July 23, 1913.[644]

The Salvation Army, which originated in London, England, in 1865, was at work in Oswego as early as 1886.[645] Based on contemporary news accounts, the community did not exactly welcome the workers with open arms:

> The Salvation Army, after several ineffectual attempts, has at last succeeded in securing a foothold in Oswego, and henceforth our citizens may expect to be treated to tambourine playing, shouting and exhortations such as but few have been permitted to listen to. . . . It is only fair to say that the army has not been received with marked favors in this community. As they have come to our city we hope the police will control the "hoodlum element" which will doubtless attend the meetings.[646]

The opposing view of the Salvationists portrayed Oswego as a modern-day Sodom and Gomorrah, as reported by an eyewitness:

> Oh! What a wicked city with all her churches and schools, yet how dark is her blackness, and unless God through the Army does something quickly, we are afraid the city will be lost. Well we are going to do something. We are pleased to see our dear friend, the War Cry, had made its appearance here again. We are ashamed to think S. A. officers could live in such a large city and not order from headquarters one War Cry. . . . Here in this bed of wickedness we had a real jubilee. A good crowd greeted us but no one would let Jesus in.

The same article contained another report: "Hallelujah to the King! We have the victory over the Devil this morning, and we are believing that many who are now living in sin in this wicked city will enter into the same liberty before long."[647] The fear that "hoodlums" would attend the meetings for the purpose of disrupting the proceedings was real, and the local newspapers reported numerous incidents where young men—some intoxicated, others simply looking for trouble—invaded the hall and proceeded to start fights or disrupt the service. To their credit, the same newspapers that condemned the Salvationists' ways were quick to defend their right to conduct services without interference: "There is evidently an organized gang who mean to give the salvationists all the trouble possible and the sooner they get a lesson the better. While the salvationists continue in their barracks they have a right to protection and will receive it."[648]

Despite all the bad publicity and harassment, the Salvation Army continued to minister in Oswego City and in 1893 finally established a citadel.[649] When Helen Purviance arrived in the city, the Salvation Army was an accepted, if not overly popular, charitable organization (figure 1.63). She set out to improve the community's perception of the Army, and by 1915 the local newspapers were noticing her efforts. In that year, for example, she organized a campaign to raise five hundred dollars for Christmas relief that received favorable press notice: "Since she has been in charge in this city, Captain Purviance has done some remarkably good work among the poor and unfortunate and a fund for relief work in her hands this winter would go farther than most people believe possible. She is in close touch with the people who need the money and knows best how to give it out in ways which will do the most good."[650]

Figure 1.63. Helen Gay Purviance's quiet pursuit of improving the lives of the poor in Oswego City resulted in increased respect among civic leaders for the work of the Salvation Army. Salvation Army National Archives.

The result of the campaign was that the Salvation Army was able to distribute sixty Christmas baskets, including twelve dozen sets of children's underwear.[651] Proof that the Salvation Army was gaining not only acceptance but also support was evidenced by the fact that several fraternal organizations, among them the Elks Club, Oswego Lodge No. 127 Free and Accepted Masons, and Lake City Chapter No. 352 OES, were actively soliciting donations on behalf of the Army.

Helen carried out her charitable efforts in quiet ways. Hearing of a destitute family, she immediately took steps to provide assistance: "[N]ot a particle of food in the house nor a bit of fuel. Three of the children were in the bed trying to keep warm and the fourth was running around in its bare feet and only partially clad." Concluded the reporter, once Captain Purviance had heard of the situation, it "was promptly taken care of."[652]

One of Helen's charitable actions pointed out a real need in the Port City. When a seventeen-year-old girl was arrested, the police had no safe place to hold her. Hearing of this situation, Helen immediately went to police headquarters and gained custody of the girl. She took her to the citadel, where she was fed and housed. Because of her action, it was proposed that Helen be offered the nonsalaried position of police matron! "It has been suggested that Captain Purcival [sic], a woman of refinement and culture, now at the head of the Army, be given the position. Chief Richardson says that a better selection could not be made and he will ask the mayor to designate, temporarily at least, Captain Purcival."[653]

A real test of Helen's commitment to "Heart to God—Hands to Humanity" came when the United States entered World War I. She received a message from Colonel W. A. McIntyre at the New York City Headquarters, soliciting her assistance: "If we should need you for war work in France, are you willing to go and to sail in the not very far distant future?"[654] By the end of August, Helen and several other Army volunteers were in Bordeaux, France.[655]

Stationed with the First Division of the American Expeditionary Forces only fifteen miles from the front, the women's job was to help the soldiers in any way they could, from sewing on buttons to feeding them coffee and sandwiches. One of the women came up with the idea of frying doughnuts for the soldiers and a legend was born. It was a story often told for the rest of Helen's life:

> Adjutant Helen Purviance of the Salvation Army, who is in charge
> of the flourishing corps in Oswego, N. Y., has many claims to

distinction and one which stands quite near the top of the list of her many achievements and reasons for a niche in the hall of fame is that she fried the first doughnut that saw service in the American Expeditionary Force. Capt. Violet McAllister of Philadelphia mixed the dough, but to the adjutant from Oswego went the honor of frying the first circle with dough around it.[656]

Helen and her companion Salvation Army workers did their best with limited resources to provide support to frontline soldiers:

We had been making fudge for the soldiers and we were trying to think of something else to make with some supplies we'd gotten from the commissary of the ammunition train. And the more we talked, it just spelled doughnuts. Margaret said, "But what about eggs?" I said I would go see the villagers about eggs. We got the eggs. When we made those first doughnuts we partitioned off the hut with a blanket so the soldiers wouldn't know what we were making until it was ready.[657]

At first the women made do with primitive equipment (figure 1.64):

Assigned to an ammunition train at Montiers-sur-saulx in the Toule sector, Miss Purviance, then an ensign, spent the next few days on her knees, not praying, but cooking doughnuts in a low, wood-burning French stove. The first doughnuts were made from dough mixed according to her mother's recipe, rolled with an empty bottle and twisted into cruller shape by hand. The first batch was wolfed down with such cries of joy that Colonel Purviance and her companion, Miss Margaret Sheldon, went into doughnut making seriously. They persuaded a local blacksmith to construct a makeshift cookie cutter out of an evaporated milk can and a camphor ice tube (the latter to cut the all-important hole in the middle) and sent for more professional equipment from the United States.[658]

Initially they could prepare only seven doughnuts at one time. Shortly thereafter, with the arrival of better equipment, production increased significantly. By war's end, Salvation Army workers were turning out thousands of doughnuts all over France every day.

Figure 1.64. Helen Purviance fried doughnuts for homesick soldiers in France during World War I. Salvation Army National Archives.

The work of the "doughnut lassies" came to the attention of Brigadier General John L. Hines, who was having trouble getting his motor transport division to carry out their duties quickly and efficiently. Suddenly he noticed a marked change in attitude and performance:

> All at once he began to see improvement. The trucks increased the number of their trips and congestion was relieved. He sought to find the reason and he called several of his officers in. "There's a little Salvation Army lassie that gets out every morning at four o'clock now and meets the boys as they go by. She gives them hot coffee and sandwiches and the boys feel more in a mood to work," the officers told him. General Hines said he wanted to see that Salvation Army lassie, and she was taken to him. It was none other than Ensign Helen Purviance, and he told her that he wanted her permanently attached to his brigade and that she was to move when they did.[659]

Life near the front lines was brutal, as Helen remembered: "That first winter, we were very, very cold. How did we keep warm? We didn't. Our feet would get frozen. We used to take candles and light them and put them close to our feet to warm them. We tried to get hot water to wash our feet. When I came back to this country I had 19 black spots on my feet where they had been frozen, thawed out and frozen again."[660]

Cold was not their only concern, as Helen wrote in a letter:

We have been on the march for more than ten days. While the battle was raging so badly we were in the town for four days. The first night we had no place to sleep excepting in an ammunition car. The following night we went to a nearby village and took possession of a house that had been vacated and expected to go back to it the next night. But we were ordered out so for two nights were in a large cave and it was a good thing for us we were there. Nine German planes were overhead at one time and bombs fell all about us. Many persons were killed and many others wounded. It was a terrible sight to see bits of flesh, piles of dead and splattered brains and blood soaked earth. It just made me weak. . . . The first night in the cave I slept well, but the second I was dreadfully nervous. The last occupants were Germans and they had used the place as a hospital and it was so much like a corner in hell that really I was frightened.[661]

Late in 1918 Helen was ordered home. She had injured her arm badly during the thousands of hours she spent making doughnuts. She recalled that her ship sailed into New York Harbor with all its lights on, a sure sign the war was nearly over. A day after she arrived, the armistice was signed. Her superiors had decided to send her on a publicity tour to raise money for the European campaign: "After 14 months at the front, the Army publicity strategists decided to introduce the original 'Doughnut Girl' to the home folks. She handed out doughnuts in a hut in Union Square, New York and toured the country, making speeches."[662]

In February 1919 Helen returned to France to assist at US Army debarkation ports. She reminisced, "It was even harder work because they were all fed up—the war was over and they wanted to get home."[663] In due time she herself went home—back to Oswego, where she was given a hero's welcome: "Many friends of Adjutant Helen Purviance were present at the reception last night held at the Salvation Army headquarters in her honor. . . . Adjutant Purviance gave a most interesting talk to her friends, telling how delighted she was to be once more back among them. She felt that she had already told them on previous occasions all things of interest and congratulated the army on the good results of their efforts here."[664] After a brief vacation in Indiana, Helen returned to Oswego and to her work. In the fall the Salvation Army sponsored a harvest festival to "furnish assistance to the wayward girls and other needy people."[665] The Army's Christmas relief program was bigger than ever, as they were "planning its greatest celebration. It is planned to distribute at least 500 dinners, as well as serviceable articles for the children."[666] The campaign's success was revealed in a statement Helen released later in the month, in which she personally thanked individuals, civic organizations, churches, and fraternal organizations for their generosity.[667]

Helen's community involvement extended beyond her charitable work for the Salvation Army. In 1919 alone she was invited to speak before several local organizations. When addressing the Knights of Pythias, she took the opportunity to detail some of the Army's plans and services, mentioning low-cost laundry service for local washerwomen. She also made an appeal for gently used clothing and shoes:

> The Salvation Army in Oswego is at your service. If you do not get something out of us, it will be your own fault. It doesn't intend to let an opportunity for service slip by unused. We are here to stay. As Pershing said in France, "Lafayette, we are here," so say we now, "Oswego, we are here." We hope that in our new quarters we may be a credit to the city. We hope to make our building one of which the city will be proud and that it will take rank as one of the show places which you will point out to your friends when you are exhibiting the lake. A successful Army institution speaks well for any city and its citizens. We feel we have a wonderful future here.[668]

Helen was also the featured speaker at a memorial service for Oswego area soldiers who died during the war.[669]

Her World War efforts did not go unnoticed by her superiors. At the closing rally of the Eastern Congress of the Salvation Army held in October 1919, Evangeline Booth, head of the Salvation Army in the United States, presented her a bronze medal "for valorous conduct" that was inscribed, "World War/For Heroic and Faithful Service/To Helen Gay Purviance/The Salvation Army/1914–1919. "[670]

When Adjutant Purviance went off to war, she was promised that she might return to Oswego even though she had already been there several years and Army officers were generally transferred to new posts every two to three years. The residents of Oswego were shocked when it was announced in 1924 that she was being sent to New York City. A campaign was begun to keep her in Oswego but in vain.[671] An editorial summarized the esteem with which she was held:

When adjutant Helen Purviance leaves Oswego in pursuance to duty's call the city will lose a woman of striking personality, unusual abilities and whose career brought distinction to the Salvation Army and to Oswego, as the city from which she hailed during the World War period. To do great, self-sacrificing things where the world will see them and applaud is one way of serving mankind; to dedicate oneself and one's life to a service whose very nature forbids publicity and personal acclaim is quite another variety of heroism and this is the sort of work to which Adjutant Purviance was drawn at any early age. To return from a world-wide war which had given her distinction as the "doughnut girl," the woman who first conceived the happy thought which brought cheer to thousands of boys at the front, and to settle down again to the grinding everyday problems of directing the work of the Salvation Army corps in Oswego, was a feat which Miss Purviance compassed with apparently no effort. She quickly forgot the thrill and terror and fatigue of the war days and began building a center for the poor, the down and out and the discouraged in this city, or those who perchance drifted this way. The present Army headquarters, two buildings in excellent repair and equipped fully for the Army needs, stand as a monument to her quiet, untiring energy. But even more eloquent would be the testimony, if it could be written, of hundreds of boys and girls, men and women to whom she has brought the concrete comforts of food and clothes and fuel and the more important comfort of an understanding heart and a helping hand. Oswego's loss of Miss Purviance will be keenly felt in many directions as yet unperceived.[672]

At a farewell gathering held the evening before Helen departed from Oswego, community leaders lauded her unstinting devotion to the cause of human charity and relief. According to F. B. Shepherd, chair of the local Salvation Army Advisory Committee,

> Eleven years ago the Salvation Army sent Miss Helen Purviance to Oswego to carry on here its work of encouragement and assistance to the weak, to the impoverished, to the broken in spirit, to the faint-hearted, and to those wearied with life—the unfortunates and the derelicts. Her coming was without flare or trumpetry and few of our citizens knew when she came—nor cared. The equipment of the Salvation Army in Oswego at that time was woefully insufficient. Its work was among the down and almost out. Few cared to be identified with it. And the Ensign quietly began her labors. As months went by busy men became familiar with a resolute face, a compelling smile and a Christian earnestness which appeared on the street, in their offices, here, there, everywhere, in the garb of a Salvation Army lass, commanding respect. There came to the women of the city reports of encouragement and assistance, wondrous kind, to the afflicted in body and spirit; of this one and of that one who had been helped by the influence and aid of Ensign Purviance. . . . Such, very briefly, is the work accomplished by Adjutant Purviance to Oswego, but it does not record, nor can we record ought of the hours of quiet, responsive helpful service which have brought to hundreds of men and women hope out of their despair, which have restored ambitions, checked wayward tendencies or sustained the faltering.[673]

Adjutant Purviance moved to her next assignment as chief side officer at Salvation Army Headquarters in New York City, where she was in charge of the women's department of the Salvation Army Training School.[674] In 1925 she was promoted to the rank of captain, and in 1928 to major. She remained in New York City until 1932, when she was sent to Buffalo, New York, as director of religion for Corps No. 1.[675] Her last position was as assistant field secretary for territorial headquarters. As such she directed the activities of eighteen hundred officers in eleven eastern states. She was also promoted to the rank of brigadier.[676] In recognition of her "outstanding work in the Salvation Army," she was promoted to lieutenant colonel in 1942.[677] On July 20, 1943, she received the Silver Star of the Long Service Order.

Lieutenant Colonel Helen Purviance left active duty in 1949 after forty-one years of devoted service.[678] Shortly before she retired, a World War I veteran wishing to pay his respects visited her. The visitor was none other than Irving Berlin, who desired to express personal gratitude for her wartime efforts:

> In this little ceremony on Broadway the other day, Berlin stopped work on his new musical, "Miss Liberty," to hand documents to Lieut. Col. Helen Purviance of The Salvation Army, who was retiring after 41 years of active service. He handed her messages from such people as Gov. Thomas E. Dewey, Elsie Janis and Perry Brown, national commander of the American Legion. Then Berlin, a quiet-speaking and quiet-moving man, shyly added his own gift. It was an autographed copy of his song, "Oh, How I Hate to Get Up in the Morning," which woke up so many of his reluctant soldier mates in their training days at Camp Upton. Berlin after many years was giving this song to the girl who had given him doughnuts in World War I and he told her that she might forget the song. But the soldiers would never forget the doughnuts which the Salvation Army brought up to moving troops when regular Army food could not get up. . . . It was nice that Broadway's ambassador, Irving Berlin, could represent the soldiers the other day to say "Thank you, Colonel Purviance."[679]

For many years after retiring Helen provided assistance to the Army on an informal basis. In 1958 she moved to St. Petersburg, Florida, and remained there until shortly before her death.

Despite all her other accomplishments as a Salvation Army officer, she was saddled with the nickname "Doughnut Girl" her entire life. In 1927 she accompanied a delegation of veterans to Paris, France, for an American Legion convention. One morning she set up her equipment outside the Legion headquarters and began to fry doughnuts: "The Paris legionnaires lined up en masse for their first taste of Yankee cooking in years, smacked their lips loudly and demanded second helpings. They kept Helen Purviance and other Salvation Army workers, veterans of the war-time front lines, busy for several hours satisfying the demand."[680] In 1964 the American Legion in Indianapolis honored her for "humanitarian service and unswerving devotion to her cause" by presenting her with a plaque decorated with a golden doughnut.[681] In 1965 she was recognized at the annual convention of the Kings County, New York, American Legion.[682] A feature story published in 1981, complete with period photos, retold the tale.[683] Despite the fact that in 1936 she confessed that she detested doughnuts and never ate them, she patiently bore the nickname and the unwanted attention.[684]

Helen Gay Purviance returned to Indiana in 1983, entering the Peabody Retirement Community in North Manchester. On February 26, 1984, she succumbed to cardiac arrest and pneumonia. She had just celebrated her ninety-fifth birthday. An obituary originally published in a Tampa Bay, Florida, newspaper was reprinted in the *Oswego County Messenger*, once again showing how beloved this small, modest woman still was to those who remembered her kindness, steadfastness to duty, and overall compassion for those suffering about her.[685]

Despite the fact that Helen Gay Purviance devoted almost a half century to the work of the Salvation Army, her monument in Mount Hope Cemetery, Huntington, Indiana alludes only to her appellation as the original Doughnut Girl of World War I (figure 1.65).

Figure 1.65. Lieutenant Colonel Helen Gay Purviance is buried with members of her family in Mount Hope Cemetery, Huntington, Indiana. Richard Earl Post, Sr., Findagrave.com.

Grace E. Lynch

Teacher, activist, historian, writer: Grace Lynch was all of these. Blessed with intelligence and humor, she contributed to the welfare and the cultural development of her native city, Fulton, New York, through her long teaching career, many newspaper columns, and civic participation.

Born on February 8, 1891, in Volney, New York, Grace was the daughter of John P. Lynch (March 1856–March 30, 1938) and Catherine A. "Kate" Frawley (March 1858–January 30, 1925). She was the second daughter in a family of four surviving siblings. Her mother immigrated from Ireland in 1873. John P. Lynch, although born in the United States, was of Irish lineage.

As a young girl Grace attended the prestigious Falley Seminary in Fulton. She graduated from Oswego Normal School in 1913.[686] She taught eighth grade at Erie School in Fulton until 1921 and then transferred to Fairgrieve Junior High School, where she taught eighth grade social studies until her retirement in June 1959.[687] During the final semester of her career, she was the principal of Fairgrieve.[688] For her longtime dedication to the children of Fulton, the State University College at Oswego honored her at the 1958 commencement "for outstanding work in behalf of schools and children in New York State."[689]

Grace's interest in education extended far beyond the classroom. She promoted teaching as a profession as an organizer of the Fulton Teachers' Association. She was elected president of the organization numerous times.[690] She also founded the Oswego County Chapter of the New York State Teachers' Association (NYSTA), serving as president. She was a member of the Central Zone of NYSTA and served as the organization's president and secretary several times, in addition to being selected as a representative to the state body.[691] Upon her retirement, she joined the New York State Retired Teachers' Association. Finally, she edited *The Report Card*, the board of education's quarterly publication.

Grace's fondness for history was exhibited in several ways. She was, for example, a member of the Oswego County Historical Society, which dedicated its *Twenty-Eighth Publication* to her for "her lifelong service to her community, to local history and to the Society." According to the dedication, her papers "presented before the Oswego County Historical Society and other groups were never dull, always clever, always interspersed with the wit and humor so characteristic of her. It was a real experience to be in her audience on such an occasion." (figure 1.66).[692]

Figure 1.66. Grace Lynch's love of history was recognized by the Oswego County Historical Society in its 1966–1967 publication. Friends of History in Fulton, New York.

The year 1962 was significant for the citizens of Fulton since it marked the sixtieth anniversary of the incorporation of the city. Community leaders contemplated a way to celebrate and decided upon the theme "Forward with Fulton." The large steering committee, which included Grace Lynch, scheduled a multiday party replete with a horse show, parade, theatrics, and a souvenir newspaper.[693] Grace became editor in chief of the special newspaper which appeared on May 30, 1962. Her command of local history was evident in her front-page article "Fulton Grows from Portage to Progressive City." After touching briefly on the earliest known information concerning the area, she continued:

> What a dramatic array of personages have followed that pathway!
> The French Jesuit Father LeMoyne was the first white man ever to
> see the Oswego Falls when in August, 1654, he "carried" around
> them on his way to try to Christianize the Onondaga tribe of the
> Iroquois. Others who came later were French, English and Dutch
> fur traders, Count Frontenac with a force of 2, 200 in 1696,

the English colonel, Bradstreet, who with young Philip Schuyler battled the French and Indians under DeVilliers in 1756 in the fight that gave Battle Island its name, Sir William Johnson, the King's Indian agent for North America, and in 1760, the largest military force ever to pass the falls, Gen. Amherst's army of 4, 000 English regulars, 6, 000 colonial troops and 600 Iroquois warriors. In the Revolution came Sir Guy and Sir John Jonson, both Tory leaders, and Gen. Barry St. Leger, who was defeated at Oriskany by the Americans under Gen. Herkimer.[694]

In the space of a page and a half she managed to encapsulate four hundred years of local history with an article both informative and entertaining.

Wit and humor were trademarks of her longtime column "The Way It Used to Be," published in the *Fulton Patriot*. She tackled many subjects, with titles such as "The Wonderful Tin Lizzie" and "The I.R.S. vs. Me."[695] Twenty-six of her essays were collected and published in book form in 1980, and twenty-two more in 1992 (figure 1.67).[696]

Figure 1.67. Many of Grace Lunch's essays were compiled into two volumes after her death. Author's collection.

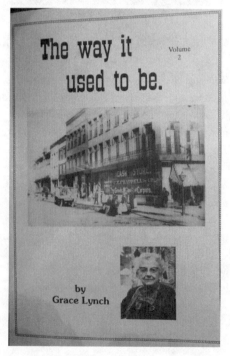

Like Francis Squires, considered Oswego County's first historian, Grace found inspiration in almost any topic. In her two hundred plus articles, she discussed local industries, early days of moving pictures in Fulton, the era of local railroad transportation, the *Old Farmers' Almanac*, Halloween, and even the month of March. A particularly entertaining piece dealt with Grace's experiences as a young teacher:

> The opening of school each year has the same effect on me that the alarm bell used to have on the fire horses in days gone by. I want to go, too. Small wonder when the years I spent as a student added to the time I taught in Fulton schools makes a grand total of 60 years. When I began teaching in the then brand new Erie Street School, Mr. James R. Fairgrieve was Superintendent of School. For him, the ideal classroom was one with forty pupils divided into A and B classes, with promotions every half year. If a child did not grasp the work, he was kept in the same class until he did or until he had put in two full years in that room. In those days teachers faced a problem that is not so familiar in today's schools. That was providing help for needy children, for the Poor Commissioner, in later years called the Commissioner of Welfare, held families in relief to a rigidly meager budget. They didn't starve but there were no extras. Besides, it was then considered a disgrace to be on the relief rolls and many parents preferred to send their children to school poorly fed and dressed in clothing ready for the rag bag rather than accept what they called "charity." So the teachers on their salaries of $450 to $500 a year did what they could to alleviate distress.[697]

When the collected works were published, a reviewer offered the following:

> No one ever had to critique anything Grace Lynch wrote. Almost 20 years ago, after many people including the publishers of The Fulton Patriot had asked Grace to put her thoughts into newspaper articles, she submitted one. It was read and published, the first of over 200. . . . Grace's well-written, personable articles didn't need "reviewing" or "critiquing." They spoke for themselves. That's the way it is with the long-awaited book of Grace's stories published this week by the Fulton Historical

Society. . . . The editors had no easy task in going through 12 years of articles and coming up with 26 for this book. They made a fine choice. If you're an "old-timer" you'll smile again at Grace's remembrances; if you numbered yourself among her many friends and acquaintances you'll remember her fondly as you peruse the pages. . . . "The Way It Used to Be" is a tribute to Fulton and most of all to Grace Lynch. We hope the new book is only the first of a continuing series.[698]

When Grace Lynch was not writing about Fulton, she was involved in it. She was appointed to a mayor's committee to study changes and revisions to the city's government. She sold war bonds during both world wars, served on the Civilian Advisory Committee of the War Rationing Board during World War II, and volunteered for the Red Cross. She was the local unit's publicity chair in 1935 and secretary in 1948. She belonged to the Fulton Women's Club and at one time served as parliamentarian. She was active in the Salvation Army's Auxiliary, and the A. L. Lee Hospital's Auxiliary.[699] A devout Roman Catholic, she was a charter member of Court Pierre LeMoyne, Catholic Daughters of America, later serving as its regent.[700]

She was a member of Fulton's Business and Professional Women's Club and, as stated above, a valued member of the Oswego County Historical Society.[701] In 1957 she became a charter member of Alpha Iota Chapter of Delta Kappa Gamma, an international educational honorary for women.[702]

Such outstanding community service was recognized in 1966 when the Fulton Rotary Club bestowed its Service Award upon her "for her many years of volunteer community service work, in addition to her long and busy teaching career as inspiring as this was in so many people of this area who were her pupils."[703] When presented with the honor on March 17, she responded: "I was born in Fulton and in all the years since I have never met with anything but kindness, friendliness and helpfulness from Fulton people."[704]

Grace E. Lynch died on August 30, 1974, in the Michaud Nursing Home, Fulton, after a long illness. According to one obituary, her writings "recalled the past intertwining her lucid philosophic interpretations of not only the time gone past but of today as well."[705]

Grace E. Lynch is buried in St. Mary's Cemetery, Fulton, with other members of her family.

Muriel Leola Jobst Allerton

Muriel Jobst Allerton made history in November 1987 when she became the first woman not only to run for the mayor's office in Fulton, New York, but also to win the election. Although a first for her and the city politically, she had been a fixture in Fulton's civic and social fabric for many years and was in fact dubbed "the mother of Fulton."

Born in West New York, Hudson, New Jersey, on November 23, 1919, she was the only child of John Jobst (November 29, 1889–June 6, 1966) and Eva L. Aten (April 16, 1896–August 8, 1968). After graduating, Muriel attended a secretarial school before entering college. She revealed to a reporter why she majored in journalism at New York University: "She said she had decided upon journalism as a college major because she realized she liked to write while she was working for Doubleday and Company, New York. She wanted to incorporate this love with employment possibilities. She added that it was rare at that time for journalists to have college training in the field."[706]

Muriel's husband, Joseph Allerton (March 17, 1919–August 9, 2018), obtained a position with the Nestlé Company in 1963 and the family moved to Fulton. Muriel reminisced about her introduction to the city's civic life:

> When we moved to Fulton in 1963, it was the custom for the wives of fellow workers at the Nestlé Company to take new-comers under their wing. It was a fortunate way to fit into a new community. Esther Hibbard opened her whole wingcage for me. We lived in a Nestlé-owned house on East Broadway. Esther was one of our first visitors which ripened into a friendship of several decades. . . . To be a protégé of Esther Hibbard was a daunting experience. You became a member of State Street Church, the Women's Club, the Hospital Auxiliary and Cancer Dressing Chairperson in Fulton with an attic loaded with hand-made dressings by a lot of good people who also stopped by on behalf of stricken loved ones.[707]

Esther's mentorship was more than repaid by Muriel's ever-increasing role in community affairs. Her journalistic career alone was extensive. She once told the story that her first editor at *New York Daily News* gave her some advice: "Be brief, keep it short, and stick to the facts." Her first piece adhered strictly to that counsel: "S. White looked up the elevator shaft to see if there was a car coming down. There was. He was 45."[708]

During the 1980s Muriel was a freelance writer for local newspapers such the *Oswego Valley News,* the *Oswego Palladium-Times,* and the fledgling, short-lived *Oswego County Messenger.* She wrote on many topics, including child abuse, life in early Fulton, a dog rescue on the Oswego River, and the dangers of rabid animals.[709] She wrote book reviews and frequently took the pictures for her articles.[710] She was a founder and first president of the Oswego County Press Club, serving later as the organization's secretary.

To say that Muriel was an innovator is understating the case. Her role in founding the Fulton Historical Society is a good example. She and several others organized the society at a meeting held at Fulton City Hall on February 15, 1979. She was elected a member of the board of directors that evening and also acted as the group's provisional treasurer.[711] When the group decided to move into the historic Pratt House, Muriel wrote about the improvements being made in the building and how the community at large might use the facility.[712]

It was Muriel and fellow society member Marie Goode who spent almost two years compiling Grace Lynch's articles published under the headline "The Way It Used to Be." The Fulton Savings Bank provided a generous grant so the articles could be compiled into a book. According to Muriel, "[W]ithout her a lot of Fulton history would never have been recorded." She further stated, "She was gone, and no one seemed to put together her material. But when the historical society was being formed I felt her presence . . . she was such a great historian."[713]

Muriel and her husband Joseph were music lovers and turned that passion into something concrete with the founding of the Oswego Opera Theater in 1978 (figure 1.68). The Allertons served on the original board of directors. The Opera Theater's initial production, Gilbert and Sullivan's *H.M.S. Pinafore,* demonstrated the ambition and enthusiasm of the fledgling organization.[714]

Realizing that hunger was a problem in Fulton, Muriel suggested opening a soup kitchen for a six-week trial at the Methodist Church. Despite the fact that no one showed up to eat on the first day, the trial turned into a permanent offering.[715] Diners were offered soup, a sandwich, dessert, and hot drinks. Anyone who wished to do so was free to return for second helpings.

In fact, there was little in Fulton that Muriel did not organize or support. When she arrived in Fulton, she discovered that there was no

Figure 1.68. Muriel and Joseph Allerton, longtime opera buffs, were among the founders of the Oswego Opera Theatre. Friends of History in Fulton, New York.

League of Women Voters in the area. She, Sally Soluri, and Norma Bartle organized a chapter in 1964.[716] She was a charter member of the Fulton Art Association in 1974; member of the SUNY Oswego College Council, 1985–1996; and member of Fulton Drug Program and Hotline, 1970–1972. She was a member of the Salvation Army's advisory board in 1984.[717] She was involved with A. L. Lee Hospital's auxiliary and did publicity for their annual Cracker Barrel Fair.[718] She was secretary for United Way, and in 1992 and 1993 chaired the annual fund drive. She chaired the Fulton Community's Christmas Tree Lighting Committee in 1999.[719]

It is as Fulton's first female mayor that Muriel Allerton will be most remembered. As she recalled on several occasions, her introduction to local politics was effected when Mayor Patrick Percy asked her to be a substitute secretary for one day. That one day turned into nine years, during which time she became knowledgeable about Fulton's history, its shortcomings, and its possibilities.[720]

When Mayor Ronald L. Woodward announced in early 1987 that he would not seek reelection, Muriel was encouraged to run for the office since she had gained valuable experience acting as Woodward's campaign manager in addition to all she had learned as Mayor Percy's secretary. The city's Democratic party unanimously endorsed her candidacy over Cosimo

Borzumate, who was endorsed by the Conservative Party and hoped for the Democratic endorsement as well.[721] Muriel and her two opponents, Cosimo Borzumate and Robert Burleigh, carried on a spirited campaign. All three candidates had definite ideas about improving the city, which had some real problems, ranging from poorly treated drinking water to the lax management of municipal equipment and the ever controversial subject of taxes. Muriel ran on a platform of rigid fiscal control, beautifying downtown Fulton, promoting a motel bed tax, and assisting the chamber of commerce in bringing events to the city.[722] One promise Allerton made was to refrain from using negative campaign tactics. Borzumate, undoubtedly smarting from the Democrats' rejection, had no such compunction.

In 1987 Muriel was sixty-eight years old, energetic and eager to meet possible constituents, whether at home or at organized events. Borzumate chided her for her perceived lack of political experience by calling her the Democrats' "last resort." He belittled her secretarial skills, reportedly stating, "Mrs. Allerton is a truly nice person and her experience in the secretarial field, working for those in elected office, gives her extensive background for the office she seeks. Unlike her predecessors, should she win, she will be able to take notes."[723] Then he made the mistake of saying publicly that she was incompetent to hold the mayor's office because of her advanced age.[724]

It is likely that Borzumate, aged thirty-six, soon regretted his statement. An attempt to soften his stand was weak: "Borzumate . . . said he wished to clarify his recent comment that 'only two candidates are young enough to stay in office enough terms to make a difference.' He said he feels that if Fulton's next mayor is to accomplish what needs to be done in the city, 'It's going to have to be done in more than two years. I've seen what the mayor goes through.' He said the voters should ask if the other candidates can accomplish what needs to be done. 'If the people feel that's so, then age is not an issue."[725] The backlash did not help his campaign and most assuredly assisted Allerton's. An editorial voiced what many Fultonians were thinking:

> It was in poor taste, to say the least, for Fulton mayoral candidate Cosimo Borzumate to bring up Democrat Muriel Allerton's age as a campaign issue during a candidates' forum Monday night. It was politically unwise as well. Fulton, and every other community, has its share of active senior citizens. Not all of them become mayor, but many work harder than any political figure half their age—and are twice as effective. Borzumate undoubtedly

offended more than one senior who believes himself or herself entirely capable of handling the rigors of office. Nowadays no political candidate should be downgraded for his age.[726]

Muriel herself struck back, declaring she was absolutely fit to be mayor:

> I can lead because I am not looking to the past for all solutions. I know generous federal and state assistance, which was used to solve present and past problems, is no longer available. I can lead because I respect the role of the technically trained in our increasingly complex technological society. I do not look for simplistic answers to tough environmental problems that were ignored through a lack of knowledge in the past, but must be faced now at great cost to the people if we are to remain a prosperous, growing city.[727]

She displayed a deep understanding of the types of problems facing Fulton in a letter thanking the International Association of Machinists and Aerospace Workers for their endorsement:

> During an election campaign it is difficult to be sure that the people realize that growth in the city of Fulton must be maintained, that the city's natural assets of lake, river and abundant water supply must be guarded in order for Fulton to prosper. The working people of Fulton understand only too well that prosperity and growth mean jobs and family security, which is the bedrock of a good life for the community . . . We cannot dwell on the mistakes of the past but must build on what we have, looking for new ways to keep our hold on the present as a safe passage to the future.[728]

When the votes were tallied on election day in November, Allerton defeated her opponents by a slim margin and was sworn in as Fulton's first female mayor in January 1988 (figure 1.69).[729] Over the next two years she endeavored to carry out her campaign promises. Taking a cue from Oswego City's very successful Harborfest, she suggested a similar festival for Fulton, dubbed Riverfest. The idea came to fruition in August 1989, and a delighted mayor was exuberant with the turnout: "It was beyond my wildest expectations. . . . Fulton has a great deal to offer. I'm not sure the people of Fulton

Figure 1.69. Muriel Allerton was elected Fulton's first female mayor. Author's collection.

or visitors know what a nice community this is. They found out and had a good time too. Now, that's hitting the jackpot."[730] Less glamorous but nevertheless as important were her support of a county recycling program, efforts to bring new business to Fulton, delivering clean water to Fulton residents, and reinvigorating the North Bay camping area.[731]

In 1989 Allerton announced she would run for a second term to build upon her achievements in maintenance of city properties and equipment and increased sales tax revenue. She again faced two opponents, Republican Frank Corsoneti and Independent Philip Blair.[732] After a lively campaign she was reelected by a narrow margin.[733]

When she decided to leave office after her second term she reflected on her accomplishments of the previous four years, reminding the interviewer, "If you remember back in my [first] campaign I never said I was going to build the Taj Mahal." She continued:

> I fulfilled all my commitments. . . . I never cared whether we were the best or had the most—so long as we had our own character. . . . Being a woman means that you look at things differently. . . . Men think of leadership as wielding a certain

amount of power. I like to solve problems but I like to do it with as few errors as possible. . . . There's been more communication and less conflict. . . . If I have a conflict with somebody, they soon know it. And I don't play games.[734]

After so many years of community service Allerton received well-deserved recognition for her efforts on behalf of the residents of Fulton. In 1989 Zonta named her their "Woman of Achievement." In announcing the award, Connie McKinstry, chair of the Amelia Earhart Committee, said, "Our honoree is chosen on the basis of her dedication to family-oriented activities, church and volunteer work, civic service and work to advance the status of women. Muriel Allerton filled the bill on each of these criteria."[735]

Fulton's Rotary honored her with its Paul Harris Award in 1992. In 2010 the New York State Senate named her a "Woman of Distinction."[736] She received the Community Recognition Award from SUNY Oswego in 2013.[737]

Muriel Allerton died on July 25, 2013. A lengthy obituary paid tribute to her long career in the service to the residents of Fulton.[738]

A long career of cultural and political activity ended only with Muriel Allerton's death. The inscription on her gravestone in Mt. Adnah Cemetery, Fulton, New York, "Mayor of Fulton," alludes to her history making election as the first female mayor of that city (figure 1.70).

Figure 1.70. Muriel Allerton is buried in Mt. Adnah Cemetery, Fulton, New York. The inscription on her monument reads, "Mayor of Fulton." Author's collection.

Virginia Louise Radley

Once apocryphally described as possessing "an ego as big as Montana," Virginia L. Radley began life in Wayne County, New York. Throughout her long career of teaching and administrative positions she left an indelible mark upon scores of students and colleagues for her unswerving devotion to honesty, integrity, and academic excellence.[739]

Born on August 12, 1927, in Marion, New York, Virginia Louise was the fifth child and only daughter of Howard James Radley (March 27, 1888–April 16, 1956) and Lula Louise Ferris (March 24, 1892–June 19, 1974). She was admittedly shy as a child, literally hanging onto her mother's skirt when they went out in public. Her four years at Russell Sage College in Troy, New York, developed her into a confident young woman, as her college "Big Sister" Betty Jean Koonz Schnurr recalled: "We did all the fun things that everyone did with their freshmen sisters in those days, and we formed a bond that's lasted 50 years. But you knew, even then, that she was going to do something important with her education."[740]

After graduation Radley obtained a position at Emily Howland Central School in Aurora, New York, where she taught English from 1949 to 1951. She later described her time there: "I first began teaching in 1949. I taught in high school—all four English, two public speaking classes, and I was the librarian, drama coach, and driver for the baseball and bowling teams. I taught over 200 students each semester—gave one composition per week for each of the four English classes. Survived? More than survival! Dewey's learning by doing!"[741] She left that position to obtain a master's degree in English from the University of Rochester in 1952.

Her next teaching position was at Chatham Hall, a private girls' school in Virginia where she amazed her students with her command of English literature and her charismatic demeanor, as Cynthia Lovelace Sears recalled: [W]e were convinced that she must have been on close personal terms with Socrates, Shakespeare, Pope, Emerson, Hardy, Hawthorn, and every poet in the Romantic era. In public we were always appropriately formal and polite. In private, among ourselves, we referred to her as 'Rads,' feigning casualness—but with a surreptitious glance cast skyward, waiting for the thunderbolt."[742] Radley left Chatham Hall in 1955 to pursue a master's degree in administration and a doctorate in English literature at Syracuse University. She was subsequently appointed assistant dean of students and assistant professor of English at Goucher College in 1957.[743] Returning to

Russell Sage in 1959, where she remained until 1969, she served successively as dean of freshmen, director of freshman composition, associate dean of the college, and finally, chair of the English Department.[744] In 1969 she accepted a position as dean of the college and professor of English at Nazareth College in Rochester, New York. Her appointment made headlines since it was the first time in Nazareth's history that a lay person had been hired for an administrative position. Sister Helen Daniel, college president, explained, "Miss Radley can bring special qualities to the post of dean, and will help importantly in our efforts to make education at the college more rewarding and inspiring."[745]

Dr. Radley made news again in 1973 when she was the first woman to be appointed provost for undergraduate education in central administration of the State University of New York. As such she was the second-highest-ranking female in the SUNY System.[746] Her responsibility was to assist in developing undergraduate curricula across the seventy-two SUNY institutions (figure 1.71).[747]

Figure 1.71. Virginia L. Radley made educational history several times in her career. SUNY Oswego Archives and Special Collections.

Her meteoric rise in the ranks of New York State's higher education continued when in 1974 she was named by the SUNY Board of Trustees to a new position of provost and executive vice president at SUNY Oswego: "Dr. Radley's appointment climaxes a year-long search by Oswego officials for a provost to help administer the growing arts and science college. Her professional rank is among the highest in State University provosts for undergraduate education with responsibilities involving all units of State University."[748]

Radley voiced her beliefs and opinions in a wide-ranging interview given shortly after arriving in Oswego. She did not advocate for the unionization of teachers, and she worried that technology would overshadow the humanistic approach to education. She viewed her role as one ensuring that Oswego students received a quality education: "I would like to see Oswego the star in the crown of four year colleges in the state university system. I have seen what colleges in the private sector can do with careful husbanding of resources."[749]

SUNY Oswego president James Perdue's decision in 1977 to accept a new SUNY central position of associate chancellor for special projects propelled Radley to the president's office, if only on a temporary basis, since a lengthy search would be undertaken for a permanent college head. Radley now had total responsibility for the operation of a ninety-three-million-dollar campus, forty academic programs offering bachelor's and master's degrees, as well as certificates of advanced study. The current enrollment stood at nearly nine thousand students and the annual budget was approximately nineteen million dollars.[750]

The college council at SUNY Oswego quickly took steps to search for a new president, and almost as quickly controversy arose when faculty members complained that they were not permitted a role in the selection process. When six finalists were named, one of them was Virginia Radley. The informal faculty committee deemed her unacceptable, favoring instead Dr. David Barry, dean of graduate studies at the University of Toledo, and Dr. James Young, president for policy and planning at SUNY Buffalo.[751]

Nevertheless, on March 22, 1978, the SUNY Board of Trustees announced that Dr. Virginia L. Radley had that morning been appointed the eighth president of the college at Oswego. She was also the first woman so appointed in any SUNY school. Mrs. Elisabeth Luce Moore, chair of the SUNY Board of Trustees, announced the board's choice: "The appointment of a person with Dr. Radley's excellent credentials, coming as she does from within our own State University system, is proof of the board's genuine effort to recognize the intellectual caliber of our staff and faculty and the competence of women as administrators and managers as well as educators."[752] Radley said of her selection, "I knew I was qualified for the job and kept hoping that people would feel we've come far enough in civilization to finally allow and recognize the abilities of a woman to hold down such a post" (figure 1.72).[753] Even she, however, grew weary of being singled out as "the first." When a reporter asked her "whether she tires of being asked how it feels to be the first woman president in the SUNY system she said, 'frankly, the question bores me.' She finds it tedious to have the question raised again and again because she is so long established in the world of education."[754]

The Radley years at SUNY Oswego were fraught with controversy. One of the biggest concerns was the annual budget. Beginning in 1980 Governor Hugh Carey proposed drastic cuts to the SUNY allocations, which in Oswego ultimately led to retrenchment of many staff members.[755] Radley vigorously campaigned for more local fiscal autonomy and did not hesitate to criticize the state when she thought its actions were detrimental to the Oswego campus. Said one reporter of her performance at a public

Figure 1.72. Virginia Radley's inauguration as SUNY Oswego's eighth president was full of pomp and circumstance. SUNY Oswego Archives and Special Collections.

function, "She spent most of the time selling the college to the community reviewing the school's past, its progress and its present situation. Then she turned on the state owned State University of New York and let them have it with both barrels. She was taking on her own boss and her boss took a very eloquent beating."[756]

Another controversy involved arming college security officers.[757] Despite student objections, Radley agreed to permit officers to carry weapons during the night shift. Radley herself was a licensed pistol owner, and at least one letter writer considered that fact something wonderful, praising her for paying no attention to those who were "smirking and jeering about the pistol totin' female acting college president." The anonymous writer continued, "Now that we have someone who is 'gutsy' enough to run a tight ship, let her get down to providing a good education for our young who wish it and let her kick out those who don't wish it. The Equal Righters say she has set Oswego back ten years. I'd say she is the brightest spot that has come over the horizon in the last ten years."[758]

Radley's own personality generated its share of negative criticism. She was deemed oppressive and overbearing, particularly by the male members of the Oswego faculty. She had no problem labeling critics "Yahoos."[759] She acknowledged that she was strict and explained the reason in a speech given for business and civic leaders at a function hosted by the Oswego Chamber of Commerce: "I don't believe as president that I should put job security over excellence of performance. I've been called strict. I do talk about acceptable behavior. . . . I believe in high quality standards and achieving them."[760]

As the head of a large public college, Virginia Radley reacted seriously to any type of behavior she deemed harmful to its future. The editors of the *Oswegonian,* the campus newspaper, found that out when they published their April Fool's Day spoof in 1984. April 1 was also the date of an open house for the parents of prospective students. Frustration and disappointment spilled out in a letter addressed to the entire campus community:

> A number of you have spoken to me of your strong reactions to the Oswegonian's April Fool's section. Your reactions have ranged among chagrin, disgust, anger, dismay, outrage, sorrow—all negative. I have not the foggiest idea why the students responsible for this section chose to publish such tasteless and offensive drivel. It may be that they misunderstand what constitutes a

free press. . . . Townspeople in the stores, barber shops, garages and on the streets have approached us with concern also. They are, of course, quite right to ask why taxpayer monies should subsidize such scatology. Those among the 800 parents who were here for Open House (and had the misfortune to pick up a copy of the paper) were incensed to the point where I do not expect to see their sons and daughters enrolled here this fall. For those of us who take pride in our college (and I include the vast majority of students here), the publication was at very least disheartening. . . . Many have said they would like to write letters to the editor but fear the nastiness of reprisal in the form of public vilification. While I can understand their reluctance, I, as your president, have the responsibility to speak forth regardless of retaliation. A fearful community is not a free community. Further, a community of scholars cannot afford to yield to such nefarious tactics. . . . This letter will not go to the Oswegonian. The last letter I wrote never got into print. Apparently, there are different standards applied for judging worth. Criticize the publication, your letter goes in the circular file. Write an anti-anything (including "excellence"), and you get the front page. Perhaps a little straightforward talk will freshen the atmosphere. It needs it.[761]

If any particular word applied to Radley's efforts during her tenure as president, it was "excellence." She tightened entrance requirements when other colleges were relaxing them (figure 1.73). For example, in 1987–1988 only 47 percent of applicants were accepted at Oswego, compared to 77 percent ten years earlier.[762] She promoted excellence in many ways, "emphasizing academic advisement, imposing a strict policy on academic disqualification, cracking down on vandalism and other uncivil behavior, instituting the first general education program on campus, creating the honors program for the best of Oswego's students, restoring traditional academic ceremonies like the annual Honors Convocation and, not least, by making an eloquent, public and incessant case for liberal education"[763]

She also advocated for and insisted upon excellence in teaching. She outlined what she meant by the phrase in a speech delivered before the American Industrial Arts Association, simultaneously managing to weave the poetry of Wordsworth, Keats, and Milton into her presentation:

Figure 1.73. Radley's office was on the top floor of Culkin Hall, affectionately known as "the tower of power." SUNY Oswego Archives and Special Collections.

EXCELLENCE IN TEACHING—We are here to honor it tonight and to recognize the efforts of those who excel. What is excellence in teaching?—Making a positive impact on both brain and behavior and, ultimately, on taste, appreciation, joy in work and living. . . . When Henry Adams said "A teacher affects eternity; he can never know when his influence stops," he uttered a truism, an eternal verity. . . . The impact of the Master teacher [is] not only on the brain and behavior, but also on taste and "Refinement"—in your field, the art and craft synthesize and culminate in taste, in discrimination.[764]

She was not afraid to say that teachers bore the responsibility if students failed to succeed. Asserting that educators uselessly blamed such things as television for Johnny's lack of basic skills, Radley continued, "If your students have a problem with reading or writing, address it directly and squarely—regardless of the subject area you are teaching. . . . Graduating from high school or college doesn't necessarily mean a person has mastered basic skills." She urged educators not to "throw up their hands and arms in despair" but rather to do whatever was necessary to upgrade their students' skills.[765]

Parents came in for a little counseling as well. Remarking on the fact that most college disciplinary actions involved young men, she offered suggestions to parents aimed at preventing such situations:

> Do not expect the college to accomplish in four years what you failed to do in 18. Begin early on to make ground rules clear to children. Yes, tell them you love them but tell them they live with you. You do not live with them (they are not cats). You are supposed to be the learned, they the learners. Do not tolerate nor condone the attention-getting device of breaking things (including rattles and toy trucks). . . . Do not sanction drug use or alcohol abuse. Cultivate a climate where good manners form the acceptable mode of deportment in your homes. It is difficult enough to exist in our troubled world without having to do so confronted with surly, churlish, boorish children who really do turn into ugly adults. . . . Early encouragement of reading, writing, ciphering, and the study of a foreign language is essential to the formulation of a civilized person. Never, never use the phrase, "Boys will be boys." We hear it all too often AFTER THE FACT, the fact of a tearful young man of 18, 20, or 22 being sent home from college, his "life" in ruins from his point of view and very likely from yours too.[766]

Good town and gown relations are always important to college administrations, and Radley was well aware of that fact. There were, however, limits to her power to control student behavior, especially if the offenses occurred off campus. In an entertaining guest editorial, Radley poked fun at herself and at townspeople's (futile) expectations of her in this area.[767]

Newspaper guest editorials aside, Virginia Radley was a serious scholar who specialized in nineteenth-century British poets. She habitually arose at 5 a.m. to use the time for personal research, knowing that no one would bother her at that early hour. In addition to numerous published articles and book reviews, she was the author of biographies of Samuel Taylor Coleridge and Elizabeth Barrett Browning (figure 1.74).[768] She was frequently called upon to deliver speeches pertaining to college governance or the role of women in university administration.[769]

She also served on many boards and committees, theorizing that her involvement permitted her to advocate for SUNY Oswego. She was a member of the board of trustees for Goucher College and for Marymount

Figure 1.74. Radley's first book was a biography of Samuel Taylor Coleridge. Author's collection.

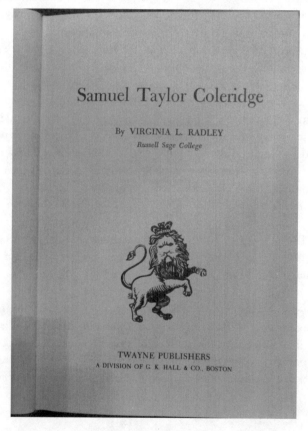

Manhattan College; the New York State Economic Advisory Council; the College Board Planning Committee; the Commission on Women, American Council on Education; and the Chamber of Commerce of Greater Oswego, Board of Directors, to name only a few. When appointed to the Board of Sentry Life she told a reporter that her new post would "entail some work" to be ready for meetings on policies, trends, ideas, and recruitment. She alluded to the fact that she was the only woman on the board: "Someone has to begin things. . . . It behooves [the companies] to have more women on the board." She said she intended to use the experience both for herself and for the students at SUNY Oswego: "It gives me more knowledge on the corporate level. . . . I can introduce students to the business and corporate world."[770]

Over the course of a career of forty-five years, Dr. Radley garnered many awards. She was the recipient of the Doris Crocket Award, Russell Sage College, in 1984; "Outstanding Educator," Oswego Chamber of Commerce, in 1982; the Galileo Medal, University of Pisa, Italy, in 1976; an honorary degree, Russell Sage College in 1981; and the distinguished alumnus award, Syracuse University in 1979, to name only a few. For her long-held view that foreign language study was imperative for a well-educated person, she was awarded the Citation as Distinguished Administrator by the New York State Association of Foreign Language Teachers in 1974. The National Organization for Women recognized her pioneer work in higher education administration in 1982 with an "Unsung Heroine" award. The New York State Legislature honored her for "achievements in higher education."[771] She was listed in *Who's Who in America, International Who's Who in Education,* and *Directory of American Scholars,* among others.

The college at Oswego celebrated its 125th anniversary in 1986, and President Radley used the occasion to reflect on her tenure. While budgets remained worrisome and complete local autonomy was still nonexistent, many advances had made the campus a better place for all. She had brought new faculty to the college and she was taking steps to bring additional minority students to provide a more diversified campus. Calling the SUNY system "the best bargain in the state," she said that she had traveled extensively recently to recruit the brightest students available, making thirty-eight addresses across the country. She proudly noted that SUNY Oswego was ranked with such private institutions as RIT and Rutgers.[772]

At the first faculty meeting in September 1987, Dr. Radley announced that she was leaving the presidency the following spring. She believed that ten years in the position was sufficient, and she had determined the time was right for her to "step out." She explained, "I've always said 10 years was long enough to be in a presidency. . . . I have been in this presidency two years longer than I planned. I've accomplished the things I wanted to see done."[773] After a short vacation/study break, she planned to return to SUNY Oswego to teach.[774] As usual, reaction to her decision was mixed. Mayor William Cahill applauded her good relations with the city. John Sullivan, chair of the College Council, alluded to her long and distinguished career and wished her well. Not so laudatory was the response of Leland Marsh of the Science Department, who complained that her administration ignored many important environmental issues.[775]

Dr. Radley spent the remainder of her career where she began the journey: in the classroom. Holding the title of "Leading Professor" at SUNY Oswego, she taught general courses in English literature as well as her specialty, the Romantic poets. In an interview given during her second year as a professor she stated, "It's a tremendous satisfaction to be back in the classroom. . . . I love to study. I love to read. I love to work with young people. This is what attracted me to the academy in the first place."[776] She elaborated in another interview, "Teaching is what it's all about. . . . A president who isn't a teacher isn't going to do very well."[777]

Radley left Oswego in January 1993, retiring to her home in Poestenkill, New York. A reporter asked her if she had "any parting words of wisdom. Dr. Radley thought for a minute, then said, 'I would like to tell my students that I've really enjoyed them.' "[778] Her alma mater, Russell Sage, invited her to be a scholar in residence, an offer she gladly accepted.[779]

On December 20, 1998, Dr. Virginia L. Radley succumbed to cancer in Poestenkill. Her death was widely reported in obituaries, which noted particularly her pioneer work in upper echelon college administrative ranks.[780]

In her monumental book *SUNY College at Oswego: Its Second Century Unfolds*, Dorothy Rogers detailed the accomplishments of the Radley era. Invited to disclose her most effective talents as an administrator, Dr. Radley said, "Every president has his or her forte, and mine is academics—I like to build monuments to the spirit and intellect. I am a combination of academician and doer; I am both a contemplative person and a person of action. You don't often find that combination in the same person. My greatest strength is that I think a lot, but I also make decisions. I am not indecisive—right, wrong, or indifferent. I make a decision, not always the perfect one."[781]

Dr. Virginia L. Radley is buried in Marion Village Cemetery with her parents and siblings.

2

Vignettes

Cora M. Ballister

Cora M. Ballister was born in Williamstown, New York, on June 16, 1879, the elder daughter of William Ballister (November 1856–September 21, 1901) and Mary V. Hanrahan (November 7, 1856–March 24, 1942).[1] Her family operated the Williamstown Hotel. Following the death of her father, Cora and her mother moved to Syracuse. Cora, a dressmaker, obtained a position at Dey Brothers Department Store in 1910 and was a longtime buyer for the company (figure 2.1). A newspaper advertisement described her position: "Miss Ballister is head of the waist department. She goes to New York markets regularly and also cooperates with our waist manufacturer in our building. The Dey waist and the Dey middy have a wide circle of friends throughout the state. Miss Ballister's energy and devotion to this exacting work have contributed much to the success of the department."[2]

Cora died unexpectedly after suffering a heart attack in her office on January 4, 1930. According to her obituary, "For the past 20 years she has been employed by Dey Bros. and had earned the esteem of her fellow employees and a vast circle of friends who were shocked to learn of her passing."[3]

Cora M. Ballister is buried in Holy Cross Cemetery, Williamstown, New York, with her parents.

Figure 2.1. Cora Ballister was a buyer for Dey Brothers Department Store in Syracuse, New York. *Syracuse Journal.*

Jessie Fairfield Gordon

Born in May 1872 in Oswego City, Jessie was the ninth and youngest child of Robert Gordon (June 29, 1828–September 27, 1891) and Sarah Jane Fairfield (May 10, 1834–December 19, 1901). Her father, who was born in Scotland, married Sarah Jane Fairfield in St. Catharines, Ontario, Canada. They came to Oswego in 1853.[4]

Jessie very early displayed an aptitude for art. In June 1896 she was awarded an arts certificate at Drexel Institute in Philadelphia, Pennsylvania.[5] She announced she would teach a class in Oswego that summer in drawing, painting, and modeling with an emphasis on outdoor sketching.[6] She garnered first prizes at the New Jersey State Fair that fall for two watercolor paintings and one bas relief, called by the newspaper "a triumph involving a substantial cash receipt and, what is more valuable than that, even substantial credit. This success confirms the opinion of numerous friends that Miss Gordon's inclination to art work is supported by undoubted aptitude for it."[7]

February 1897 saw Jessie traveling to New York City to study at the Art Students' League under the direction of "noted" sculptor Augustus Saint Gaudens: "Miss Gordon has done exceptionally fine work in her chosen line, her productions evidencing the possession of great talent."[8]

For much of the rest of her life Jessie lived in Philadelphia, although she returned to Oswego long enough to graduate from the normal school with a degree in English in 1901.[9]

She became an expert potter and her works were exhibited throughout the United States. In 1910, for example, she displayed her pottery at the Third Annual Exhibition sponsored by the Arts and Crafts Society of Portland, Oregon.[10] Her wares were exhibited at an arts and crafts show sponsored by the Arts and Crafts Guild of Philadelphia in 1915.[11]

Jessie operated a pottery in Philadelphia for twenty-eight years.[12] In 1922 she was appointed the pottery instructor at the School of Industrial Art, to succeed Charles Thomas Scott, who had been killed in a railroad accident.[13]

Her talents extended beyond simply throwing, firing, and decorating pottery. She was interested in researching the finest materials available to use in her creations:

> In the hall cases there is pottery by Jessie Fairfield Gordon, of Chestnut Hill, who has pioneered in artistic fields hitherto believed unsuited for modern Americana. She built her own potter's wheel, searched out her own red clay deposits, after vainly endeavoring to import suitable clay from Europe and from the Middle West. She made her own molds and perfected her own glazing and tinting formulae. Her work was first begun as a relaxation and as a means for personal artistic expression, but her creations have found such favor that Gordon ceramics are now in constant demand.[14]

Jessie was most noted for creating the tiles in the pergola of the Pan-American Building in Washington, DC, and the tiles located in the Bok Singing Tower in Lake Wales, Florida. After living in Philadelphia for most of her adult life, she returned to Oswego on account of ill health a year before her death on December 10, 1942.[15]

Although she had long lived away from her hometown, Oswego, Jessie Fairfield Gordon chose to be buried in Riverside Cemetery, Scriba, New York (figure 2.2)

Figure 2.2. Jessie Fairfield Gordon is buried with her parents in Riverside Cemetery, Scriba, New York. Author's collection.

Ida Louise Griffin Keating

Ida Louise Griffin had the distinction of being the first woman elected to the position of school commissioner (superintendent) in Oswego County. It is probable she was also the first woman elected to any office in the county.

Born on July 9, 1856, in Henderson, Jefferson, New York, Ida was the second of three children born to Henry L. Griffin (1822–September 9, 1875) and Lovina Gilman (1827–March 9, 1893). Her father was a soldier in Company B, 186th Regiment, during the Civil War. The family lived in Henderson, Jefferson County, in 1865 but had moved to Volney by 1870.

After graduating from Mexico Academy at the age of seventeen, Ida taught school for several years, reportedly to help pay her late father's debts. She enrolled in the Oswego Normal School and graduated from the elementary English program in February 1880.[16] She subsequently taught in several places, notably Phoenix, New York, and Greenport, Long Island. She was teaching in Marcellus, Onondaga County, in 1887 when approached by local Democratic leaders about running for the office of school commissioner for the Third Oswego District. A recent change in New York State's education law permitted women to run for this office even though they could not vote for candidates.

Ida was no shrinking violet, and when her opponent issued misleading and false statements about her, she did not hesitate to write a letter to the editor of a local newspaper refuting the charges.[17] When the votes were counted, Ida had made history by defeating her Republican opponent, Jay B. Cole of Williamstown, by roughly five hundred votes. Her victory, considered by many a step forward towards female suffrage, was not viewed with elation in all quarters. Cole, insisting votes for her be discounted since she was "ineligible to run on account of her sex," filed a petition to have the election declared null and void. He abandoned the suit only when informed that he would not be installed in her place even if he won the argument. The local Republican newspaper, the *Oswego Daily Times*, decried her election, basing its claims on the false notion that she was only twenty-one years old when she was actually thirty-two: "No girl twenty-one years of age is fit for the office of School Commissioner. She may be bright, vivacious and well educated, but she has not the experience, the knowledge of business affairs and the judgment which are necessary for a School Commissioner of one of our country districts."[18]

For the next three years Ida competently carried out her duties, attending and speaking at teachers' conventions, visiting the local rural schools, scheduling teacher examinations, and licensing teachers (figure 2.3). By all accounts she acquitted herself well.[19] She encouraged local schools to participate in Arbor Day celebrations, and because of her advocacy, in 1889 the Third Oswego District placed second in the state, with 518 trees planted on school grounds.[20] Ida was elected the first president of the Third District Teachers' Association in 1888, and vice president of a new School Principals and Commissioners' Council in the same year.[21]

Renominated for school commissioner in 1890, Ida lost a close race to her opponent, Frederick L. Smith, by a vote of 1, 544 to 1, 532.[22] In September 1891 she secured a position in the senior department of Mexico Academy.[23]

On November 25, 1891, Ida married Daniel Keating, school commissioner for the Second Madison County District.[24] She gave birth to their first daughter, known only as Miss Keating, on November 21, 1892. The baby died on January 29, 1893.[25] Ida and Daniel had two more daughters, Ida Marian (September 27, 1894–October 1, 1967) and Josephine B. (September 18, 1895–1966).

Ida died on December 11, 1897, after suffering from heart disease for more than two years.[26]

Figure 2.3. Ida L. Griffin's election as the first female education commissioner in Oswego County was big news and reported in many newspapers. *Frank Leslie's Illustrated Newspaper.*

Ida Griffin Keating was buried with her infant daughter in St. James' Catholic Cemetery, Cazenovia, Madison, New York. Her husband, Daniel Keating, is also buried there.

Rhea Claire Wilder LaVeck

Born in Syracuse, Onondaga, New York, on November 5, 1914, Rhea Claire Wilder LaVeck spent most of her adult life in Pulaski, Oswego County. Emerging from personal tragedy suffered as a young wife, she courageously met the challenges of single motherhood, professional career, and community service.[27]

Rhea was the eldest of four children born to Tracy Hartwell LaVeck (March 11, 1890–October 27, 1973) and Lois Belle Parsons (February 2, 1895–April 8, 1995). Musically gifted, she studied piano from an early age. After graduating from East High School, Syracuse, in 1929, she attended Westminster Choir College in Princeton, New Jersey, where she studied organ. For many years she served as the organist in local churches in Syracuse and Pulaski. She was in constant demand as a musical accompanist for wedding ceremonies.

Rhea married Marion Edward LaVeck (January 26, 1911–May 13, 1948) in 1936. The couple became the parents of four sons, David Edward (January 17, 1937–November 6, 2011), James William (February 6, 1938–May 9, 2012), Philip Thomas (April 13, 1939–December 8, 2013), and Steven Henry (February 1944–). Marion was a soldier during World War II and was reported missing in Italy for two months in 1944.[28] After the war, he worked as a carpenter.

It is probable that Rhea never considered that her life would extend beyond her home and family, but all that changed on May 13, 1948, when Marion was accidentally killed after falling from scaffolding in the belfry of St. Stephen's Church in Oswego City.[29] Left with four small boys to support, she suddenly faced having to make her own way in the world, and found a position as a music teacher in Pulaski High School. She obtained a bachelor's degree at Oswego State Teachers College in 1954 and a master's degree from the Crane School of Music at Potsdam State Teachers College in 1959 (figure 2.4).

Figure 2.4. Rhea LaVeck was in constant demand as a musician for local weddings. Courtesy Shawn Doyle and Half-Shire Historical Society.

Rhea's parents were very active members of Pulaski Chapter No. 159 the Order of the Eastern Star in Pulaski.[30] With their encouragement she petitioned for membership and was initiated on November 23, 1948. Advancement came quickly. She was elected Pulaski Chapter's worthy matron for 1955–1956 and appointed Oswego's district deputy grand matron for 1960–1961, with Bruce Merritt as her district grand lecturer.[31] She officially visited eleven chapters that year.[32]

Harry M. Stacy, past grand patron of the Order of the Eastern Star in New York State, invited her to consider pursuing the position of grand matron, the order's highest office. She served a two-year term as commissioner of appeals in 1963 and 1964, then was successively elected associate grand conductress for 1964–1965, grand conductress for 1965–1966, and associate grand matron for 1966–1967.[33] She was formally installed as grand matron on October 12, 1967, at the Conrad Hilton Hotel in New York City, with John K. France as her grand patron.[34] She was the first and only Oswego County woman ever to be elected grand matron (figure 2.5).

Figure 2.5. Rhea LaVeck was the first and only woman from Oswego District to be elected grand matron of the Order of the Eastern Star in New York State. Courtesy Steven T. LaVeck.

The Order of the Eastern Star is the largest fraternal organization for women in the world, and at the time Rhea became grand matron New York State was divided into forty-nine districts, containing eight hundred chapters and 145,000 members. Rhea took a year's leave of absence from her teaching job in order to make an official visit to each district.[35]

She made numerous social visits.[36] She also dedicated two chapter rooms in Oswego District.[37] Whenever possible, she visited chapters in Oswego District, accompanying Florence Grant, the district deputy grand matron.[38]

As grand matron Rhea automatically became the chair of the Eastern Star Home and Hall Foundation, and one of her duties involved fundraising for the Home at Oriskany, New York. She was instrumental in the campaign to enlarge the facility to accommodate more residents.

Rhea LaVeck was a gifted speaker, and her enthusiasm for the order was ever present in her speeches. In fact, she was known for a recitation called "Entusiasm" and was always happy to perform it. She was very proud of Oswego District and wherever she spoke always referred to it as "the biggest little district in the state."

Rhea LaVeck returned to Pulaski Academy in the fall of 1968, but her accomplishments of the previous several years were not forgotten. In 1969 the Pulaski Junior Civic League named her its "Woman of the Year."[39]

In 1973 Rhea retired from teaching. She remained active in her chapter, serving as musician for many years. She was the recognized head of Oswego District Order of the Eastern Star, the trusted confidant and advisor to numerous district leaders and worthy matrons. She enjoyed attending meetings around the district and state. In 2001 she moved to the Eastern Star Home in Oriskany. The members of Oswego District organized a surprise party to celebrate her eighty-eighth birthday in 2002.

Rhea Wilder LaVeck died at the Eastern Star Home on February 18, 2008, at the age of ninety-four and was buried in Pulaski Village Cemetery next to her husband.

Semantha "Almira" Reynolds McLean

The daughter of Alonzo S. Reynolds (1815–June 12, 1871) and Minerva L. Mason (November 1819–November 27, 1904), Semantha Reynolds McLean chose to spend a good portion of her adult life among the Shakers, first in New York State and later in Massachusetts.

Semantha, generally known as Almira, was born on April 18, 1842. According to her death certificate, she was born in Cooperstown, Otsego, New York. Little is known about the first seven years of her life, but in 1850 she was living in the Shaker community in New Lebanon, Columbia, New York. In 1855 she was living with her father and his second wife, Sarah Parmiter (January 17, 1819–June 27, 1887) in Ira, Cayuga, New York.

In 1865 Almira resided in Oswego City with her husband, James Alexander McLean (October 24, 1831–July 18, 1915). James was a veteran of the 81st Regiment NYSV (New York State Volunteers), serving from October 21, 1861 to October 31, 1864. They probably had not been married very long. Their first child was Alonzo Francis (June 1867–January 30, 1941). In 1875, the family lived in Parish, New York, and three more children had been born: Ruby C. (1869–May 17, 1884), Irving Norwood (May 18, 1871–1946), and William Theodore (August 16, 1872–January 11, 1952).

When the 1880 census was taken, James and the boys were living in Williamstown, and Almira, her mother Minerva, and Ruby were with the Shakers in Canaan, Columbia County. The couple never lived together again (figure 2.6).

Figure 2.6. Almira Reynolds McLean lived for many years in Shaker communities in New York State. She became an eldress in the Harvard Community in Massachusetts. Courtesy Douglas McLean Wilson.

The members of the United Society of Believers in Christ's Second Appearing were commonly called Shakers on account of their ritualistic dancing, which they thought "shook off" sin. The sect came to America in the late eighteenth century, and by the middle of the nineteenth century had established many communities across the nation. They believed in pacifism, simplicity of life, and celibacy. They were known for, among other things, their distinctive furniture. Their prohibition on marriage and sex resulted in a decline in membership, since only by recruiting could their ranks be replenished.[40]

When the Harvard Shaker Community in Massachusetts experienced such a decline, Almira McLean was one of the people who moved there from Mount Lebanon Community in New York State, reportedly arriving on April 13, 1887.[41] She served as ministry eldress from 1912 until 1918, when the Harvard Community closed.

Although James McLean claimed in 1900 that he was divorced, such was not the case. After his death in 1915, Almira applied for and obtained a widow's pension and thus was able to provide for herself when the Harvard Community disbanded. She died in Boston on September 30, 1923, and her body was taken to the Harvard Shaker Cemetery for burial. In September 1938 a hurricane flooded the cemetery, washing away many grave markers, including hers.[42] The graves today are decorated with metal markers affectionately known as lollipops on account of their unusual shape.[43]

Almira's grave in Harvard Shaker Cemetery is located in row seven, number thirty-eight. Her husband, James McLean, is buried in Fairview Cemetery, Williamstown, New York.

Mary Austen Oliver

Born in Norwalk, Fairfield, Connecticut on November 27, 1851, Mary Austen was the daughter of John Austen (1820–June 24, 1874) and Ann Matilda Wood (1825–May 13, 1902). She became a well-known artist, specializing in still life paintings. She was best known for her rose watercolors.

In 1850, her father, John, a native of England, called himself a Daguerreian, and by 1870 he was a professional photographer in Oswego City. Little is known about Mary's early life. A somewhat fanciful article purporting to be autobiographical appeared in 1921:

> Mrs. Oliver is a painter of roses. At the age of ten years a friend showed her how to make paper flowers and that was the

beginning. Encouraged by her father, who was an art dealer, she began her study of art, intending it only as a pleasing diversion. A few years later necessity forced her to make her avocation a profession. Widowed only a short time, she lost a large sum of money and, as is not unusual in such cases, "sat down and cried." Then she took up the painting of roses and "has never cried a day since."[44]

Mary is reputed to have studied art in New York City: "Mrs. Oliver received most of her art education in New York city, studying at the Art League and in the private studios of Walter Satterlee, Bronche, Shumway, Mrs. E. M. Scott, the rose painter, and others among the leaders of the profession."[45]

She probably became acquainted with her future husband, Francis William "Frank" Oliver (July 8, 1845–November 12, 1882), because he was a partner in her father's photography business in Oswego. They were married September 12, 1871, and their first child, Alice Josephine "Allie Joe," was born in 1873. They were also the parents of Francis William, Jr. (February 15, 1876–January 14, 1968), and Mary Eugenia "Gene" (May 7, 1881–January 14, 1975). Frank died unexpectedly of heart disease, leaving Mary with three small children to support.[46] In March 1883 she delivered a baby that died shortly thereafter.[47]

Mary's artistic talent was showcased at the Oswego Fair in September 1889 (figure 2.7):

> The private art exhibit made by Mary A. Oliver, a well known Oswego lady, cannot be too highly commended for the artistic talent it portrays. It was one of the features of the fair, and has been highly praised by those whose knowledge allows them to speak with confidence upon such subjects. The collection includes a portrait of Mr. Robert Oliver's venerable features and a family group of six of H. D. McCaffrey's children which are complete exhibits in themselves.[48]

Mary moved to Syracuse, where her daughters attended Syracuse University, and opened a portrait studio in her home at 611 Irving Avenue.[49] In 1894 Mary and Kate E. Miller opened a studio at 7 Hendricks Place (figures 2.8 and 2.9).

Figure 2.7. Mary A. Oliver painted this portrait of her father-in-law, Robert Oliver, Sr. Author's collection.

Figure 2.8. Mary A. Oliver was a well-known artist who specialized in painting roses. *Syracuse Sunday Herald.*

Figure 2.9. Mary A. Oliver and Kate E. Miller advertised their Syracuse studio in local newspapers. *Oswego Daily Palladium.*

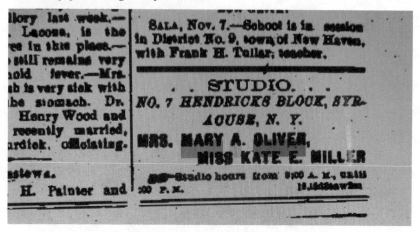

One of the new studios opened this Fall is that of Mrs. Mary A. Oliver and Miss Katherine Miller, who have a charming place in the Hendricks block. Although there are many women artists in the city, their studios are as a rule at their homes. This is one of the very few down town ladies' studios, and was a venture on the part of Mrs. Oliver and Miss Miller, but they express themselves as being immediately pleased with the results. Mrs. Oliver's specialty is portrait painting in water colors. After working in crayon for many years she decided that while the gradation of values produces artistic effects in crayon portraits, they are not faithful representations of life. They lack the warmth of flesh coloring, beauty and expression sacrificed for want of color character. She has therefore made a close study of color from life, working under some of the best instructors in New York city. Delicacy of coloring, combined with pure, clear brush work are the chief characteristics of her portrait work.[50]

Mary's talent was further recognized in a feature article published the following year: "Water-color painting, portraits from life-size to miniatures on ivory, and flowers, particularly roses, are the special lines of work pursued by Mrs. Oliver, and in these branches she has met with flattering success. Among her portraits are many reproductions of Syracusans."[51] Of particular notice was a miniature Mary created of Professor Unni Lund:

A miniature in oils, painted on ivory by Mrs. Mary A. Oliver, has been exhibited at Hendrick's & Co.'s store during the past week and has attracted a great deal of attention. Mrs. Oliver has worked with considerable skill at this very difficult line of portraiture, and its old time popularity seems likely to be revived here, as it has revived in New York since the recent celebrated exhibition of the portraits of women. The subject of Mrs. Oliver's latest miniature is Professor Unni Lund of the vocal department at the University. The likeness is admirable and the general treatment, particularly of the dress, is in the best of taste.[52]

In 1900 Mary lived in Otselic, Chemung County, but by 1902 she and Gene were living in Geneva, Seneca County. A local newspaper announced that she had been awarded a silver medal by the American Art Society of Boston for two watercolor paintings on exhibit there. In 1905 her prize-winning watercolors were exhibited in the Beard Gallery in Minneapolis.[53]

During the 1920s Mary was a resident of Laguna Beach, Orange, California, and active in the Laguna Art Association.[54]

Mary Austen Oliver died on June 2, 1930, in Ramsey County, Minnesota.[55]

Although Mary Austen Oliver died in Ramsey County, Minnesota, her body was returned to Oswego for burial in Riverside Cemetery, Scriba (figure 2.10).

Figure 2.10. Mary A. Oliver is buried in Riverside Cemetery, Scriba, New York, with her husband, Francis. Author's collection.

Caroline E. Waugh

Born in Scriba, New York, Caroline E. "Carrie" Waugh was the eldest child in a family of six siblings born to Alexander Waugh (June 1, 1808–March 27, 1853) and Amanda Malvina Stone (November 12, 1814–April 6, 1908).[56] The Waughs were devout Baptists, and one of Carrie's brothers, Hial Eugene (June 11, 1844–April 19, 1930), became an ordained Baptist minister. Although barred from the ministry, Carrie felt "called" to some sort of missionary work (figure 2.11). She herself told the story fifty years later:

> In answer to your question of what led me into the mission work I shall have to go back to the 40's or 50's when the great pro-slavery and anti-slavery agitation was causing so much trouble in our land. My father was one of the strong abolitionists of that day and I a young girl at the time the fugitive slave law was passed by Congress, and I still remember one day asking father, "If a black slave should come to our house would you hide him?" and his reply was "Certainly." It was a thousand dollars fine or imprisonment to harbor a runaway slave, and my child's heart was often troubled lest my father should be sent to prison. Always at the family altar was the slave remembered in prayer "as bound with him" and my sympathy and love for the poor slave began to grow in my childhood. Then came the soul stirring "Uncle Tom's Cabin" and the four years of Civil War and the smoke of battle had not cleared away when God called me to go to the Freedmen. Meantime, my father died when I was sixteen, leaving my mother a widow with six children, I the eldest. I felt I could not leave her, but the call grew louder and stronger and God's word continuously rang in my heart, "He that loveth father or mother more than me is not worthy of me," until I answered, "Yes, Lord, anywhere I will go.'" I told my pastor of my call and he applied to the Freedmen's Aid Society of New York who were sending out teachers to the Freedmen. I was appointed by them in the fall of '65 and then had to wait till March '66 for a vacancy. My first school was in Raleigh, North Carolina. In June when vacation came I was asked to go down the country to a plantation which Chaplain Horace James of Boston had rented, as teacher for the school he wished to have for the hands that worked his land. I went and

taught both day and night school for two years and six months. Then I was sent to James City to help in school there. I taught there three years and then the Freedmen's Aid Society disbanded and turned all their schools over to the Presbyterian Board of New York, and after a year ours was discontinued. I then asked the Baptist Home Mission, but they had all the teachers they needed. Then the Congregational Society of New York employed me for five years, two in Georgia and three in North Carolina. Seeing the great need of more work in the homes, I resigned and entered the missionary work under the Woman's Baptist Home Mission Society of Chicago. This is a brief account of how the Lord has guided me these fifty years. Most wonderfully has he led all the way; as one door would shut another would open, and to Him be all the glory.[57]

Figure 2.11. Caroline Waugh was "called" to teach former slaves in southern states after the Civil War. *Missions.*

MISS CARRIE WAUGH

Caroline E. Waugh died at the family homestead in Scriba on August 22, 1921.[58] A memorial tribute published several months later quoted Carrie's response to a question about her experiences: "I cannot describe the experiences, but I feel that I am walking in the footsteps of Jesus and where he leads me I will follow."[59]

Hillside Cemetery, located in Scriba, New York is the final resting place of Baptist missionary, Caroline E. Waugh (figure 2.12).

Figure 2.12. Caroline E. Waugh is buried in the family plot in Hillside Cemetery, Scriba, New York. Author's collection.

Notes

Preface

1. See Natalie J. Woodall, "Edwin Winslowe Clarke: Abolitionist and Humanitarian," *Oswego Palladium-Times*, July 23, 2022, 1.

2. Harriet Thompson Sampson had to wait until 1869 to learn the fate of her husband, Peter, who was killed on June 25, 1863, by a Confederate soldier as he lay in a hospital bed in Brashear City, Louisiana. See Natalie Joy Woodall, *Men of the 110th Regiment: Oswego's Own* (Denver, CO: Outskirts Press, 2016), 449–450.

3. Natalie Joy Woodall, *Notable Civil War Veterans of Oswego County, New York* (Albany, NY: SUNY Press, 2023), 215–216.

4. See Crisfield Johnson, *History of Oswego County, New York, 1789–1877* (Philadelphia, PA: L. H. Everts, 1877), 159–160. See also John Churchill, *Landmarks of Oswego County, New York* (Syracuse, NY: D. Mason, 1895), 456.

5. Churchill, *Landmarks*, 457–458.

Introduction

1. "Women's Rights Convention," *New York Evening Express*, August 7, 1848; rpt. *Rochester Democrat*.

2. The convention was widely but not immediately covered in the press. See, for example, "Woman's Rights Convention," *National Reformer*, August 3, 1848; "Women's Rights Convention," *North Star*, August 11, 1848, 1; "Woman's Rights," *New York Evening Post*, August 12, 1848, 2; "A Woman's Rights' Convention," *Weekly Memphis Eagle*, August 24, 1848, 3. Each of these, except the first, included the Declaration of Sentiments in full.

3. "Women's Rights Convention," *North Star*.

4. Deposition of January 17, 1870.

5. Woodall, *Men of the 110th Regiment*, 520–521.

6. Letter to Mrs. Georgia Cooter from J. L. Davenport, commissioner of pensions, dated August 22, 1912, located in Josiah Cooter's pension file.

7. See "Charges Will Be Made," *Oswego Daily Palladium*, November 30, 1897, 5; "Charges Were Preferred," *Oswego Daily Palladium*, December 1, 1897, 5; "Against Dr. Manwaren," *Oswego Daily Palladium*, December 17, 1897, 5; "Denies All Charges," *Mexico Independent*, January 12, 1898, 1; "Found the Doctor Guilty," *Oswego Daily Palladium*, April 30, 1898, 8; "Manwaren No Longer a Mason," *Oswego Daily Times*, May 4, 1898, 1. See also Natalie J. Woodall, "Dr. Ernest Manwaren: A Masonic Scandal," *Oswego Palladium-Times*, October 22, 2022, 1.

8. Natalie Joy Woodall, *Of Blood and Battles: Oswego's 147th Regiment* (Denver, CO: Outskirts Press, 2019), 528–530.

9. See Woodall, *Men of the 110th Regiment*, 279.

10. Woodall, *Of Blood and Battles*, 477–479.

11. Much has been written about Dr. Walker and Elmina Spencer. See, for example, Sharon Harris, *Dr. Mary Walker: An American Radical, 1832–1919* (New Brunswick, NJ: Rutgers University Press, 2009), and Joyce Cook, *Elmina Spencer: Oswego's Civil War Battlefield Nurse* (Syracuse, NY: Avalon Document Services, 2017). See also Woodall, *Notable Civil War Veterans,* 181–190 and 217–227.

12. Johnson, *History of Oswego County,* 159.

13. Churchill, *Landmarks,* 457–458.

14. "Dr. Mary Walker at Polls," *New York Sun*, November 8, 1880, 1.

15. "Woman Suffrage," *Los Angeles Sunday Times*, May 17, 1896, 26. The propounder of such an attitude, Professor H. H. Powell, was actually speaking before a women's congress in Los Angeles.

16. "Richard Croker on Women in Politics," *Oswego Daily Times*, November 28, 1908, 1.

17. The role of women in the Muslim faith depends upon the time period and cultural perspective.

18. See "Women Are Given Right to Preach," *Lowville Journal and Republican*, April 24, 1930, 1.

19. See Anne Seagraves, *Daughters of the West* (Hayden, ID: Wesanne, 1996), for excellent examples of women who made their mark on society in the western part of the United States. Particularly illustrative is the story of Kittie Wilkins (18–23). For an overview of American women's history, see Sara M. Evans, *Born for Liberty*, 2nd ed. (New York: Free Press Paperbacks, 1997).

Chapter 1

1. North America, Family Histories No. 2029, Ancestry.com; "Mexico hill" may be a corruption of Mexicoville. See also "Death of Orson Ames," *Mexico Independent,* February 21, 1867; T. A. Weed, "History and Reminiscences of the

Town of Mexico, No. 3," *Mexico Independent,* June 1, 1870, 3; and "Interesting Notes on Early History of Mexico Village," *Mexico Independent,* June 1, 1939, 3.

2. Margaret Simpson, *Mexico: Mother of Towns* (Mexico: Mexico Independent, 1985), 251.

3. "Meeting of Old Settlers' Association," *Mexico Independent,* August 30, 1882.

4. "Meeting of Old Settlers Association."

5. Simpson, *Mexico,* 468.

6. Simpson, *Mexico,* 468.

7. "Biographical," *Northern Christian Advocate,* March 1852, 52. See also "A Historical Discourse on the Origin and Progress of the M. E. Church in Mexico, N.Y.," *Deaf-Mutes' Journal,* February 8, 1877, 1.

8. "Mexico Schools Part of Civic Life," *Mexico Independent, Centennial Issue, 1861–1961,* 11; Simpson, *Mexico,* 435–436.

9. Simpson, *Mexico,* 437–438.

10. "Dr. Jas. V. Kendall's Address," *Deaf-Mutes' Journal,* September 21, 1876, 1.

11. James Strong and John McClintock, *The Cyclopedia of Biblical, Theological, and Ecclesiastical Literature* (New York: Harper and Brothers, 1894), 9:155.

12. S. P. Gray, "Rev. Wm. W. Rundell," *Minutes of the Fourth Session of the Northern New York Conference of the Methodist Episcopal Church* (Watertown, NY: Kenyon & Holbrook, 1876), 30; see also Strong and McClintock, *Cyclopedia,* 155.

13. J. H. Myers, "Mrs. Harriet P. Rundell," *Minutes of the Twenty-Fifth Session of the Northern New York Conference Methodist Episcopal Church* (1897), 74.

14. Edgar Luderne Welch, *Grip's Historical Souvenir of Mexico* (Syracuse, NY: Grip, 1904), 37.

15. "Homeopathic Medical Society," *Mexico Independent,* October 12, 1870.

16. "Homeopathic Medical Society," *Mexico Independent,* June 19, 1889, 1.

17. Johnson, *History of Oswego County,* 128.

18. "James V. Kendall's Address."

19. No headline, *Deaf-Mutes' Journal,* June 28, 1877.

20. "The Heroic Dead," *Mexico Independent,* July 24, 1862. The first battle of Bull Run occurred on June 21, 1861. See also Nelson Ames, "A History of Battery G," *Mexico Independent,* December 2, 1896, 3. Battery G saw action in many of the Civil War's bloodiest and costliest battles, among them Malvern Hill, Antietam, Fredericksburg, Chancellorsville, Gettysburg, Wilderness, and Cold Harbor.

21. Simpson, *Mexico,* 376.

22. *Deaths of Volunteers,* Ancestry.com. The writer of "The Heroic Dead" claimed he had succumbed to typhoid fever.

23. Myers, "Mrs. Harriet P. Rundell," 74; Simpson, *Mexico,* 471.

24. *Grip's Souvenir of Mexico,* 44.

25. See "Anniversary Exercises," *Deaf-Mutes' Journal,* November 7, 1872; see also "Woman's Foreign Missionary Society," *Oswego Daily Times,* October 6, 1877.

26. *Grip's Souvenir of Mexico,* 44. See also "The Anniversary of the Woman's Foreign Missionary Society," *Mexico Independent,* April 6, 1892, 3.

27. "Soldiers' Aid Society," *Mexico Independent,* June 30, 1864.

28. For information on the Old Settlers' Association, see Woodall, *Notable Civil War Veterans,* 193.

29. "Semi-Centennial Reunion of Mexico Academy," *Deaf-Mutes' Journal,* August 24, 1876. Another reunion was held in December 1889 with which Harriet was also personally involved. See "Mexico Academy Alumni Reunion," *Mexico Independent,* January 1, 1890.

30. "Rev. Wm. W. Rundell," 30; "Briefs," *Mexico Independent,* March 30, 1876.

31. "Harriet Rundell," *Mexico Independent,* March 21, 1935, 13.

32. *Grip's Souvenir of Mexico,* 44.

33. "Death of Mrs. Dr. Rundell," *Mexico Independent,* August 12, 1896, 5. See also "November 1871–November 1896. 25 Years W. F. M. Society," *Mexico Independent,* November 18, 1896, 5: "A touching memorial for Mrs. Dr. Rundell, our honored president for many years, was given by Mrs. Ella Ball. While listening, we loved to think of Sister Rundell, with others who had gone from us, that their influence still lingers"; "Harriett Rundell," *Mexico Independent,* March 21, 1935, 13; "Under the Town Clock," *Mexico Independent,* February 22, 1940, 2.

34. Myers, "Mrs. Harriet P. Rundell," 74.

35. "Woman's Home Missionary Society," *Mexico Independent,* April 14, 1897, 5.

36. "Has Taught Nearly Fifty Years," *New York Daily Tribune,* January 28, 1902; "Born Near Rome," *Rome Daily Sentinel,* April 28, 1909, 5.

37. See Churchill, *Landmarks,* 435–441, for the early history of education in Oswego.

38. Churchill, *Landmarks,* 441.

39. Churchill, *Landmarks,* 442; see also "The Pride of Oswego," *Oswego Daily Palladium,* December 31, 1887, 4, which provides an excellent summary of the development of the Oswego City school system.

40. No headline, *Eagle River Review,* March 29, 1902.

41. "World of Women," *Utica Herald-Dispatch,* April 8, 1903.

42. See Dorothy Rogers, *Oswego: Fountainhead of Teacher Education* (New York: Appleton-Century-Crofts, 1961), 58–61, for a good description of early teacher qualifications.

43. Oswego County outside of Oswego City was divided into three educational districts, each headed by a commissioner who was in charge of in-service teachers' institutes, teacher examinations, and teacher licensing. The position was also political, and the local machine nominated candidates, initially all male. They might or might not have had a baccalaureate degree. See, for example, Natalie J. Woodall, "Harvey Irving Pratt: Oswego's Scholar Shoe Salesman," *Palladium-Times,* February 4, 2023, A-7; Natalie J. Woodall, "Willis Gaylord Chaffee: Business Education Pioneer," *Palladium-Times,* March 18, 2023, A-7.

44. William A. Pope, *A History of the First Half Century of the Oswego State Normal and Training School, Oswego, New York* (Oswego, NY: Radcliffe Press, 1913), 227.

45. "Board of Education," *Oswego Daily Palladium,* March 6, 1867; "Forty-Six Years," *Oswego Daily Palladium,* September 30, 1899, 1.

46. See "A Wandering Watch," *Syracuse Daily Standard,* October 9, 1882.

47. "Miss Bruce and Her Gold Watch," *Oswego Morning Express and Times,* October 16, 1882. See also "Ellen Bruce's Watch," *Syracuse Sunday Herald,* October 8, 1882; "Onondaga County," *Utica Morning Herald,* October 10, 1882. The boys were released because Miss Bruce declined to prosecute. See "Miss Bruce's Watch," *Oswego Daily Palladium,* October 11, 1882.

48. "Stricken with Paralysis," *Oswego Daily Times,* April 27, 1899, 4.

49. No headline, *Eagle River Review,* March 29, 1902.

50. "Tonight's School Anniversary," *Oswego Daily Times,* June 26, 1903, 2.

51. "Miss Ellen M. Bruce Dead," *Oswego Daily Palladium,* April 28, 1909, 3. Miss Bruce did not deliver her prepared speech at the celebration. Miss Minnie Doran, a close friend, read it for her. See "Schools Opened Fifty Years Ago," *Oswego Daily Times,* June 27, 1903, 4.

52. See "Has Taught Nearly 50 Years," *New York Tribune,* January 28, 1902, 4; "Has Taught Nearly Fifty Years," *Sandy Creek News,* February 10, 1902, 2; "One of the Faithful," *Buffalo Review* February 21, 1902, 4; "General News," *Camden Advance-Journal,* March 6, 1902; "World of Women," *Utica Herald-Dispatch,* April 8, 1903; "Half Century of Schools," *Syracuse Post-Standard,* May 13, 1903, 10.

53. "Has Taught Nearly Fifty Years"; "One of the Faithful."

54. "Sanitary State of the Schools," *Oswego Daily Times,* August 16, 1898, 4.

55. "Schools Opened Fifty Years Ago," *Oswego Daily Times,* June 27, 1903, 4.

56. See "Deserves a Pension," *Oswego Daily Times,* February 24, 1902, 4; "New York State News," *Ontario Repository-Messenger,* June 25, 1903, 2.

57. "Miss Bruce Retires," *Oswego Daily Palladium,* June 24, 1905, 8.

58. "Oswego's Little Brown Schoolhouse Closed and the Aged Teacher Is Discharged," *Syracuse Sunday Herald,* June 25, 1905, 27. See also "Passing of Landmark," *Syracuse Sunday Herald,* January 22, 1912, B9.

59. "For Monument and Scholarship," *Oswego Daily Palladium,* November 25, 1902, 4.

60. "Miss Ellen M. Bruce Dead."

61. Rebeka Marshall was Lorenzo Dow's sister. She married Chauncey Devendorf, brother of Peter Devendorf, father of Henry Clay Devendorf.

62. See Woodall, *110th Regiment Biographical Supplement,* 127.

63. For more information on the 110th Regiment, see Woodall, *Men of the 110th Regiment,* 3–29.

64. Lieutenant Alonzo Cooper, a soldier in the 12th New York Cavalry, was taken prisoner at the battle of Plymouth, North Carolina. His wife, Mary Kirk Cooper, who was also there, barely escaped capture. See Lunette Cooper Lane,

"The Story of Lieut. A. Cooper," *Thirteenth Publication of the Oswego Historical Society,* 1950, 65–66.

65. Letter to Sidana Hoyt dated August 27, 1864, located in Hoyt's pension file; italics added.

66. "Boys in Blue and an Officer's Wife Contradict Arnold's Story of Cruelty at the Dry Tortugas," *Syracuse Sunday Herald,* January 18, 1903, 30.

67. *Chicago City Directory.*

68. Churchill, *Landmarks* "Biographical" 66.

69. "Our Near Neighbors," *Syracuse Morning Standard,* March 24, 1883, 1.

70. "County Politics," *Oswego Daily Palladium,* September 5, 1883.

71. The chartering date for Waterbury Post No. 55 WRC has not been discovered. See "Central Square," *Syracuse Daily Journal,* January 8, 1898, 8.

72. "Two More Conventions," *Rome Daily Sentinel,* May 19, 1899, 1.

73. "The Women's Relief Corps," *Utica Daily Press,* May 24, 1900, 6.

74. "Central Square," *Oswego Daily Times,* February 12, 1915, 6; "Central Square," *Oswego Daily Times,* January 11, 1916, 6.

75. See, for example, "W. R. C. Elects Officers," *Oswego Daily Palladium,* December 11, 1920, 3.

76. Henry was a member of Central Square Lodge No. 622 Free and Accepted Masons. See "Central Square," *Syracuse Daily Journal,* January 4, 1897, 8; see also "Death of Maj. H. C. Devendorf," *Mexico Independent,* January 13, 1897, 5.

77. Although the *Baltimore American* copyrighted the memoir, it was serialized all over the United States. See, for example, "Arnold's Story of Lincoln Conspiracy," *Philadelphia Inquirer,* December 7, 1902, 18; "Arnold's Story of the Lincoln Plot," *New Haven Morning Journal and Courier,* December 19, 1902, 3; "Daring Conspiracy to Kidnap Lincoln," *Lincoln Evening News,* December 19, 1902, 3; and "Arnold Ends His Confession of Lincoln Conspiracy," *Salt Lake Tribune,* December 21, 1902, 25.

78. "The Lincoln Conspiracy—Samuel B. Arnold's Story of the Dry Tortugas," *Syracuse Sunday Herald,* December 14, 1902, 38.

79. "Boys in Blue and an Officer's Wife"; see also "Prisoners at Dry Tortugas," *Oswego Daily Palladium,* January 20, 1903, 4. Charles Clements, a soldier in Battery L, 5th US Artillery, was stationed at Fort Jefferson from July 1865 to July 1868. He too refuted Arnold's charges. See "Arnold's Story Branded Untrue," *Philadelphia Inquirer,* December 30, 1902, 2. Arnold, who died on September 21, 1906, maintained until his death that his memoir was completely factual.

80. "Family Records," *Enterprise and News,* February 14, 1934, contains birth and death dates that Armonella compiled in a notebook. There is no mention of a daughter.

81. See "Central Square Honors Leaders," *Oswego Palladium-Times,* November 28, 1931, 3.

82. Several accounts falsely claim Armonella Devendorf was a charter member. See, for example, "In Memoriam," *Empire State Universalist,* November 1927.

83. "In Memoriam."

84. "Gave Birthday Dinner," *Oswego Daily Palladium*, May 29, 1923, 5; see also "Mrs. Armonella Devendorf Celebrates Ninetieth Birthday," unsourced article.

85. "Mrs. Armonella Devendorf," *Christian Leader*, November 5, 1927, 1438; see also "A Tribute to Mrs. Armonella Devendorf," unsourced testimonial.

86. Her only known sibling was Martha Olivia Lee (January 12, 1828–November 29, 1898), who married Alfred Lawrence Loveland (November 12, 1825–September 22, 1884) in 1850. She was the mother of four children.

87. Pope, *History*, 75–76.

88. "Dr. Mary V. Lee Pioneered Physical Education Program at Oswego Normal," *Oswego Palladium-Times*, November 10, 1959, 12; Pope, *History*, 76.

89. Pope, *History*, 77.

90. Much has been written about the Pestalozzian Method. For Sheldon's adoption of it, see Rogers, *Fountainhead*, 5–6.

91. "Normal School Anniversary," *Oswego Daily Palladium*, February 28, 1906, 5.

92. Pope, *History*, 77; "Dr. Mary V. Lee Pioneered Physical Education Program."

93. Pope, *History*, 77. Lee's religious convictions were evident in her speeches and in her actions. She was a member of Christian Endeavor and the Women's Christian Temperance Union. See "Christian Endeavor," *Oswego Daily Times*, May 30, 1890; "Gymnastics in the Normal School," in *Historical Sketches Relating to the First Quarter Century of the State Normal School at Oswego, N.Y.* (Oswego, NY: R. J. Oliphant, 1888), 97–102; "Temperance Workers in Council," *Oswego Daily Times*, October 14, 1892, 5.

94. See "Died," *New York Evening Post*, January 4, 1870, 3; "Died," *Winona Daily Republican*, January 5, 1870; "Working Women's Mutual Aid Society," *New York Herald*, January 7, 1870, 5; "News of the Week," *Red Wing Argus*, January 20, 1870, 3.

95. Pope, *History*, 77.

96. "Oswego County," *Jefferson County Journal*, November 4, 1874, 1. She eventually abandoned her medical practice to concentrate on teaching.

97. Pope, *History*, 77; "Personal Mention," *Oswego Daily Palladium*, August 17, 1880; "Personal," *Oswego Morning Express*, June 3, 1882; "Returning from Europe," *Oswego Daily Palladium*, June 16, 1882; "Notes from Reporters' Books," *Oswego Daily Palladium*, June 19, 1882.

98. "Lectures," *Oswego Daily Times*, March 9, 1875.

99. "Sermon on the Mount," *Oswego Daily Times*, April 3, 1880.

100. "Teachers' Institute," *Lowville Journal and Republican*, October 6, 1887. See also "Northern Central Counties," *Utica Weekly Herald*, October 25, 1887, 3.

101. "Teachers Institute," *Mexico Independent*, May 15, 1889, 3. Note the Pestalozzian influence in her suggestions.

102. See www.delsarteproject.com, "A Brief History of Delsarte," The Delsarte Project.

103. "Gymnastics in the Normal School," 97, 100. The text is supplemented with parenthetical material indicating that Dr. Lee employed pictures and various movements throughout the presentation to illustrate her thoughts.

104. "Normal School Gymnastics," *Oswego Times-Express,* July 3, 1886, 5. See also "Gymnastics Training," *Oswego Times-Express,* July 15, 1886.

105. "Gymnastics for Children," *Oswego Times-Express,* July 17, 1886, 8.

106. "Teacher's Institute," *Sandy Creek News,* April 9, 1891.

107. "Away with the Garters!" *Watertown Daily Times,* October 6, 1890, 5.

108. See, for example, "The Garter Must Go," *Utica Weekly Herald,* October 7, 1890, 2; "The Order of the Garter," *Washington Evening Star,* October 8, 1890, 9; "No Heels, No Stays, No Garters," *New York Weekly Press,* October 15, 1890, 5; "Fashion in Garters," *New York Sunday Press,* November 2, 1890; "The Ways of Woman Fair," *New York Evening World,* December 20, 1890.

109. No headline, *The Homer* [LA] *Guardian-Journal,* October 15, 1890, 2.

110. "Common Sense Manners," *Oswego Daily Palladium,* January 9, 1892.

111. "Dr. Lee Ill," *Oswego Daily Palladium,* April 22, 1892, 5.

112. "Dr. Lee Improving," *Oswego Daily Palladium,* April 25, 1892, 5. Dr. Elvira Rainier was a close friend of Dr. Lee. See her story elsewhere in this book.

113. "Dr. Lee's Funeral," *Oswego Daily Palladium,* July 26, 1892, 8. See also "Dr. Lee's Funeral," *Oswego Daily Palladium,* July 27, 1892, 1.

114. "Death of Dr. Mary V. Lee," *Oswego Daily Times,* July 25, 1892, 5.

115. "The Dr. Mary V. Lee Memorial Fund," *Oswego Daily Times,* December 2, 1892, 5.

116. "Brilliant Irish Poet to Lecture Here, May 1," *Oswego Daily Times,* March 19, 1925, 3.

117. "Tablet to Dr. Lee," *Oswego Daily Palladium,* March 25, 1914, 8; italics added.

118. Churchill, *Landmarks,* 413.

119. Churchill, *Landmarks,* 414.

120. Natalie J. Woodall, "John McNair: Plotting Oswego's Future," *Oswego Palladium-Times,* July 16, 2022, 28–31; see also "The Macs," *Danville Advertiser,* August 15, 1878, 1. This article quotes in its entirety Julia's recollection of her family tree.

121. Richard M. Wright, Jr., "William Janes Wright," Findagrave.com.

122. Frances E. Willard and Mary A. Livermore, eds., *A Woman of the Century* (Buffalo, NY: Charles Wells Moulton, 1894), 804. See also Thomas William Herringshaw, ed., *Herringshaw's National Library of America,* vol. 5 (Chicago, IL: American Publishers' Association, 1914), 784.

123. Julia McNair Wright, "The Life-Labor of Jean Garston," *Ladies' Repository* 19 (November 1859): 679–683.

124. Note by Philip Whitcomb on Ancestry.com, posted by Connie McNeill on September 23, 2016.

125. Professor D. S. Gage, "William Janes Wright, D. D.," *Christian Observer*, October 10, 1903, 10.

126. D. S. Gage," A Remembrance of Julia MacNair Wright," *Christian Observer*, October 14, 1903.

127. "Personal," *Anaheim Gazette*, July 29, 1876, 6.

128. See "The Disaster on Saturday," *Oswego Commercial Times*, December 23, 1851; "Peril and Rescue," *Rochester Daily Democrat*, December 25, 1851; "Reward of Heroism," *Oswego Daily Palladium*, January 27, 1852.

129. "Current Literature," *Albany Evening Journal*, September 19, 1870.

130. "Women Lecturing to Promiscuous Assemblies," *Valley Sentinel*, April 20, 1877, 5.

131. Gage, "Remembrance of Julia MacNair Wright."

132. Willard and Livermore, *Woman of the Century*, 804.

133. Programme," *Juniata Herald*, October 27, 1887, 2; rpt. of letter written by Julia McNair Wright to the *Home and Farm* magazine, published in Louisville, Kentucky.

134. Advertisement appearing in *Mower County Transcript*, April 15, 1880, 2.

135. Julia McNair Wright, *The Complete Home: An Encyclopedia of Domestic Life and Affairs, Embracing All the Interests of the Household* (Philadelphia: J. C. McCurdy), 1879, 560.

136. See, for example, Irene Chase, "Breezy Bits," *Morning Pioneer*, January 21, 1973, 12, in which the writer describes the text as "my favorite old reference book." See also "What Makes a Happy Home in Pages of a Dusty Book," *Kansas City Star*, August 9, 1931, 5, and Minnie Hite Moody, "An Old-Fashioned Book," *Newark Advocate*, August 10, 1968, 12.

137. Julia McNair Wright, *Sea-Side and Way-Side, No. 1* (Boston: D. C. Heath), 1888.

138. Gage, "Remembrance of Julia MacNair Wright."

139. Note by Philip Whitcomb posted on Ancestry.com.

140. Gage, "Remembrance of Julia MacNair Wright."

141. See, for example, "Mrs. Julia McNair Wright," *New York Evening Post*, September 3, 1903, 7; "Julia M'Nair Wright Dead," *Spokane Chronicle*, September 3, 1903, 6; "Mrs. Julia Wright Dead," *Butte Intermountain*, September 3, 1903, 8; "Noted Author Dead," *Harrisburg Patriot*, September 4, 1903, 5; "Julia M'Nair Wright Dead at Advanced Age," *Colorado Springs Gazette*, September 8, 1903, 4; "Condensed Intelligence," *Northern Christian Advocate*, September 9, 1903, 532; no headline, *Vermont Tribune*, September 11, 1903, 3.

142. Gage, "Remembrance of Julia MacNair Wright."

143. No headline, *Coldwater Sentinel*, August 3, 1869, 3.

144. "Female Physicians," *Philadelphia Times,* March 16, 1877, 2; "Lady Physicians," *Philadelphia Inquirer,* March 16, 1877, 2; Churchill, *Landmarks,* Part III "Family Sketches," 307.

145. "Elvira Rainier," *Oswego Daily Palladium,* October 13, 1902, 4.

146. "Annual Meeting of the Oswego County Medical Society," *Mexico Independent,* June 19, 1878.

147. See, for example, "Officers Elected," *Oswego Daily Palladium,* May 15, 1901, 8.

148. See, for example, "News in Brief," *Oswego Daily Palladium,* October 18, 1899, 5.

149. "A Novel Lecture," *Oswego Daily Palladium,* November 21, 1887.

150. "Church Notices," *Oswego Daily Palladium,* March 19, 1892, 6; "News in Brief," *Oswego Daily Palladium,* March 29, 1892, 5.

151. "Our City Almshouse," *Oswego Daily Palladium,* March 6, 1902, 4.

152. "King's Daughters," *Oswego Daily Times,* November 13, 1897, 8.

153. "Officers Elected," *Oswego Daily Palladium,* April 22, 1898, 8; "Grace Church Fair," *Oswego Daily Times,* December 9, 1899, 5.

154. "The Outlook Club," *Oswego Daily Times,* September 20, 1902, 5.

155. "Fountain for Park," *Oswego Daily Times,* May 5, 1900, 5.

156. "Sanitary State of the Schools," *Oswego Daily Times,* August 16, 1898, 4; "Health in Schools," *Oswego Daily Times,* August 17, 1898, 4. The latter article was written by Reverend Philip Nelson Meade, rector of Christ Episcopal Church.

157. "Indulged in Personalities," *Oswego Daily Palladium,* September 3, 1898, 5; "Outlookers Want Evils Remedied," *Oswego Daily Times,* September 3, 1898, 4.

158. "Address to Taxpayers," *Oswego Daily Times,* October 18, 1898.

159. "Taxpayers' Special Election," *Oswego Daily Times,* October 14, 1898, 3; "The Special Election," *Oswego Daily Times,* October 17, 1898; "In Common Council," *Oswego Daily Times,* November 8, 1898, 6.

160. "Department of Fire and Police," *Oswego Daily Palladium,* October 18, 1899, 6.

161. "Department of Fire and Police."

162. "On Duty—The Ambulance," *Oswego Daily Times,* October 18, 1898; "Ambulance Accepted," *Oswego Daily Times,* March 22, 1900, 4; "The Ambulance," *Oswego Daily Palladium,* March 22, 1900, 5.

163. Pope, *History,* 80–82; "Mrs. Emma Dickerson Straight," *Oswego Daily Times,* March 29, 1890. Her maiden name was incorrectly spelled in the headline.

164. "Major Willard Straight Dead," *Oswego Daily Palladium,* December 2, 1918; Mary E. Cunningham, "An Oswego Man Opens the Door of China," *Ninth Publication of the Oswego Historical Society* (Oswego, NY: Palladium-Times, 1945), 83–91, especially 85–91; Ann Reeves, "This Oswegonian Was a Straight Shooter," *Palladium-Times,* February 22, 1992, 14. Willard married Dorothy Payne Whitney (1887–December 14, 1968) in 1911. They were the parents of three children. After

his death, Dorothy paid to have Willard Straight Hall erected at Cornell University. She married Leonard K. Elmhirst in 1925 and moved to London, England.

165. "Mrs. Hazel Straight Sanborn," *Oswego Daily Palladium,* February 22, 1922; "Death of Hazel Henrietta Straight," posted on Ancestry.com by emilymae13 on October 4, 2007. This story originated with "Aunt Peg," Margaret Morley Sanborn Day (March 18, 1916–April 13, 1987).

166. "Dr. Elvira Rainier," *Oswego Daily Times,* October 13, 1902, 4.

167. "Elvira Rainier, M. D.," *Oswego Daily Palladium,* October 13, 1902, 4. See also "The Late Doctor Rainier," *Oswego Daily Palladium,* October 22, 1902, 3 (resolutions by Trustees of Oswego Hospital); "A Prominent Physician Dies," *Warren Sheaf,* October 16, 1902, 7; "In Memory of Doctor Rainier," *Oswego Daily Palladium,* October 15, 1902, 6 (resolutions by Woman's Outlook Club); "Funeral of Doctor Rainier," *Oswego Daily Palladium,* October 15, 1902, 4.

168. "Mr. Straight Gives $1,000," *Oswego Daily Times,* October 23, 1915, 4; "For Bigger and Better Work," *Oswego Daily Palladium,* March 17, 1916; "Oswego Y.M.C.A. Burns Mortgage," *Syracuse Post-Standard,* March 17, 1916, 13.

169. "For Bigger and Better Work." The tablet which was mounted in the main parlor of the YMCA was inscribed thus: "This tablet commemorates a gift to the Oswego Y. M. C. A. in loving and grateful memory of Dr. Elvira Rainier, 1847–1902. Faithful friend and beloved physician devoted to all good work. Willard D. Straight, donor."

170. "Death of Author Recalls Tears of 'Way Down East,' " *Cincinnati Post,* January 7, 1937, 17.

171. Some modern biographers have mistakenly claimed she was born in 1858, but in 1855 she was two years old, and in 1860 she was seven. Lottie's sister, Margaret, died in infancy. In 1870 George Blair married Eliza A. Danbury (1841–April 8, 1916). After Blair's death she married Captain Stephen Lefaiver (1837–October 20, 1917) on July 5, 1898. All are buried in Rural Cemetery, Oswego Town.

172. Pope, *History,* 222.

173. "Lottie Parker's Play," *Oswego Daily Palladium,* October 21, 1899, 6.

174. See "Some of the Plays Written by Lottie Blair Parker," *Richmond Item,* February 27, 1904, 12.

175. See Lida Penfield, "Charlotte Blair Parker, Actor, Author, Playwright," *Ninth Publication of the Oswego Historical Society* (Oswego, NY: Palladium-Times, 1945), 44. Penfield based much of her article on reminiscences of local residents who had known the Blair family as well as newspaper clippings collected by Frederick Wright. See also Woodall, *Men of the 110th Regiment,* 434. Anna Randall's first husband, Lieutenant Valorus Randall, was killed at the Battle of Port Hudson on June 14, 1863. She later married Israel Diehl, diplomat and clergyman.

176. "A Woman Playwright's Success," *Washington Evening Star,* January 2, 1904, 23.

177. "Successful Woman Playwright Writing a Novel of Rural Life," *New York Evening World,* November 18, 1901, 8.

178. "'Way Down East' Author, 78, Dies," *Brooklyn Times-Union*, January 6, 1937, 38.

179. "Woman Playwright's Success."

180. "Successful Woman Playwright Writing a Novel of Rural Life."

181. "Some of the Plays Written by Lottie Blair Parker."

182. Penfield, "Charlotte Blair Parker."

183. "Way Down East," *Buffalo Courier*, September 8, 1901, 2.

184. "Woman Playwright's Success."

185. "A Play that Lost $40,000 the First Year and Made Millions in Next 21," *Milwaukee Journal*, January 19, 1937, 10. See also "'Way Down East' Another Stage Hit That Seemed Doomed as a Failure," *Kansas City Times*, February 2, 1937, 18.

186. "A Long Island Dramatist," *Brooklyn Daily Eagle*, January 17, 1897, 23.

187. "Author of 'Way Down East' Likes Drinks and Smokes," *Albany Times-Union*, December 28, 1935, 13. Martha Morton (October 10, 1865–Febraury 18, 1925) was born and died in New York City. The first successful American female playwright, she wrote thirty-five plays, many of which were successfully produced despite overtly demonstrated male prejudices. Because women were not permitted to join the American Dramatists' Club, she founded the Society of Dramatic Authors, opening membership to women and men alike.

188. "Death of Author Recalls Tears."

189. See Woodall, *Notable Civil War Veterans*, 25–29.

190. Talbot Lake, "Meet the Author of 'Way Down East,'" *Las Vegas Evening Review-Journal*, November 7, 1935, 4.

191. "Author of 'Way Down East' Likes Drinks and Smokes."

192. Lottie Blair Parker, "My Most Successful Play," *Green Book Album*, July 1911, 879–881.

193. "A Play That Lost $40,000." To be fair, Lottie describes the year (1897) spent in rehearsing and trying the play in various cities. The article in *The Green Book Album* proves, however, that she did not lose all control of the script simply because she had sold the rights to Brady.

194. "Miss Parker Defends 'Under Southern Skies,'" *New York Times*, November 15, 1901, 8. The play was made into a movie starring Mary Fuller in 1915.

195. "Successful Woman Playwright Writing a Novel." See also "Lottie Blair Parker in Town," *Wilkes-Barre Times*, February 5, 1902, 5.

196. Charles Frederic Goss, *The Redemption of David Corson* (Indianapolis, IN: Bowell-Merrill Company, 1900). The stage version ran in New York City on January 8–19, 1906.

197. "Successful Woman Playwright Writing a Novel."

198. "Lottie Blair Parker in Town."

199. "Some of the Plays Written by Lottie Blair Parker."

200. "By Mrs. Parker," *Topeka State Journal*, September 17, 1903, 6.

201. "Some of the Plays Written by Lottie Blair Parker."

202. "Successful Woman Playwright Writing a Novel."

203. "Lottie Blair Parker in Town." "Syrchester" was a combination of Syracuse and Rochester. She used the false name to indicate obliquely the location of Oswego City.

204. Lottie Blair Parker, *Homespun* (New York: Henry Holt), 1909; "Homespun," *New York Times,* August 14, 1909, 24.

205. No headline, *Richmond* [MO] *Democrat,* December 7, 1882.

206. "Lottie Blair Parker," *Neenah Daily Times,* September 8, 1904, 1.

207. "Dog Catcher Too Active," *New York Times,* August 18, 1910, 4. See also "Gives Her Dogs Sea Bath," *New York Tribune,* August 18, 1910, 4.

208. "Women Carry Election," *Brooklyn Daily Eagle,* August 4, 1910, 5.

209. "Noted Woman Playwright Pays Visit to Washington," *Washington Times,* March 19, 1908, 8.

210. John W. Leonard, ed., *The Woman's Who's Who of America* (New York: American Commonwealth Co., 1914), 3:621.

211. " 'Way Down East' Authoress Weds," *San Francisco Chronicle,* May 21, 1912. What response, if any, Lottie and Harry made is unknown.

212. "Harry Doel Parker Dies," *New York Evening World,* April 19, 1921, 11; "Body of Harry D. Parker on Way Here for Burial," *Chicago Tribune,* April 24, 1921, 14. Harry's parents were Lewis Harris Parker (April 13, 1836–June 13, 1910) and Mary Ellen McDoel (July 22, 1838–May 15, 1926).

213. See, for example, "Author of 'Way Down East' Dies," *New York Sun,* January 6, 1937, 25; "Lottie B. Parker, Author of 'Way Down East,' Dies," *St. Louis Post-Dispatch,* January 6, 1937, 23; "Author of Play 'Way Down East' Dies in New York," *Saskatoon* [Canada] *Star-Phoenix,* January 8, 1937; "Way Down East," *Ogdensburg Journal,* January 11, 1937, 8; "Mrs. Lottie Parker, 78, Playwright, Is Dead," *Fort Worth Star-Telegram,* January 6, 1937, 3.

214. See, for example, Sally Lewis, "Pettycoat Lane," *Buffalo Evening News,* January 11, 1937, 7.

215. Pope, *History,* 324.

216. "Board of Education," *Oswego Daily Palladium,* September 16, 1872, 3.

217. "Board of Education," *Oswego Daily Times,* August 19, 1873, 4.

218. "Teacher of 55 Years Retires," *Watertown Daily Standard,* September 12, 1927, 2.

219. "The Normal School Commencement," *Oswego Daily Palladium,* June 26, 18991, 1; Pope, *History,* 324.

220. "Miss Harriet E. Stevens," *Oswego Palladium-Times,* June 4, 1931, 11.

221. "Will Be Great Week for Teachers," *Syracuse Daily Journal,* September 17, 1904, 8.

222. "Teachers at Pulaski," *Sandy Creek News,* September 22, 1904, 1. See also "Miss Stearns Spoke," *Oswego Daily Times,* September 18, 1915, 4. The headline

should have read "Miss Stevens." This was a reprint of an article which appeared in the *Auburn Citizen* the previous day.

223. Her sisters, Frances Adelle and Florence Grace, were also DAR members.

224. "Mrs. Riggs Re-Elected," *Oswego Palladium-Times,* May 14, 1926, 5.

225. "Memorials to Be Erected," *Syracuse Post-Standard,* March 13, 1908.

226. "Boulder Will Mark Old Fort George Site," *Syracuse Post-Standard,* September 11, 1909.

227. "Boulder Was Unveiled with Fitting Ceremonies," *Oswego Daily Times,* October 14, 1909, 4.

228. "Montcalm Park Developed, Preserved by DAR Chapter," *Oswego Palladium-Times,* January 17, 1962, 5.

229. "The Park Bill Is Approved," *Oswego Daily Times,* April 10, 1912, 4; see also "New Park Bill Almost a Law," *Oswego Daily Times,* March 22, 1912, 5.

230. "Plans Made for the Dedication," *Oswego Daily Palladium,* September 12, 1913, 5; "Historians Open Sessions Today," *Syracuse Post-Standard,* September 29, 1913.

231. "Impressive Ceremonies Signalize Dedication of Montcalm Park," *Oswego Daily Times,* September 30, 1913, 6.

232. "Montcalm Park Developed, Preserved by DAR Chapter."

233. "Local Historians," *Oswego Daily Times,* March 1, 1916, 6.

234. See, for example, "District Historians Organize and Elect," *Auburn Citizen,* December 6, 1926.

235. "Honor Miss Stevens," *Oswego Palladium-Times,* December 6, 1926, 7.

236. For information on the origins of the Oswego County Historical Society, see Natalie J. Woodall, "William Pierson Judson: Father of the Oswego County Historical Society," *Oswego Palladium-Times,* December 17, 2022, A-7; Natalie J. Woodall, "John D'Auby Higgins, Oswego's Mighty Mayor," *Oswego Palladium-Times,* March 24, 2023, A-7. See also Edwin M. Waterbury, "Oswego Historical Society Yet Strong after Fifty Active Years," *Tenth Publication of the Oswego Historical Society* (Oswego, NY: Palladium-Times, 1946), 112–155.

237. Waterbury, "Oswego Historical Society," 123. Many men were members of both clubs, among them John D'Auby Higgins and William Pierson Judson.

238. "Kingston Hosts Greet Historians," *Oswego Daily Times,* October 2, 1913, 4.

239. Waterbury, "Oswego Historical Society," 130–131. Other women who became members that night included Mrs. Frederick Leighton and Lida Scovil Penfield, for whose story see below.

240. "Famed 'Oswego' Medal Gift to Historical Society by Son of Theodore Irwin, Sr.," *Oswego Palladium-Times,* July 16, 1946, 7.

241. "Miss Harriet Stevens Selected Historian," *Syracuse Daily Journal,* September 4, 1919, 18. In 1921 the New York State Legislature passed a law mandating a historian for each village, city, town, and county.

242. "History of Oswego in World War," *Oswego Daily Palladium*, April 6, 1923, 6. The article was reprinted as "Stevens Story of World War I Is Preserved," *Oswego Palladium-Times*, November 20, 1945, 4.

243. "History of Oswego in World War."

244. "History of Oswego in World War."

245. "Oswego's Fine Showing," *Oswego Palladium-Times*, October 19, 1925, 10.

246. "Oswego Should Provide Place for Keeping Historic Records, Dr. A. C. Flick Tells Audience," *Oswego Palladium-Times*, April 21, 1925, 5.

247. "Fathers' Night Great Success," *Oswego Daily Palladium*, March 6, 1925, 5; "The Mothers' Club," *Oswego Daily Times*, March 3, 1906, 4; "County History Given at the D.A.R. Meeting," *Oswego Daily Palladium*, April 16, 1921, 6; "Miss Stevens to Speak," *Oswego Palladium-Times*, May 12, 1925, 8.

248. "Great Patriotic Parade Planned," *Oswego Daily Times*, November 27, 1917, 4.

249. "Old Home Week," *Oswego Daily Palladium*, January 24, 1922.

250. "News of Politics and Other Chat," *Oswego Palladium-Times*, September 13, 1927. She listed twelve in all.

251. "Plan Display of History Relics," *Oswego Daily Palladium*, January 17, 1925, 4.

252. "Miss Harriet E. Stevens," *Oswego Palladium-Times*, June 4, 1931, 11.

253. Sunday School Is Prospering," *Oswego Daily Times*, March 21, 1907.

254. "Oswego Teachers Want More Pay," *Syracuse Post-Standard*, November 4, 1904; "Teachers After More Pay," *Syracuse Daily Journal*, November 4, 1904.

255. "Board of Education," *Oswego Daily Times*, February 9, 1876; "Board of Education," *Oswego Daily Times*, January 27, 1879.

256. "The Big Tour Contest Has Come to an End," *Oswego Daily Times*, August 17, 1910, 1.

257. See, for example, "Times' European Tourists Have Pleasant Voyage," *Oswego Daily Times*, September 14, 1910, 5; "Times Tourists Delighted with Paris, the Beautiful," *Oswego Daily Times*, September 24, 1910, 5; "Versailles Palace and Gardens Indescribable," *Oswego Daily Times*, September 24, 1910, 4; "Will Arrive Home Tomorrow," *Oswego Daily Times*, September 28, 1910, 5; "Times Guests Home from Europe," *Oswego Daily Times*, September 30, 1910, 6.

258. Pope, *History*, 95.

259. "An Appreciation," *Oswego Palladium-Times*, June 6, 1931. The encomium was signed by Marietta Odell, Lida S. Penfield, and Richard K. Piez.

260. Emma's exact date of birth has not been discovered. It does not even appear on her death certificate.

261. Diane Doyle Parrish, *The Story of the Columbian Dolls: How the Adams Sisters Saved the Family Farm* (New Haven, CT: CreateSpace, 2013), xviii.

262. In 1890, when the law was changed to include almost every Union soldier or sailor, William Adams made successful application for a pension. At the time of his death he was receiving twelve dollars per month.

263. For a description of the Battle of Cedar Creek, see "Memories of the War," *Oswego Daily Palladium,* April 6, 1898, 6. Himan Dutcher, a veteran of the 184th Regiment, recollected the retreat and subsequent advance of the regiment under the personal leadership and encouragement of General Philip Sheridan.

264. "Fulton Fair," *Oswego Daily Times,* September 21, 1878.

265. Parrish, *Columbian Dolls,* 41–42.

266. Parrish, *Columbian Dolls,* 42.

267. Pope, *History,* 213. Cornelia's teaching career was short-lived. When she became insane is unknown, but she was a patient in the State Hospital, Ogdensburg, St. Lawrence County, in 1900. She remained confined there until her death on February 5, 1915.

268. "Resolutions," *Oswego Daily Times,* September 15, 1894, 2.

269. "Oswego Center," *Oswego Daily Times,* March 8, 1897, 8.

270. Parrish, *Columbian Dolls,* 42. See also "Emma E. Adams," *Oswego Daily Times,* July 28, 1900, 4.

271. "Oswego Center," *Oswego Daily Times,* September 25, 1894, 6.

272. Parrish, *Columbian Dolls,* 41.

273. "Oswego Center," *Oswego Daily Times,* August 11, 1894, 2.

274. Parrish, *Columbian Dolls,* 69. See also "Handmade Rag Dolls," *Utica Herald-Dispatch,* January 27, 1906, and "A Unique Enterprise," *Northern Christian Advocate,* July 10, 1901, 44.

275. Parrish, *Columbian Dolls,* 69.

276. Parrish, *Columbian Dolls,* 127. Parrish does not provide the original source for the article, and it is possible that the clipping was not properly cited.

277. "A Doll Manufactory," *Oswego Daily Times,* March 30, 1897, 5.

278. Parrish, *Columbian Dolls,* 69.

279. Parrish, *Columbian Dolls,* 126.

280. Esther Ruttan Doyle, "The Columbian Doll Story," *Thirty-Third Annual Publication of the Oswego County Historical Society* (Oswego, NY: Beyer Offset, 1972), 72. Esther Ruttan Doyle was the daughter of Emma's sister, Marietta, and the mother of Diane Doyle Parrish. See also "How the Making of Rag Dolls Developed Into an Industry," *Detroit News Tribune,* May 13, 1906, 59.

281. "Oswego Woman Honored," *Oswego Daily Times,* March 6, 1900. See also "A Doll Collection," *San Diego Union and Bee,* August 11, 1901, 6, which revealed how Mrs. Horton's six-hundred-doll collection began.

282. "'Miss Columbia' Stolen," *Oswego Daily Times,* March 10, 1900, 4.

283. "Miss Columbia Starts," *Oswego Daily Times,* March 29, 1900, 3.

284. "Delights the Children," *Los Angeles Times,* July 15, 1900, 33.

285. "A Globe Trotting Doll," *Rome Daily Sentinel,* January 27, 1903, 6. The article was printed in several newspapers. See, for example, "A Globe Trotting Doll," *Canajoharie Courier,* January 31, 1903.

286. "Oswego Center," *Oswego Daily Times,* July 13, 1899; "Oswego Center," *Oswego Daily Times,* July 25, 1899.

287. See, for example, "Obituary Notes," *Poughkeepsie Daily Eagle,* July 20, 1900; "Death of an Artist," *Buffalo Courier,* July 29, 1900; "Recent Deaths," *Boston Evening Transcript,* July 30, 1900, 5; "Telegraphic Briefs, *Ottawa Citizen,* July 31, 19006, 6.

288. "Originator of Columbian Dolls Dead," *Rochester Democrat and Chronicle,* July 29, 1900, 8.

289. "Emma E. Adams," *Oswego Daily Times,* July 28, 1900, 4.

290. Audrey Lewis, "Traveling Doll," *Utica Observer-Dispatch,* February 16, 1975, 2C.

291. "Columbian Doll Cards Ready," *Oswego Palladium-Times,* December 5, 1997, 10.

292. Natalie Woodall, "Columbian Doll Exhibit Provides Interesting Contrast," *Oswego Palladium-Times,* August 19, 2000, 2A.

293. An earlier version of this piece, "Charlotte Lund: An Unforgotten Oswego Treasure," appeared in the *Oswego Palladium-Times,* on December 24, 2019, 1.

294. Charlotte's birth date is a matter of debate since she, like many female artists of the time, frequently alleged she was younger than she actually was. She did not appear on the 1870 census taken on July 27, 1870, but was five in 1875.

295. See "Unni Lund Chosen," *Syracuse Evening Herald,* January 4, 1893, 4; "Prof. Unni Lund Dead," *Oswego Daily Times,* November 16, 1901, 1; "Obituary," *Troy Daily Times,* November 18, 1901; "Funeral of Miss Lund," *Syracuse Evening Herald,* November 19, 1901, 9; "Banked by Flowers," *Syracuse Daily Journal,* November 19, 1901; "News of the Week," *Baldwinsville Gazette and Farmers' Journal,* November 21, 1901, 1; "Miss Lund's Death," *Oswego Daily Times,* January 2, 1902, 1; "Miss Lund Said She Did Not Believe in Doctors," *Thrice-A-Week World,* January 3, 1902, 7.

296. "Oswego Singer's Debut in Paris," *Syracuse Post-Standard,* May 4, 1908.

297. Pope, *History,* 283.

298. "Funeral of Mrs. Looney," *Oswego Daily Palladium,* October 7, 1897, 8.

299. "Personal," *Oswego Daily Times,* July 1, 1895, 4. According to the passenger list located on Ancestry.com, they arrived in New York City aboard the *Alesia* on August 27, 1895.

300. "Dolgeville," *Little Falls Journal and Courier,* November 21, 1896. See also "Fairfield," *Little Falls Journal and Courier,* June 22, 1896.

301. "Beyond All Expectations," *Oswego Daily Palladium,* May 28, 1898, 5. See also "Miss Charlotte Lund's Festival," *Oswego Daily Times,* May 20, 1898, 1; "Miss Lund's Concert," *Oswego Daily Palladium,* May 26, 1898, 6. Not everyone was delighted with the program. Teachers complained that they were being forced to assist with rehearsals. Rumors abounded that Charlotte planned to pocket all

the receipts for herself. See "Miss Charlotte Lund's Festival," *Oswego Daily Times,* May 20, 1898, 1. See also "Hard Racket on the Board," *Syracuse Evening Journal,* April 15, 1899.

302. "Her Services No Longer Required," *Oswego Daily Times,* September 6, 1898. The headline does not refer to Lund. See also "Hard Racket on the Board" and "Investigating Slowly," *Syracuse Post-Standard,* September 23, 1898.

303. "Our Music Teacher Appreciated," *Oswego Daily Palladium,* July 19, 1898. See "Hard Racket on the Board." A board of inquiry established by Mayor John D'Auby Higgins into the activity of the board of education investigated Charlotte's motives in ordering new music books. She originally recommended books published by Silver Burdette then changed her mind and suggested those published by the American Book Company. Although the change looked suspicious, given the fact that the latter company hired her as an instructor that summer, Charlotte asserted that she had paid her own traveling and board expenses, and the committee found the accusations against her "unproven and undisclosed."

304. "Miss Lund Graduated," *Oswego Daily Times,* August 23, 1899; "Miss Lund a Graduate," *Oswego Daily Palladium,* August 28, 1899, 5.

305. "Mr. Bullis Will Make No Changes," *Oswego Daily Times,* June 24, 1899, 5; "Oswego's Teachers," *Syracuse Post-Standard,* June 25, 1899. In the days before collective bargaining education commissioners could and did arbitrarily determine what each teacher would receive. See the stories of Ellen M. Bruce and Harriet E. Stevens, for example.

306. "Miss Lund's Position," *Oswego Daily Palladium,* July 12, 1899, 5.

307. See "School Controversy," *Oswego Daily Times,* September 6, 1899, 1; "A Real Old-Fashioned Fight," *Oswego Daily Palladium,* September 6, 1899, 3; "Miss Lund Teaching," *Oswego Daily Times,* September 7, 1899, 8; "Bullis and Lund," *Syracuse Sunday Herald,* September 10, 1899, 1899, 22; "Teachers' Meeting," *Oswego Daily Times,* September 9, 1899, 4; "Board Deadlocked," *Oswego Daily Times,* September 29, 1899, 4; "Pay Still Held Up," *Oswego Daily Times,* October 4, 1899, 4; "Democrats Still Hold Up Salaries of Teachers," *Oswego Daily Times,* October 10, 1899, 4; "Salaries of Teachers Paid," *Oswego Daily Times,* October 18, 1899, 4.

308. See, for example, "Miss Lund to Sue the City," *Oswego Daily Palladium,* February 12, 1900, 8; "The Papers Are Served," *Oswego Daily Palladium,* February 17, 1900, 5; "The Lund Case," *Oswego Daily Palladium,* February 28, 1900, 3; "Pretty Teacher's Fight," *Syracuse Evening Herald,* March 10, 1900, 6; "Department of Education," *Oswego Daily Palladium,* May 15, 1900; "Will Be Postponed," *Oswego Daily Times,* November 12, 1900, 8.

309. "Miss Lund's Suit," *Oswego Daily Palladium,* November 12, 1900, 8.

310. "Syracuse University," *Oswego Daily Palladium,* April 12, 1900, 6; "WEAF," *The Chat,* January 26, 1924, 16; "Radio Broadcasting News," *Brooklyn Citizen,* January 29, 1924, 10.

311. See "Miss Lund's Suit."

312. See, for example, "Music and Musicians," *Harrisburg Telegraph,* October 17, 1903, 7; "In Music's Realm," *Passaic Daily News,* April 11, 1904, 4; "It Was a High Class Concert," *Montclair Times,* December 3, 1904, 5; "The Century Theatre Club," *New York Dramatic Mirror,* December 30, 1905, 10.

313. See "Charlotte Lund to Sing," *Montclair Times,* October 19, 1912, 1.

314. "Personal," *Oswego Daily Times,* May 30, 1906, 4.

315. "New Soprano," *Philadelphia Inquirer,* May 2, 1908, 7; "Oswego Singer's Debut in Paris," *Syracuse Post-Standard,* May 4, 1908. See also "Miss Charlotte Lund Hailed as New Soprano," *New York Sunday Herald,* May 3, 1909, 10; "Miss Lund Sings," *Oswego Daily Times,* May 4, 1908, 5; *Sunday Herald,* May 3, 1909, 10; "Miss Lund Sings," *Oswego Daily Times,* May 4, 1908, 5.

316. "Another Invasion," *New York Herald,* May 10, 1908, 10.

317. "Miss Lund in Rome, Italy," *Oswego Daily Times,* June 9, 1909, 8. See also "Daughter of Oswego in Grand Opera," *Syracuse Sunday Herald,* August 29, 1909, 6–B; "Miss Lund in Concert," *Oswego Daily Palladium,* February 2, 1911, 8.

318. "Charlotte Lund: Prima Donna Soprano," J. B. Pond Lyceum Bureau (Iowa City), 3; "Charlotte Lund a Brilliant Artiste," *Oswego Daily Times,* October 31, 1913, 6.

319. "A Splendid Success," *Oswego Daily Palladium,* December 7, 1918, 3. See also "Saengerbund Concert," *Hartford Courant,* January 11, 1914, 4.

320. "Charlotte Lund Pleases Audience," *Altoona Tribune,* November 8, 1927, 4.

321. May Stanley, "Musical Critics Artist's Best Friends, Says Charlotte Lund," *Musical America,* June 17, 1916, 13.

322. "Miss Lund's Tour," *Oswego Daily Palladium,* November 29, 1911, 8.

323. "Miss Lund Gives Recital," *New York Daily Tribune,* March 29, 1916, 11.

324. "Charlotte Lund Gives a Delightful Recital," *New York Evening World,* December 21, 1911, 29.

325. "Radio Fans Are to 'See' Grand Opera," *Oswego Daily Palladium,* March 21, 1925, 9.

326. "Woman Impresario Hopes to Train Children to Know Opera," *Denver Post,* January 27, 1930, 10. See also Rosalie Espenscheid, "Grand Opera for Children," *Brooklyn Daily Eagle,* September 13, 1931, 87.

327. "Woman Impresario."

328. "Opera 'Thais' Numbers Will Be Presented Here," *Palladium-Times,* July 21, 1932, 14.

329. "Charlotte Lund Gives Lecture on Opera for Children," *Stamford Advocate,* April 20, 1934, 21.

330. "The School Post Box," *New York Evening Post,* October 15, 1932, 6.

331. "Symphony Orchestra in Pleasing Program," *Springfield Daily News,* April 16, 1913, 8.

332. "Noted Artists to Sing Here for Charity," *Jersey Journal,* May 14, 1913, 2; "A Musical Treat," *Bayonne Herald and Greenville Register,* May 17, 1913, 4.

333. "The Music Festival," *Peekskill Highland Democrat,* July 28, 1917, 2.

334. "Oscawana Station," *Peekskill Highland Democrat,* July 21, 1917, 10.

335. "Mme. Lund, Famous Prima Donna, Will Sing Tonight for Boys of Battery E," *Cedar Rapids Evening Gazette,* August 25, 1917, 7.

336. "Sung to the Soldiers," *Toronto Star,* April 18, 1918, 5.

337. "Christmas at the Bowery Mission," *New York Evening Post,* December 20, 1919, 13; advertisement, *New York Herald,* December 20, 1919, 10.

338. "Music Lovers Out in Force," *Syracuse Post-Standard,* October 27, 1909, 10. See also "Miss Lund's Triumph," *Oswego Daily Times,* October 27, 1909, 7. The event, adjudged "the musical event of the season," was heavily publicized. See "Miss Lund Will Give Concert," *Oswego Daily Times,* October 15, 1909, 10; "Miss Lund's Concert Tomorrow," *Oswego Daily Times,* October 25, 1909, 4. A large display advertisement appeared in the *Oswego Daily Times,* October 23, 1909, 6.

339. "Renders a Concert in Her Home City," *Syracuse Post-Standard,* October 30, 1913, 2.

340. "Charlotte Lund a Brilliant Artiste."

341. "Opera 'Thais' Numbers Will Be Presented Here."

342. "Charlotte Lund to Sing Tonight," *Oswego Daily Times,* December 9, 1924.

343. See, for example, "Normal Reunion Held Saturday Great Success," *Oswego Palladium-Times,* May 17, 1932, 3.

344. "New Memorial to Dr. Sheldon at Oswego Normal," *Oswego Palladium-Times,* October 4, 1934, 5.

345. "Madame Lund Is Heard at Normal," *Oswego Palladium-Times,* October 2, 1934, 9.

346. "Charlotte Lund, An Author," *Oswego Daily Times,* May 26, 1924, 3. Prices for a complete set of the paperback version today can run from twenty-five to sixty-nine dollars. A hardback set has been advertised for $180.00; "Nordica Sang Miss Lund's Song," *Oswego Daily Palladium,* December 9, 1905. Lillian Norton "Nordica" (December 12, 1857–May 10, 1914) was an American-born opera singer whose talent earned her international fame.

347. "Charlotte Lund Heads the World's Smallest Opera Company," *Musical Observer* 24, no. 5 (May 1925), 38. It appears that the novel was never published.

348. "What to Do with the Girl with a Voice," *Inter Ocean,* March 12, 1911, 30.

349. "Madame Lund in New Role," *Brooklyn Daily Eagle,* March 10, 1919, 3; "In New Role," *Oswego Daily Palladium,* March 11, 1919, 13. See also "Push Peekskill," *Peekskill Highland Democrat,* March 15, 1919, 3.

350. No headline, *Saginaw News,* June 18, 1918, 2.

351. "Chiropean Has Fine Meeting on Child Welfare," *Brooklyn Times Union,* November 21, 1924, 5.

352. "Radio Broadcasting News." To date no one by that name who might have been old enough to be her teacher in 1878 has been identified.

353. "Mrs. Andrew Lund Dead," *Syracuse Post-Standard,* February 11, 1910, 12; "Purchased the Lund Residence," *Oswego Daily Palladium,* February 26, 1910, 4.

354. Deaths," *New York Tribune,* January 22, 1921; "Funeral of Andrew Lund," *Oswego Daily Palladium,* January 22, 1921, 10.

355. "Miss Unni Lund to Be Married," *Syracuse Evening Telegram,* November 20, 1900, 2.

356. Miss Lund Engaged," *Oswego Daily Times,* November 10, 1900, 4.

357. See "Rites Held for Geo. W. King," *Auburn Citizen,* October 1, 1930, 10.

358. "Walks and Talks," *Atlanta Constitution,* June 28, 1893, 6.

359. "Police Find Attorney Dead in His Apartment," *Washington Times,* March 1, 1921, 9; "Thomas Harrison Raines Found Dead in His Room," *Washington Evening Star,* March 1, 1921, 19; "Raines Found Dead in Washington Home," *Memphis Commercial Appeal,* March 2, 1921, 7; "Newton County Man Dies in Washington," *Newton Record,* March 3, 1921, 1; "T. R. Raines' Body Moved," *Washington Evening Star,* March 3, 1921, 21. Raines's name was given incorrectly in several notices. See also "Describes His Trip," *Washington Sunday Star,* March 13, 1921, 4. Raines was buried in Hickory Cemetery, Hickory, Mississippi.

360. César Saerchinger, *International Who's Who in Music and Gazetteer* (New York: Current Literature Publishing, 1918), 385.

361. Social Security Applications and Claims Index, Ancestry.com.; *Who's Who of New York City and State* (New York: Lewis Historical Publishing, 1947), 656 and 1208.

362. "Charlotte Lund Heads the World's Smallest Opera Company."

363. Stanley, "Music Critics Artist's Best Friends."

364. See "Mme. Lund in City," *Oswego Palladium-Times,* July 18, 1944, 4.

365. "Music and Musicians."

366. See, for example, "WEAF," *The Chat,* January 26, 1924, 16; "Radio Broadcasting News."

367. *International Who's Who in Music,* 385.

368. See, for example, "Charlotte Lund, Opera Director," *Brooklyn Daily Eagle,* July 17, 1951, 7.

369. Stanley, "Music Critics Artist's Best Friends."

370. "Death of Joel B. Penfield," *Oswego Daily Times,* July 8, 1873. See also "Death of Samuel B. Johnson," *Oswego Daily Times,* September 29, 1891, 5. Joel's first wife was Mary Olcott Pitkin (January 27, 1814–May 28, 1866).

371. "Newton W. Nutting," *Oswego Daily Palladium,* October 16, 1889; "Judge Nutting's Funeral," *Oswego Daily Times,* October 16, 1889; "N. W. Nutting's Funeral," *Oswego Daily Times,* October 17, 1889; "The Late Judge Nutting," *Oswego Daily Times,* October 17, 1889; *Memorial Addresses on the Life and Character of*

Newton W. Nutting (A Representative from New York) (Washington, DC: Government Printing Office, 1890).

372. "Mrs. C. A. Nutting," *Sandy Creek News,* February 21, 1929, 6.

373. "Tribute to an Oswego Young Lady," *Oswego Daily Times,* June 11, 1894, 4; rpt., "Known in Auburn," *Auburn Bulletin,* June 9, 1894. See also W. S. Maxwell, *General Alumni Catalogue of Boston University,* 38. Phi Chapter of Kappa Kappa Gamma was the oldest Boston University's sorority. See "Its 15th Annual Banquet," *Boston Globe,* May 22, 1897, 2; "Boston University Class Day," *Boston Evening Transcript,* June 4, 1894, 2.

374. UK and Ireland incoming passenger lists and arrivals in New York City, located on Ancestry.com.

375. "Personal," *Oswego Daily Times,* November 16, 1895, 5.

376. "*Oswegonian* Dedicated to Dr. Penfield by Students on Eve of Her Retirement," *Oswegonian,* April 29, 1940, 1; "Right and Left," *Oswego Daily Times,* April 9, 1898, 2. She was there in 1899 when called home on account of Judge Nutting's illness and death.

377. "*Oswegonian* Dedicated to Dr. Penfield."

378. See, for example, "Solving the Maid Problem," *Cincinnati Post,* March 24, 1905, 4; "Women and Their Work," *Cleveland Leader,* October 4, 1905, 7; "Linguist Asks for Char Work," *Cleveland Plain Dealer,* August 18, 1907.

379. "Miss Penfield in Charge at Y.W.C.A.," *Scranton Tribune-Republican,* September 27, 1910, 3.

380. "High School Girls in Athletic War," *Scranton Tribune-Republican,* November 3, 1910, 1.

381. "Y.W.C.A. Reports Excellent Year," *Scranton Tribune,* May 24, 1912, 4. See also "'Open House' as New Year Started," *Scranton Tribune,* January 2, 1913, 5; "Y.W.C.A. Classes," *Wilkes-Barre Times, Leader,* February 16, 1912, 12.

382. "Evening Chat," *Scranton Truth,* January 20, 1914, 7. See also "City Business Women Rally in Bible Class," *Scranton Truth,* April 25, 1914, 3.

383. New York State employment cards, located on Ancestry.com. See also "Big Class at The Normal," *Oswego Daily Times,* September 9, 1914, 4; "Teachers in Normal Are Designated," *Albany Argus,* September 25, 1914, 3.

384. "Girls' Honorary [Taps] 16 for Membership," *Oswego Palladium-Times,* May 7, 1942, 4.

385. "Teachers' Conference," *Jefferson County Journal,* November 15, 1916, 1.

386. "Teachers' Conference," *Jefferson County Journal,* November 14, 1917, 5.

387. See Rogers, *Fountainhead,* 195. See also "Graduation Exercises and Torch-light Ceremony Bring to Close the College Year," *Oswegonian,* May 17, 1943, 1.

388. "D.A.R. Leaders Visit Pulaski," *Oswego Palladium-Times,* June 14, 1935, 15.

389. Lida Scovil Penfield, *Stories of Old Oswego* (Oswego, NY: Oswego Normal School Print Shop, 1919).

390. "*Oswegonian* Dedicated to Dr. Penfield."

391. "Lest We Forget," *Sixth Publication of the Oswego Historical Society* (Oswego, NY: Palladium-Times, 1942), vii. For more information see Waterbury, "Oswego Historical Society," especially 123, 129–131. For information on the Pageant of Oswego, see Josephine Wilhelm Wickser, *Pageant of Oswego: Commemorating the Two Hundredth Anniversary of First Settlement in Oswego by the White Man* (Oswego, NY: Palladium-Times, 1925), for which Lida Penfield wrote the foreword.

392. For details on Morgan Robertson, see "Dr. Penfield Will Address Society," *Oswego Palladium-Times,* March 6, 1942, 5.

393. Contained in *Seventh Publication of the Oswego Historical Society* (Oswego, NY: Palladium-Times), 1943, 18–26. See also "Many Recall Ned Lee and Mission on First Street," *Oswego Palladium-Times,* March 17, 1943, 3.

394. Contained in the *Ninth Publication of the Oswego Historical Society* (Oswego, NY: Palladium-Times), 43–51.

395. "College President Named on Board of Historical Society," *Oswego Palladium-Times,* January 14, 1948, 7.

396. "Club Will Hear Scriba History," *Oswego Palladium-Times,* January 25, 1933, 5.

397. "Woman's Society Meets," *Oswego Palladium-Times,* March 6, 1942, 5.

398. "Bretz to Talk at Historians' Meeting Here," *Ithaca Journal,* April 28, 1933, 9. For more information on Willard Straight, see the chapter on Dr. Elvira Rainier.

399. "College Women Held Their Annual Meeting," *Oswego Daily Palladium,* May 14, 1917, 5. The organization was completing its first year of existence and boasted a membership of twenty-four.

400. "AAUW Celebrates 70 Years," *Oswego Palladium-Times,* September 30, 1988, 2. See also Ann Marie French, "Lida Penfield," *Remarkable Women in New York State History,* Helen Engel and Marilynn Smiley, eds. (Charleston, SC: Arcadia Press, 2013), 206–207.

401. "Mrs. Kideney New President of State University Women," *Buffalo Evening News,* May 16, 1942, 5.

402. "Winter Club to Resume Meetings," *Oswego Palladium-Times,* January 4, 1946, 3; "Program for Year Has Been Charted for Winter Club," *Oswego Palladium-Times,* January 5, 1952.

403. See "Supper Club Members Hold Christmas Party," *Oswego Palladium-Times,* December 8, 1942, 5; "Adjutant Howells to Speak," *Oswego Palladium-Times,* December 30, 1940, 5; "Unusual Display of Hobbies Seen at Large Throng," *Oswego Palladium-Times,* November 5, 1943, 5; "In Memoriam Mrs. Mary Egan O'Brien," *Oswego Daily Times,* May 5, 1917, 4; "Entertained at Tea," *Oswego Palladium-Times,* September 24, 1941, 5; "University Women Urged to Aid Defense Program," *Oswego Palladium-Times,* February 20, 1942, 5.

404. "Pine Twig Elects," *Oswego Palladium-Times,* September 29, 1925, 5.

405. See, for example, "To Do Summer School Work," *Oswego Daily Times,* July 1, 1918, 6.

406. "Reception, Tea Will Be Held by College Alumni," *Oswego Palladium-Times,* June 6, 1949, 3; "Sidelights of B. U. Graduation," *Boston Globe,* June 13, 1938, 7.

407. Rogers, *Fountainhead,* 201.

408. She shared the honor with Dr. Lucien B. Kinney. See "To Honor Retiring Faculty Members," *Oswego Palladium-Times,* April 12, 1940, 11. As noted above, the staff of the *Oswegonian* dedicated its April 29, 1940, issue to her.

409. This building is now known officially as Grace Ellingwood Rich Hall. See "SUCO Names New Buildings," *Fulton Patriot,* May 16, 1968, 6.

410. "Ground Broken at SUC for 2 New Buildings," *Syracuse Post-Standard,* May 19, 1966, 19.

411. "Women Have Played Role in Development of SUCO," *Oswego Palladium-Times,* December 4, 1978, 2.

412. Rogers, *Fountainhead,* 201.

413. "Dr. Lida S. Penfield," *Oswego Palladium-Times,* July 5, 1956, 14.

414. "An Appreciation," *Oswegonian,* April 29, 1940, 2.

415. "Una Clayton Was Once a Utica Girl," *Utica Herald-Dispatch,* November 17, 1910.

416. "Spear Comedy Company," *Portland Daily Press,* March 10, 1898, 5.

417. "The Una Clayton Company," *Selma Times,* September 22, 1900.

418. Letter dated May 2, 1902, posted on Ancestry.com by Patricia Kimber on December 26, 1912, transcribed by Sharon Davey LaDuke. See also "World of Players," *New York Clipper,* June 14, 1902, 346; "Little Miss Military," *Knoxville Journal and Tribune,* March 21, 1902, 6.

419. See "Warned by Son, but Drank Wood Alcohol," *Utica Herald-Dispatch,* April 1, 1904, 4; "Utica News," *Rome Daily Sentinel,* April 1, 1904; "The Matter of Mrs. Keyes," *Utica Herald-Dispatch,* April 2, 1904, 4. Van Rensselaer and Julia Davey Keyes are buried in Happy Valley Cemetery, Williamstown, New York.

420. Marriage certificate found on Ancestry.com.

421. See "Two Terms of Supreme Court," *Utica Herald-Dispatch,* November 3, 1909; "In Supreme Court," *Utica Daily Press,* November 11, 1909; "Final Decree of Divorce," *Utica Herald-Dispatch,* March 3, 1910, 8.

422. "Utter-Mckinley," *South Gate Press,* May 11, 1944, 4. The funeral home announced that it had conducted services for Halsey "during the past week." What happened to his body is as yet unknown.

423. "Kasoag," *Sandy Creek News,* June 26, 1902.

424. "Una Clayton," *Augusta Chronicle,* October 20, 1900, 8.

425. "Crowded House Last Night," *Raleigh Morning Post,* January 16, 1902, 6.

426. "Una Clayton at the Colonial with Her Company," *Virginian Pilot,* October 16, 1908, 10.

427. Una Clayton, "Human Interest the Greatest Style," *New York Dramatic Mirror,* March 15, 1919, 381.

428. See, for example, "Tomorrow Night," *Columbia* [SC] *State,* December 16, 1900, 7.

429. "A Grand Production," *Sunbury Sun,* January 19, 1899, 1.

430. "The Una Clayton Company," *Wilmington Morning Star,* January 18, 1902, 1.

431. "United States Jazz Band on New Proctor Bill Which Starts Today," *Yonkers Statesman and News,* March 6, 1924, 4.

432. "Woman Writer Has 26 Plays on Stage," *Boston Journal,* July 19, 1911, 6.

433. "About Una Clayton—By Herself," *New York Dramatic Mirror,* March 15, 1919, 381. See also "Mrs. Griffen to Return to Radio," *The News,* July 21, 1942, 28. Her surname is incorrectly spelled in the headline.

434. "Woman Writer Has 26 Plays on Stage."

435. "Una Clayton Has Exciting Trip," *New York Dramatic Mirror,* February 15, 1908, 13.

436. "Couldn't Bear It," *Lewiston Daily Sun,* November 23, 1906, 6.

437. "Had the Desired Effect," *Journal and Tribune,* March 27, 1902, 5.

438. "Act 'Milk' at the Elliott," *New York Times,* November 18, 1914, 11. See also "Orpheum Act Will Be Plea for Pure Milk," *Harrisburg Daily Independent,* January 21, 1915, 6; "Primrose Four and 'Milk' in the Vaudeville," *Syracuse Daily Journal,* March 23, 1915, 8; "Miss Una Clayton Plays for School Girls," *Buffalo News,* March 17, 1915, 7; "Makes Strong Plea for Infants," *Detroit Free Press,* June 13, 1915, 66.

439. "Una Clayton to Speak at 'News' Cooking School," *Buffalo Evening News,* March 17, 1915, 14.

440. "'Bird of Paradise' Coming," *Newark Star-Eagle,* January 4, 1913, 12. According to the article, this would be Herbert's first local appearance.

441. "Una Clayton Married," *Billboard,* February 27, 1915, 6. See also "Actress Weds Milk Play Hero," *Chicago Daily Tribune,* February 19, 1915, 1.

442. Cook County, Illinois Marriage Index, located on Ancestry.com.

443. "Mrs. Griffen to Return to Radio."

444. Una had been a member of the Order of the Eastern Star as early as 1908 but where she held her original membership is unknown. See Walter Browne and E. De Roy Koch, *Who's Who on the Stage* (New York: B. W. Dodge, 1908), 89–90.

445. See "Eastern Star of Little Falls has 4th Anniversary," *Little Falls Herald,* March 27, 1930, 1. See also, for example, "Eastern Star to Present Frolic at Theatre," *Mountain View Herald,* November 1, 1928, 1.

446. "Woman's Club Plans Benefit Show for Christmas Gifts," *Paterson Morning Call,* October 23, 1943, 6.

447. "Herbert Griffin, Aqueduct Checker, Dies Suddenly," *Paterson Morning Call,* November 19, 1949, 19; "Herbert L. Griffin," *Passaic Herald-News,* November

19, 1949, 2; "Last Rites for Herbert Griffin," *Paterson Evening News,* November 21, 1949, 23.

448. "Mrs. Herbert Griffin," *Otsego Farmer,* April 11, 1968, 6.

449. Sarah Pullar Gagne, *Five Generations of an American Family* (Sarah Pullar Gagne, 2015), 172. An undated marriage announcement in the *Rome Citizen* stated the wedding date was July 15.

450. "Died," *Utica Weekly Herald,* February 20, 1866, 5.

451. Helen Fish Taylor married Robert Pullar after teaching for several years. They lived in New York City, where Pullar was employed in banking and stock brokerage firms. They were the parents of Robert, Jr. (March 23, 1908–November 29, 1983), the father of Sarah "Sally" Pullar Gagne.

452. Gagne, *Five Generations,* 179–180.

453. "Petitioning for Their Rights," *Oswego Daily Palladium,* January 4, 1909, 5. See also "Suffragists to Celebrate," *Oswego Daily Times,* September 6, 1898, 4; "Equal Suffrage," *Oswego Daily Palladium,* May 24, 1905, 6. Delia was vice president of the Oswego County Political Equality Club and a delegate to its state convention. See also "Mrs. Delia Cezarine Fish Taylor," *Oswego Daily Palladium,* April 1, 1916, 5.

454. Gagne, *Five Generations,* 302.

455. Gagne, *Five Generations,* 187. Isabel was Newton's second wife. He first married Jeanette Ogden (1868–February 11, 1893) on February 27, 1892, in Chicago. See "Jeanette Ogden Macmillan," *Daily Inter Ocean,* February 12, 1893, 6; "Funeral of Mrs. Jeannette Macmillan," *Daily Inter Ocean,* February 14, 1893, 2.

456. "Hiram Taylor," *Oswego Daily Palladium,* August 12, 1898, 6; "Funeral of Hiram Taylor," *Oswego Daily Palladium,* August 13, 1898, 5. See also "Mannsville," *Jefferson County Journal,* August 16, 1898, 1.

457. "Esteemed Contemporaries," *Buffalo Express,* January 5, 1898, 4; "At Its Old Tricks," *Oswego Daily Times,* May 15, 1901, 2.

458. Despite a brilliant career as journalist, playwright, columnist, and editor, Newton Macmillan became an "invalid," to use the euphemism found in his obituaries. Gagne states that her mother told her Newton was an alcoholic. See Gagne, *Five Generations,* 303. Newton entered the New York City Home for the Aged and Infirm on August 11, 1919, and remained there until his death from a cerebral hemorrhage. His obituaries mistakenly but probably purposefully claimed he died at home in order to prevent embarrassment for the family. His body was transported to Oswego and he was buried in Riverside Cemetery. See "Newton Macmillan," *Oswego Daily Palladium,* December 9, 1920, 2, and "Was Formerly Editor of the Oswego Times," *Oswego Daily Times,* December 10, 1920, 2; "Newton Macmillan's Funeral," *Oswego Daily Palladium,* December 10, 1920.

459. "Personal Mention," *Oswego Daily Palladium,* August 3, 1893, 5.

460. Gagne, *Five Generations,* 304. Isabel set up a practice in the family home at 30 East Oneida Street.

461. "Sanitary State of the Schools," *Oswego Daily Times,* August 16, 1898, 4.

462. "Topic Will Be Art," *Oswego Daily Times,* August 22, 1903, 4; "Woman's Outlook Club," *Oswego Daily Times,* November 4, 1903, 5. Isabel was a member of the program committee in 1903.

463. See, for example, "Woman Suffrage Convention," *Albany Argus,* October 1, 1901, 5. Isabel was on the entertainment committee for this convention.

464. "50th Anniversary Is Celebrated by Fort Oswego DAR," *Oswego Palladium-Times,* November 9, 1954, 3. It appears that Isabel had become a member of the DAR several years earlier, probably in Chicago.

465. "Dr. Isabel Taylor Macmillan," *Oswego Palladium-Times,* March 27, 1935, 23. See also "Medical Women as Lecturers," *New York Press,* January 9, 1911, 8.

466. "News of Women's Clubs," *New York Evening Post,* January 25, 1911, 6.

467. "Burial in Riverside," *Oswego Palladium-Times,* April 2, 1935, 4. Isabel's death was widely noted. See, for example, "Dr. Isabel T. Macmillan," *New York Sun,* March 27, 1935, 23; "Dr. I. T. Macmillan Dies in New York," *Rome Daily Sentinel,* March 27, 1935, 9; "Dr. Isabel Taylor Macmillan," *Oswego Palladium-Times,* March 27, 1935, 4.

468. Gagne, *Five Generations,* 306.

469. Gagne, *Five Generations,* 309.

470. "Students on the Stage," *Oswego Morning Post,* February 2, 1883.

471. Pope, *History,* 328; "The Normal Alumni," *Oswego Daily Times,* June 28, 1894, 5.

472. "Public Exercises," *Oswego Daily Palladium,* April 28, 1887.

473. "Board of Education," *Oswego Daily Palladium,* February 7, 1888.

474. "Suspended the Teacher," *Oswego Daily Palladium,* November 14, 1908, 5. There seem to have been no great repercussions related to this matter because Grace returned to teaching after her suspension. It is ironic that Verna herself became a teacher.

475. "World's Fair Lessons," *Oswego Daily Times,* November 14, 1893.

476. "Suffragists to Celebrate."

477. "A Chautauqua Again This year," *Oswego Daily Palladium,* March 6, 1917, 4.

478. See, for example, "News in Brief," *Oswego Daily Palladium,* September 15, 1892, 5. See also "Guardian of Children," *Oswego Daily Palladium,* December 21, 1895, 5.

479. "The Humane Society," *Oswego Daily Palladium,* March 1, 1895, 3.

480. See chapter on Dr. Elvira Rainier for more information about this organization.

481. "The Normal Alumni," *Oswego Daily Times,* June 28, 1894, 5.

482. "Gets Leave of Absence," *Oswego Daily Palladium,* September 9, 1911, 1.

483. Gagne, *Five Generations,* 309.

484. "Dept. of Education Held Meeting," *Oswego Daily Times,* September 10, 1913, 1.

485. "Salary of Teachers and Superintendent Raised," *Oswego Daily Times,* January 22, 1918, 8; "Teachers Get Their Increase," *Oswego Daily Palladium,* January 22, 1918, 5. The name of her new home was erroneously given as Cold Harbor in the newspaper article.

486. "Miss Taylor's War Garden," *Oswego Daily Palladium,* May 27, 1918, 4.

487. "Grace Taft Taylor," *New York Daily News,* February 7, 1949, 208; "Miss Grace T. Taylor Dies[;] Was Oswego Suffrage Leader," *Watertown Daily Times,* February 7, 1949, 3.

488. "Suffrage Leader Dies," *Auburn Citizen-Advertiser* February 7, 1949, 8. The editor of the *Oswego Daily News* was John Barclay Alexander. See also "Miss Grace Taft Taylor," *Buffalo Evening News,* February 7, 1949, 26; "Grace Taft Taylor," *New York Daily News,* February 7, 1949, 208.

489. "Oswego High School," *Oswego Daily Times-Express,* January 29, 1886.

490. Pope, *History,* 328.

491. Gagne, *Five Generations,* 311; "Mrs. Treadwell, Educator, Dead; Rites Tomorrow," *Chicago Tribune,* December 15, 1931, 30.

492. "Gives Andrews a Rebuff," *Chicago Tribune,* November 10, 1899, 1.

493. "Puzzled by School Board," *Chicago Tribune,* October 2, 1905, 5.

494. "Trial of Platoon System Analyzed," *Chicago Daily News,* February 17, 1925, 4.

495. "Scanlon School in Crusade for Health," *Chicago Daily News,* October 27, 1924, 4.

496. These books are available online. Many are still in print. Margaret Free and Harriette Taylor Treadwell were colleagues at Forestville Elementary School.

497. "Construction Work," *Oswego Daily Times,* January 25, 1900, 2. See also "Famous Women," *Minneapolis Journal,* April 17, 1906, 10.

498. "Woman's Cure for All Evils," *Houston Chronicle,* April 6, 1910, 1. See also "Woman Gives Eleven Cures for the Present-day Evils," *Chicago Daily Tribune,* April 3, 1910, 6.

499. "Woman Tears Lining out of the United States Supreme Court," *Day Book,* October 13, 1913, 1; "Woman Attacks Supreme Courts," *Chicago Daily Tribune,* October 13, 1913, pt. 2, 1. Harriette delivered this speech in front of the newly organized Forum and Sunday Afternoon Club. She was promoting the election of Arthur Shay to the Illinois Supreme Court because she and others feared his opponent, who opposed female suffrage, would doom the suffrage bill.

500. "New President of Equality League," *Chicago Tribune,* May 5, 1913, 9.

501. "Instruction in Public Speaking," *Chicago Tribune,* October 5, 1913, 38; "English Creed for Better Speech Week," *Breckenridge News* [Hardinsburg, KY], November 5, 1919, 4; "Calumet P. T. A. Protests School Hall Rental Fee," *Southtown Economist,* January 18, 1927, 10.

502. "Both Sexes Vie for Honors at Pankhurst Talk," *Inter Ocean,* November 1, 1913, 1; "Who Welcomed Her," *Chicago Daily Tribune,* November 2, 1913, 2; "Mrs. Pankhurst Defends Woman's War in England," *Chicago Daily Tribune,* November 3,

1913, 1. It is odd that John Ostrander, Mrs. Pankhurst's manager, would demand she be introduced by a (male) public official. Perhaps he was more committed to making money than in helping the suffrage movement. His obstinacy in this matter caused considerable consternation among the local organizers.

503. "Women Law Makers," *Chicago Daily Tribune,* December 29, 1916, 1.

504. "Marion Drake, in Anger, Quits Equality League," *Chicago Daily Tribune,* October 5, 1914, 13. See also "Trout Forces Win Delegates," *Chicago Sunday Tribune,* October 4, 1914, 10. The subheadline reads "Mrs. Harriette Taylor Treadwell Charged with Using Steam Roller Methods." See also "Mrs. Treadwell Re-Elected," *Chicago Sunday Tribune,* May 3, 1914, 3.

505. "Old Suffrage Society Ends Its Life at Banquet," *Chicago Daily Tribune,* October 8, 1920, 7.

506. "Treadwell-Taylor," *Syracuse Daily Journal,* July 5, 1897, 3.

507. "Post-Wedding Reception," *Oswego Daily Palladium,* July 23, 1893, 8; "Reception Last Evening," *Oswego Daily Times,* July 23, 1893.

508. "Famous Women."

509. "Funeral of Dr. Treadwell," *Oswego Daily Palladium,* March 28, 1918, 10. For more information of the Treadwell family, see Natalie J. Woodall, "Charles H. Treadwell: Long-Time Oswego Educator and Masonic Leader," *Oswego Palladium-Times,* August 16, 2022, 1.

510. "Easter Brings New Home, New Name, New Parents to Small Boy," *Inter Ocean,* April 19, 1908, 3. See also "Treadwells Adopt a Child," *Chicago Sunday Tribune,* April 19, 1908, 4. Charles (Smith) Humphrey Treadwell (July 3, 1902–May 3, 1960) married Mae Adele Slobig (July 16, 1906–March 30, 1993) and became the father of one son and five daughters. He and Mae separated sometime after 1940. He is buried in Olivewood Cemetery, Riverside, California. She is buried in Eternal Hills Memorial Park, Oceanside, San Diego.

511. " 'Tearless' Funeral for Mrs. Treadwell Will Be Held Today," *Chicago Daily Tribune,* December 16, 1931, 26.

512. "Mrs. Harriette Taylor Treadwell," *Oswego Palladium-Times,* December 14, 1931, 15; "Mrs. Treadwell, Educator, Dead; Rites Tomorrow," *Chicago Daily Tribune,* December 15, 1931, 30; "Mrs. Harriette Taylor Treadwell," *Oswego Palladium-Times,* December 18, 1931; "Principal Dies on His [*sic*] Way Home," *Muncie Times,* December 14, 1931, 1.

513. " 'Tearless' Rites Follow Wish of Mrs. Treadwell," *Chicago Daily Tribune,* December 17, 1931, 28.

514. "Woman's Club to Honor Memory of Mrs. Treadwell," *Chicago Sunday Tribune,* December 27, 1931, 12.

515. "Friends to Hold Mrs. Treadwell's Memorial Today," *Chicago Sunday Tribune,* January 3, 1932, 2.

516. "Pupils to Plant Tree in Memory of Principal," *Chicago Sunday Tribune,* April 9, 1933, 59.

517. "Oswego High School," *Oswego Daily Times,* June 25, 1896, 5. See also "Diplomas for 43," *Oswego Daily Palladium,* July 1, 1896, 6.

518. "An Attractive Program," *Oswego Daily Palladium,* August 5, 1891, 4.

519. "Won at Last," *Oswego Daily Times,* August 23, 1895, 4.

520. "Miss Taylor's Triumph," *Oswego Daily Times,* July 24, 1897, 5. See also "Amateurs Make Merry," *Oswego Daily Times,* July 27, 1897, 4.

521. "A Benefit Tuesday," *Oswego Daily Times,* September 20, 1900, 4.

522. "Rehearsal Last Evening," *Oswego Daily Times,* August 1, 1902, 5. See also advertisement, *Oswego Daily Times,* August 4, 1902, 5.

523. "'Kettle of Fish' a Great Success," *Oswego Daily Times,* August 15, 1903, 4.

524. "Miss Jane Taylor's Success," *Oswego Daily Times,* June 3, 1898, 4.

525. "A Talented Oswego Girl," *Oswego Daily Palladium,* February 19, 1900, 6. See also "Stage Notes," *Minneapolis Star Tribune,* March 4, 1900, 2.

526. "Jane Taylor Coming," *Oswego Daily Times,* December 29, 1900, 7.

527. "At the Richardson," *Oswego Daily Times,* October 21, 1902.

528. Quoted in Gagne, *Five Generations,* 321.

529. Quoted in Gagne, *Five Generations,* 321–322.

530. Gagne, *Five Generations,* 320–322.

531. See "Carmel Captured by School Marms," *Putnam County Courier,* October 28, 1910, 1.

532. Gagne, *Five Generations,* 322.

533. "Vassar College Reopens with Services in Chapel," *Poughkeepsie Eagle News,* September 26, 1922, 10.

534. Judy Duchan, *A History of Speech-Language Pathology,* available at www.ascu.buffalo.edu. According to Duchan, Jane received a master's degree from Columbia in 1937.

535. "Speech Improvement Group Elects Officers," *New York Sun,* December 22, 1936, 34. See also "Speech Teachers Plan Dinner-Meeting," *New York Sun,* February 9, 1938, 38.

536. "Hunter Teachers to Attend Speech Confab," *New York Sun,* March 28, 1940, 26.

537. "Hunter Girls Now Hear Own Speech," *New York Sun,* February 24, 1940, 25.

538. Duchan, *History of Speech-Language Pathology.*

539. "Travel Club to Make Tour of Europe," *Oswego Palladium-Times,* May 8, 1926, 5. See also "Will Conduct Tours," *Oswego Palladium-Times,* April 19, 1927, 5.

540. Gagne, *Five Generations,* 323.

541. Gagne, *Five Generations,* 323–324.

542. Gagne, *Five Generations,* 323–325.

543. "Weddings of a Day," *New York Times,* December 11, 1902, 7. See also "Weddings—Past and to Come," *New York Tribune,* November 21, 1902, 8; "Weddings," *New York Tribune,* December 11, 1902, 8.

544. See "Edgar D. Johnson," *Oswego Daily Palladium,* July 24, 1918, 3.

545. See "Colonel John T. Mott," *Oswego Palladium-Times,* February 22, 1936, 5. See also "The Mott Dynasty," *Oswego Palladium-Times,* February 25, 1936.

546. "50th Anniversary Is Celebrated by Fort Oswego DAR," *Oswego Palladium-Times,* November 9, 1954, 3. See also "D. A. R. Holds First Meeting in Oswego," *Oswego Daily Times,* June 23, 1904, 5.

547. "Oswego County News," *Sandy Creek News,* August 7, 1913, 3.

548. "Suffragists Organize," *Oswego Daily Times,* September 9, 1914, 6; "First Guns Fired," *Sandy Creek News,* July 24, 1913, 1; same page, "Suffrage Meetings."

549. The event was widely reported. See, for example, "Women in Big Pageant, Unprotected, Battle through Avenue Mobs," *Washington Herald,* March 4, 1913, 1; "Indignant at Authorities," *Washington Herald,* March 6, 1913, 6; "Big Sensation Is Expected in Police Inquiry," *Washington Herald,* March 10, 1913, 1. The women demanded and obtained hearings in the Senate on the lack of adequate protection.

550. "Picked to Put Suffrage Question Up to Congress," *Syracuse Daily Journal,* January 29, 1914, 3.

551. "Plans Complete for Suffrage Convention," *Syracuse Daily Journal,* May 11, 1915, 21.

552. "Local Women to Attend Conference," *Poughkeepsie Evening Enterprise,* February 23, 1916, 6.

553. "Shall Women Have Justice?" *Sandy Creek News,* October 21, 1915, 6.

554. "The Franchise Franklin," *Sandy Creek News,* July 8, 1915, 1.

555. "Mrs. Mott's Statement," *Fulton Patriot,* April 26, 1917, 2.

556. "Sacrifice Week for Suffrage Workers," *Oswego Daily Times,* September 18, 1917, 5. The campaign to which she referred was the second attempt to pass the state suffrage amendment. See also "Sacrifice Day for Suffrage," *Oswego Daily Times,* August 12, 1917, 8.

557. "Called to the White House," *Oswego Daily Times,* October 26, 1917, 3.

558. "Five Women on G. O. P. Committee," *Knickerbocker Press,* October 6, 1918, 3.

559. "Mrs. Luther W. Mott Comes Out in Favor of Speaker Sweet," *Fulton Patriot,* October 8, 1919, 1.

560. "Glynn Names His Committee," *Watertown Daily Times,* May 17, 1920.

561. "Y.W.C.A. Raises $25,085," *Washington Evening Star,* April 26, 1922, 2.

562. "Mrs. Ruth Mott, 89, Dies; Civic Leader in Oswego," *Syracuse Post-Standard,* January 18, 1971.

563. No headline, *Sandy Creek News,* May 12, 1921, 1.

564. See, for example, "Mrs. Mott Entertains in Washington," *Oswego Daily Palladium,* February 18, 1914, 6; "Mrs. Luther W. Mott Hostess," *Syracuse Post-Standard,* April 22, 1916; "Mrs. Mott Entertained," *Oswego Daily Palladium,* February 14, 1917, 2; "Washington News," *Oswego Daily Palladium,* April 16, 1917, 1.

565. "Proposed Grant of $7,500 for Mrs. Mott," *Watertown Daily Times*, April 3, 1924, 1.

566. "House Ways Committee Roster Reads Like Financial Who's Who," *Atlanta Constitution*, June 25, 1922, 4.

567. See, for example, "Congressman Luther Mott Died at His Home Here This Noon Today," *Oswego Daily Palladium*, July 10, 1923, 1; "Representative Luther W. Mott Dead," *Buffalo News*, July 10, 1925, 1; "Brief Illness Ends Career of Congressman," *Syracuse Daily Journal*, July 10, 1923, 7; "Luther W. Mott Dead in Oswego," *Amsterdam Evening Recorder*, July 10, 1923, 7. See also "Obituary Notices," *Quarterly Journal of the New York Historical Association*, January 1924, 71; "Luther W. Mott," *Memorial Addresses Delivered in the House of Representatives in Memory of Luther Mott* (Washington, DC: Government Printing Office), 1925.

568. "Congressman Mott Died Poor Man," *Syracuse Daily Journal*, September 25, 1923, 5. See also "Luther Mott Died Poor Man Will Reveals," *Watertown Daily Standard*, September 25, 1923, 14.

569. "Landon to Join Staff of The Times," *Watertown Daily Standard*, July 23, 1923.

570. Information contained in an e-mail dated December 19, 2023.

571. "Widow May Get Seat in Congress," *Naples Record*, July 18, 1923, 8. See also "Mrs. Mott Is Considered for Congress," *Ogdensburg Republican-Journal*, July 12, 1923, 8; "Mrs. Mott May Seek Her Husband's Seat," *Utica Saturday Globe*, July 21, 1923, 6.

572. "A Foolish Political Practice," *Goshen Democrat*, July 27, 1923, 4.

573. "T. C. Sweet for Mott's Place If He Wishes," *Watertown Daily Standard*, July 13, 1923; "T. C. Sweet Can Be Congressman If He Desires," *Oswego Daily Palladium*, July 14, 1923, 4.

574. "Party Leaders in Accord in Making Next Postmaster," *Oswego Daily Palladium*, July 16, 1923; "Mrs. L. W. Mott Seeks Post Office Appointment," *Lowville Journal and Republican*, October 4, 1923, 7; "Oswego Woman Seeks Place as Postmistress," *Syracuse Daily Journal*, November 22, 1923, 1.

575. "Mrs. Mott's Appointment," *Oswego Daily Palladium*, February 25, 1924, 5.

576. It should be noted, however, that Mary I. Place Alexander, one of Ruth's friends and fellow member of the DAR, had previously been deputy postmaster under her father, John Place, and later, under her husband, John Barclay Alexander.

577. "Delegation Pays Honor to Mrs. Mott," *Oswego Daily Palladium*, March 15, 1924, 4.

578. "Sends Mrs. Mott's Name to Senate," *Oswego Palladium-Times*, March 4, 1932, 14. See also "Mrs. Mott Guest," *Oswego Palladium-Times*, July 16, 1936, 5.

579. "Mrs. Ruth Woolsey Mott," *Oswego Palladium-Times*, January 18, 1971, 2; "Mrs. Luther Mott Dies," *Watertown Daily Times*, January 19, 1971, 25.

580. "Miss Mott to Graduate," *Oswego Daily Palladium*, June 11, 1928.

581. See *Oswego City Directory* 1937.

582. "Home from Europe," *Oswego Palladium-Times,* March 7, 1938, 7.

583. "Red Cross," *Oswego Daily Times,* July 16, 1919, 7.

584. "First Report in Campaign Shows $6,792 Pledged," *Oswego Palladium-Times,* January 21, 1942, 4; "Will Take Course at Red Cross Headquarters," *Oswego Palladium-Times,* February 2, 1942, 12; "Three Have Resigned from Relief Bureau," *Oswego Palladium-Times,* February 4, 1942, 4; "Red Cross News," *Oswego Palladium-Times,* February 23, 1942, 3.

585. " 'War Pantries' Are Suggested," *Oswego Palladium-Times,* March 14, 1942, 5.

586. "Returns from Okinawa," *Oswego Palladium-Times,* December 15, 1945.

587. "Marion C. Mackin Given Red Cross Executive Post," *Oswego Palladium-Times,* February 23, 1943, 18.

588. Edwin Charles Tifft, Jr. earned a doctorate in chemistry from Syracuse University and at the time of his death was executive vice president of O'Brien and Gere in Syracuse, New York. He married Karen Churchill (May 16, 1945–?) on November 30, 1968, and became the father of two sons and a daughter. See "Miss Churchill, E. C. Tifft, Jr. Vows Solemnized, in Syracuse," *Oswego Palladium-Times,* November 30, 1968, 4. He died in March 1995 of Lou Gehrig's disease and was buried in Greenlawn Memorial Park, Warners, New York. See "Edwin C. Tifft, 50, Environmental Scientist," *Syracuse Herald-Journal,* March 16, 1995; "Dr. Edwin C. Tifft, Jr., Executive Vice President of O'Brien and Gere," *Valley News,* March 20, 1995, 9.

589. See, for example, "Business Men Speakers," *Oswego Palladium-Times,* April 19, 1940, 11; "Dinner Held by College Women," *Oswego Palladium-Times,* September 18, 1941.

590. "Bridge Matches to Start Today," *Oswego Palladium-Times,* August 28, 1939, 5.

591. See, for example, "Woman's Club to Give Concert at Oswego Theatre," *Oswego Palladium-Times,* March 3, 1941, 5.

592. See "Won Golf Prizes," *Oswego Palladium-Times,* July 10, 1940, 8; "Rose Dailey Again Has Highest Bowling Scores," *Oswego Palladium-Times,* November 2, 1943, 10; "Business & Professional Women Bowlers Hold Annual Banquet," *Oswego Palladium-Times,* May 8, 1944, 5.

593. "Community Chest Announces More Campaign Workers," *Oswego Palladium-Times,* October 13, 1950; "Launch Red Feather Campaign," *Oswego Palladium-Times,* October 18, 1950, 3.

594. "Community Chest Budget Committee," *Oswego Palladium-Times,* June 4, 1951, 12.

595. "Alice Mott Tifft," *Oswego Palladium-Times,* February 15, 1985, 2.

596. "E. C. Tifft, Welfare Head, Dies," *Syracuse Post-Standard,* November 1, 1971.

597. "Alice Mott Tifft."

598. "Miss Mott Honored," *Oswego Daily Palladium,* October 8, 1927, 8.

599. "To Tutor in Budapest," *Oswego Palladium-Times,* July 19, 1935, 14.

600. "Dorothy Mott to Seek Commission in Marines," *Oswego Palladium-Times,* April 6, 1943, 5. See also "Parade in Step to Honor Women Vets from WWII," *Oswego Palladium-Times,* June 28, 1995, 13.

601. "Miss Mott Retiring after 25 Years' Service at SUCO," *Oswego Palladium-Times,* May 25, 1971, 2.

602. "Miss Mott Retiring." See also "Captain Mott Commands Depot," *Oswego Palladium-Times,* June 13, 1944; "Is Commanding Officer," *Oswego Palladium-Times,* June 17, 1944, 7; "Given Promotion to Rank of Major," *Oswego Palladium-Times,* September 30, 1944, 5; "Oswego Woman Is Ranking Officer in Marine Corps," *Oswego Palladium-Times,* August 6, 1945, 5; "Dorothy Mott to Become Dean of College Women," *Oswego Palladium-Times,* August 23, 1946, 4.

603. "D-Day Ceremony Will Give Women the Glory," *Oswego Palladium-Times,* April 6, 1004, 9.

604. "Dorothy Mott to Become Dean."

605. "Miss Mott to Retire at SUCO," *Syracuse Post-Standard,* May 27, 1971, 6; "Dorothy Mott," *Oswego Palladium-Times,* November 27, 2000, 5.

606. "DAR Celebrates Its Centennial," *Oswego Palladium-Times,* October 20, 1990, 3.

607. "DAR Honors OHS Senior," *Oswego Palladium-Times,* December 11, 1993, 5.

608. "New Zonta Club Gets Charter at Dinner Thursday," *Oswego Palladium-Times,* June 10, 1955, 3.

609. "New Members of Zonta Inducted at Annual Party," *Oswego Palladium-Times,* December 17, 1966, 5; "Zonta Club Hears Lecture by College Art Professor," *Oswego Palladium-Times,* March 13, 1968, 5.

610. "Dedication," *Thirty-First Publication of the Oswego County Historical Society* (Phoenix, NY: Phoenix Press, 1970), v. The entire publication was dedicated to the Mott family, "[i]n recognition of countless contributions to the work of the society through three generations of activities."

611. "Salvation Army Flag Now Flies in 97 Countries," *Oswego Palladium-Times,* October 18, 1947, 3; "Salvation Army Auxiliary Will Help Children," *Oswego Palladium-Times,* June 21, 1949, 3. See also "Auxiliary Forms Advisory Board," *Oswego Palladium-Times,* January 21, 1950, 10.

612. See "Elect Miss Mott to Direct Group," *Oswego Palladium-Times,* May 18, 1950, 24, and "Winter Club Closes Season," *Oswego Palladium-Times,* April 23, 1965, 14. See also "President Dice Accorded Honor at YMCA," *Oswego Palladium-Times,* March 17, 1964, 4.

613. "Miss Dorothy Mott First Woman Elected to Christ Church Vestry," *Oswego Palladium-Times,* December 4, 1962, 3; "Christ Church Vestry," *Oswego*

Palladium-Times, December 7, 1962, 7. See also "Dr. Eric Croucher Chosen as Warden at Christ Church," *Oswego Palladium-Times,* November 29, 1955, 4.

614. "Take City Housing Posts," *Oswego Palladium-Times,* June 2, 1952, 3.

615. "Mayor Gould Postpones Affixing Signature to State Housing Contract," *Oswego Palladium-Times,* January 16, 1953, 12; "Housing Authority Seeks Court Order Compelling Mayor to Sign Contracts," *Oswego Palladium-Times,* February 4, 1953, 4; "Mayor Suspends Two of Housing Authority Body," *Oswego Palladium-Times,* May 20, 1953, 9; "Mayor's Suspension of Two Housing Authority Members Creates Furore," *Oswego Palladium-Times,* May 21, 1953.

616. "Expect Court to Rule on Show Cause Proceedings," *Oswego Palladium-Times,* June 2, 1953, 9; "Justices End Hassle over the Housing Loan," *Rome Daily Sentinel,* June 30, 1953, 9.

617. "Report Stay on Reinstatement May Be Sought," *Oswego Palladium-Times,* July 18, 1953, 3; "To Hear Arguments on Reinstatement Stay," *Oswego Palladium-Times,* August 3, 1953, 12; "Stay of Reinstatement of Housing Authority Members Denied by Court," *Oswego Palladium-Times,* August 7, 1953.

618. "Public Invited to Hamilton Homes Dedication," *Oswego Palladium-Times,* November 26, 1956, 2.

619. "Mayor Conway Lists Need for New DPW Garage as His Main Concern for 1971," *Oswego Palladium-Times,* December 31, 1970, 2.

620. "Mrs. Shapiro Appointed to Oswego Housing Unit," *Oswego Palladium-Times,* May 14, 1976, 1.

621. "Dorothy Mott," *Oswego Palladium-Times,* November 27, 2000, 5.

622. Quotation excerpted from e-mail message from Nancy Mott Frank to the author on December 20, 2023.

623. Churchill, *Landmarks* "Biographical" 15. See also Natalie J. Woodall, "Thomas Smith Mott: A Man 'Made of Sterner Stuff,'" *Oswego Palladium-Times,* May 6, 2023, 7.

624. "Polio Case in City," *Oswego Palladium-Times,* August 17, 1942, 5.

625. "Mott Children in Respirators," *Oswego Palladium-Times,* August 19, 1942, 4; "Another Polio Case Reported," *Oswego Palladium-Times,* August 31, 1942, 5.

626. "Wright Mott, 8, Dies of Polio in Oswego," *Syracuse Herald-Journal,* August 20, 1942, 18; "Funeral Held for Oswego Polio Victim," *Syracuse Herald-Journal,* August 21, 1942, 18. See also "Polio Fatal to Grandson of Dr. D. H. Young," *Attica News,* August 27, 1942, 4.

627. "Bailey Mott Is Slightly Better," *Oswego Palladium-Times,* August 14, 1942, 10. See also "Mott Girl Recovering from Polio; Taken Home," *Syracuse Herald-Journal,* September 5, 1942, 18; "Bailey Mott Goes Home," *Oswego Palladium-Times,* September 4, 1942, 4.

628. The Ithaca Reconstruction Home opened in 1920 for the express purpose of caring for polio victims. So outstanding was its program that President

Franklin D. Roosevelt praised it. Today the facility is known as Beechtree Center for Rehabilitation and caters largely to the elderly.

629. E-mail message from Nancy Mott Frank to the author dated December 20, 2023.

630. "Bailey Mott Is Honored; Judge Penney Speaker," *Oswego Palladium-Times,* February 21, 1956, 4.

631. "Oswego School News," *Oswego Palladium-Times,* March 13, 1954, 5.

632. "To Enter Business College," *Oswego Palladium-Times,* September 25, 1956.

633. "Dowd, Harrington, Oswego Landmark Notes 50th Anniversary," *Oswego Shopper* November 7, 1984.

634. "Mrs. Bodwich Presides over Insurance Meeting," *Oswego Valley News,* April 7, 1966; "County I. W. A. Installation of Officers," *Oswego Shopper* August 13, 1975.

635. "Harrington Heads Insurance Agents," *Oswego Palladium-Times,* December 10, 1963, section 2, 9.

636. See, for example, "Plan Annual Fashion Show," *Oswego Palladium-Times,* March 3, 1961, 5; "Card Caper Planned by Women of Oswego Episcopal Church," *Oswego Valley News,* April 7, 1966.

637. "Mrs. Frank Sayer Heads Auxiliary," *Oswego Palladium-Times,* January 19, 1960, 7.

638. "Zonta's Honors Go to Bailey E. Mott," *Oswego Palladium-Times,* December 27, 1975, 4.

639. "Oswego and Area Obituaries," *Oswego Palladium-Times,* May 5, 1976.

640. "Local and County History Competition," *Oswego Shopper* March 2, 1977. See also "Historical Society Slates Meeting," *Oswego Palladium-Times,* September 14, 1978, 2.

641. "Donations Needed for Hospital Bazaar," *Oswego Shopper* October 27, 1978.

642. E-mail message from Nancy Mott Frank to the author dated December 23, 2023.

643. Jeff Testerman, " 'Doughnut Girl' Helped Give Doughboys a Taste of Home," *Tampa Bay Times,* November 30, 1981, 53.

644. Helen Purviance's curriculum vitae provided by the Salvation Army National Archives.

645. See "Empowered from Above, William Booth Leaves His Mark," *Oswego Palladium-Times,* August 1999, 5.

646. "The Salvation Army," *Oswego Daily Palladium,* October 23, 1886. The established churches in the area were none too sympathetic to the ministry of the Salvation Army. Father Farley, a Roman Catholic priest in Fulton, New York, denounced the work of the Salvation Army, arguing that its method "divests religion of its dignity and sacredness." See "Go-As-You-Please-Religion," *Oswego Daily Palladium,* February 9, 1888, 1.

647. "Oh, This Wicked City," *Oswego Daily Palladium,* November 22, 1887, 1.

648. "Trouble in the Army," *Oswego Times-Express,* December 20, 1886, 5.

649. "Salvation Army Golden Jubilee to Be Observed," *Oswego Palladium-Times,* May 17, 1943, 5. See also "Active Ministry Successful in Port City," *Oswego Palladium-Times,* August 1999, 7.

650. "To Raise Funds for Relief of Poor," *Oswego Daily Times,* December 18, 1915, 6.

651. "The Christmas Charities," *Oswego Daily Times,* December 27, 1915, 7.

652. "Real Charity at Christmas Time," *Oswego Daily Times,* December 23, 1915, 10.

653. "Police Matron Is Wanted," *Oswego Daily Palladium,* February 19, 1914, 3. Helen's surname was misspelled throughout the article. There is no indication that she considered accepting the job.

654. Mario Christaldi, "Doughnuts: A Holy Mission," *Oswego Palladium-Times,* October 29, 1986, 1. See also "Miss Purviance Volunteers for Work in France," *Syracuse Herald,* August 4, 1917; "Leaves for War Zone," *Fulton Times,* August 7, 1917, 4.

655. "Ensign Purviance Reaches France," *Oswego Daily Times,* August 25, 1917, 4.

656. "This Lassie Fried First Doughnut," *Watkins Express,* May 5, 1920, 8.

657. Marian Nott, "The Creation of a 'Holy' Mission," *Oswego Palladium-Times,* August 1999, 2.

658. "Original Doughnut Girl Tells about Her Work," *Lakeland Evening Telegram,* January 21, 1919, 3.

659. "General Hines Enlists Ensign Helen Purviance," *Oswego Daily Palladium,* September 25, 1918, 5.

660. Nott, "'Holy' Mission."

661. "Likens German Cave to Little Corner in Hell," *Syracuse Herald,* August 19, 1918, 12.

662. "AEF's Original 'Doughnut Girl' Prays That We Keep Out of War," *Atlanta Journal,* September 22, 1939, 27.

663. "AEF's Original 'Doughnut Girl.'"

664. "Big Crowd at Reception," *Oswego Daily Palladium,* July 25, 1919, 5.

665. "Help Salvation Army Tomorrow," *Oswego Daily Palladium,* October 10, 1919, 7.

666. "Christmas for the Poor," *Oswego Daily Palladium,* December 8, 1919, 3.

667. "Salvation Army Grateful," *Oswego Daily Palladium,* December 30, 1919, 6.

668. "Adjutant Purviance Spoke to Pythians Last Evening," *Oswego Daily Times,* December 3, 1919, 4. See also "Southwest Oswego," *Oswego Daily Times,* September 30, 1919, 7; "To Speak at Scriba," *Oswego Daily Palladium,* October 27, 1919, 5.

669. "Exercises Tomorrow," *Oswego Daily Palladium,* September 27, 1919, 3. Helen's service is recorded in Harriet Stevens's massive volume on Oswego's soldiers and sailors.

670. "Evangeline Booth Gets Congressional Medal," *New York Tribune,* October 20, 1919, 16; "Adjutant Purviance Gets Medal," *Oswego Daily Palladium,* October 27, 1919.

671. "Making Effort to Retain Adjutant Purviance," *Oswego Daily Times,* August 23, 1924, 2.

672. "Oswego's Welfare Work Suffers a Distinct Loss," *Oswego Daily Times,* August 18, 1924, 6.

673. "Farewell to Adjt. Purviance, Who Left Today," *Oswego Daily Palladium,* September 2, 1924, 6.

674. "Adjutant Purviance Promoted to Staff of Training College of Salvation Army," *Oswego Daily Times,* August 19, 1924; "Doughboy's Doughnut Girl Will Teach in New York," *Richmond Times-Dispatch* September 28, 1924, 46.

675. "Salvation Doughnut Girl of War Here," *Buffalo Evening News,* October 6, 1932, 33.

676. "Helen A Brigadier," *New York Sun,* February 17, 1937, 20; "Given Promotion," *Oswego Palladium-Times,* February 18, 1937, 12.

677. "Given Promotion," *Oswego Palladium-Times,* January 15, 1942, 12.

678. See "Original Doughnut Girl Will Retire," *York Dispatch,* May 26, 1949, 37; "Doughnut Girl of World War I Will Pay Visit to Huntington," [Fort Wayne] *News-Sentinel,* May 30, 1949, 1.

679. Mark Barron, "Berlin Gives Song in Exchange for Doughnuts," [Uniontown, PA] *Morning Herald,* June 20, 1949, 4.

680. "Salvation Lassie Starts the Fat 'Aboiling,' " *Buffalo Evening News,* September 6, 1927, 1.

681. "Doughnut Girl Honored," [Uniontown, PA] *Morning Herald,* October 25, 1964, 1.

682. "Legion Honors Tonite for a 'Doughnut Girl,' " *New York Daily News,* June 18, 1965, 547.

683. Jeff Testerman, " 'Doughnut Girl' Helped Give Doughboys a Taste of Home," *Tampa Bay Times,* November 20, 1981, 53.

684. " 'Sick of Doughnuts,' Says Girl Who First Made them for A. E. F," *Gettysburg Times,* May 16, 1936, 6.

685. "Lt. Colonel Helen Purviance," *Oswego County Messenger,* March 6, 1984, 7; rpt. of "Helen Purviance, Salvation Army 'Doughnut Girl,' " *Tampa Bay Times,* February 29, 1984, 36.

686. "List of New Normal Students," *Oswego Daily Times,* September 25, 1911, 4; "Alumni of Oswego Normal School Pay Tribute to Dr. Richard Piez at Annual Meeting and Luncheon," *Oswego Palladium-Times,* June 7, 1941, 12.

687. "Miss Lynch's Book Unveiled," *Fulton Patriot,* November 4, 1980, 2.

688. "Miss Lynch Assumes Principalship at Fairgrieve," *Oswego Palladium-Times,* January 31, 1959, 5.

689. "Writer, Historian Succumbs in Fulton," *Oswego Palladium-Times,* August 31, 1974, 10.

690. "Grace Lynch Honored," *Fulton Patriot,* April 25, 1968, 1.

691. "Miss Lynch Honored," *Fulton Patriot,* October 25, 1951, 1.

692. "Dedication," *Twenty-Eighth Publication of the Oswego County Historical Society 1966–1967,* v.

693. See "Committee Now in High Gear as Forward Days Draw Near," *Oswego Valley News,* March 29, 1962; "Fulton Plans Huge Anniversary Program," *Syracuse Post-Standard,* May 6, 1962, 26; "Festive Atmosphere Hovers over City as Forward Fulton Day Draws Near," *Oswego Valley News,* May 24, 1962; "Old Newsboys to Sell 'Forward' Papers Saturday," *Fulton Patriot,* May 24, 1962, 1.

694. "Fulton Grows from Portage to Progressive City," *Forward with Fulton,* May 30–June 3, 1962, 1.

695. See Grace Lynch, "The Wonderful Tin Lizzie," *Fulton Patriot,* February 1, 1962, 2; Grace E. Lynch, "The I.R.S. vs. Me," *Fulton Patriot,* February 4, 1971.

696. "Miss Lynch's Book Unveiled," *Fulton Patriot,* November 4, 1980, 2. For more information, see Muriel Allerton's story.

697. Grace Lynch, "Early Teaching," *Fulton Patriot,* September 17, 1962, 2.

698. "The Way It Used to Be," *Fulton Patriot,* November 11, 1980, 2A.

699. "Miss Grace E. Lynch Will Get Fulton Rotary Service Award," *Oswego Palladium-Times,* March 2, 1966, 14.

700. "Writer, Historian Succumbs."

701. See, for example, "Women's Club to Hear Miss Lynch," *Oswego Palladium-Times,* February 17, 1967, 8. See also "Grace Lynch Honored," *Fulton Patriot,* April 25, 1968, 1.

702. "DKG Honors Charter Members in Session at Hewitt Union," *Oswego Palladium-Times,* November 24, 1967, 16.

703. "Miss Grace E. Lynch Will Get Fulton Rotary Service Award."

704. "Miss Grace Lynch Receives Rotary Service Award," *Oswego Palladium-Times,* March 18, 1966.

705. "Grace Lynch Dies after Long Illness," *Fulton Patriot,* September 4, 1974, 1. See also "Miss Grace E. Lynch, Teacher, Historian Succumbs to Illness," *Oswego Valley News,* September 4, 1974.

706. Natalie Woodall, "She's the 'Mother of Fulton,'" *Oswego Palladium-Times,* March 31, 1999, 7A.

707. "State St. UMC Plans Memorial Service for Esther Hibbard," *Oswego Valley News,* March 5, 1998, 8.

708. Carol Thompson, "Oswego County Press Club Honors Muriel Allerton," *Oswego Valley News,* July 2, 1998, 3.

709. See Muriel Allerton, "Sheriff's Deputy Scruton Rescues Dog on Ice," *Oswego County Messenger,* March 13, 1981, 1; Muriel Allerton, "A Look at Life in

Oswego Falls," *Oswego County Messenger,* December 8, 1983, 13; Muriel Allerton," Neglect and Abuse of Children on Increase," *Oswego County Messenger,* December 21, 1983, 1; Muriel Allerton, "Beware of Unusually Friendly Wild Animals," *Oswego County Messenger,* January 16, 1984, 3.

710. Two excellent examples are "Coming to Fulton," *Oswego County Messenger,* July 13, 1983, 9, and "School Boards Haven't Changed Much," *Oswego County Messenger,* August 23, 1983, 2. See also "Deputy Scruton Rescues Dog."

711. Mike Familo, "Fulton Historical Society Launched at Meeting," *Oswego Palladium-Times,* February 16, 1979, 4.

712. Muriel Allerton, "Historical Society Settles into Pratt House," *Oswego Palladium-Times,* April 24, 1980.

713. Doreen Carroll, "Editors Worked Nearly Two Years Compiling Lynch Book," *Oswego Valley News,* November 18, 1980, 7.

714. "Oswego Opera Set for Season," *Oswego Palladium-Times,* October 18, 1978, 10.

715. Marion Ciciarelli, "Soup's On! But Who Will Come to Eat?" *Oswego Palladium-Times,* June 4, 1985, 1; "Kitchen Fills a Need," *Oswego Palladium-Times,* December 23, 1985, 2.

716. Woodall, "Mother of Fulton."

717. "Salvation Army Observes 100th Anniversary at Dinner," *Fulton Patriot,* October 16, 1984, 9.

718. See, for example, Muriel Allerton, "Cracker Barrel Fair Dates Set for Sept. at Fulton," *Oswego County Messenger,* March 20, 1984, 7.

719. "Chili Cook-Off Contest Is Scheduled," *Oswego Palladium-Times,* November 10, 1999, 3A.

720. Woodall, "Mother of Fulton"; "Mayor Sees Commercial Growth in '72," *Oswego Valley News,* January 5, 1972, 1.

721. Cecilia Paiz, "Allerton to Run for Mayor in Fulton," *Oswego Palladium-Times,* June 27, 1987, 1. See also "Woodward's Plea," *Oswego Palladium-Times,* October 24, 1987, 6.

722. "Allerton Presents Mayoral Platform," *Oswego Palladium-Times,* July 20, 1987, 12.

723. "Mayoral Platform."

724. Cecilia Paiz, "Age Factor Resurfaces," *Oswego Palladium-Times,* October 28, 1987, 1.

725. "Muriel Allerton Is Democrats' Candidate," *Fulton Patriot,* June 30, 1987, 1.

726. "Tasteless Criticism," *Oswego Palladium-Times,* October 22, 1987, 4. See also "Amused," *Oswego Palladium-Times,* October 24, 1987, 4, for a voter's response to Borzumate's criticism.

727. "Age Factor Resurfaces."

728. "Grateful," *Oswego Palladium-Times,* October 30, 1987.

729. Cecilia Paiz, "Allerton Makes History," *Oswego Palladium-Times,* January 2, 1988, 1.

730. "Enthusiasm Overflows at Riverfest," *Fulton Patriot,* August 15, 1989, 1.

731. See, for example, Ken Little, "Citizens Pitch In," *Oswego Palladium-Times,* April 12, 1988, 3.

732. "Mayor Begins Campaign," *Fulton Patriot,* September 19, 1989, 5.

733. Alison Kanaley, "Allerton Is Returned to Office," *Oswego Palladium-Times,* November 8, 1989, 1. See also "Allerton's Fulton: Small-Town Flavor, with Services of a City," *Oswego Palladium-Times,* "Progress," March 31, 1990, 50.

734. Alison Kanaley, "First Lady Has No Regrets," *Oswego Palladium-Times,* December 4, 1991, 9.

735. "Muriel Allerton Named Zonta 'Woman of Achievement,'" *Oswego Valley News,* September 25, 1989, 11.

736. "Senate Honors Muriel Allerton as 2010 Woman of Distinction," www.nysenate.gov.

737. "Muriel Allerton to Receive Community Recognition Award," *Valley News,* April 10, 1995, 3.

738. "Muriel Allerton, 93," Oswegocountytoday.com, July 26, 2013.

739. For the sake of complete transparency, the author acknowledges that she was acquainted with Dr. Virginia L. Radley. Some information provided in this biography may be based upon personal remembrances.

740. "Teacher, Scholar, Pioneer, Friend," *Russell Sage Connections* (Spring 1998): 1.

741. "President Radley Addresses AIAA," *Oswego Department of Industrial Arts & Technology Newsletter* (Spring 1981): 2.

742. "Victoria Regina: Celebrating Virginia Radley," *Chatham Chat* (Spring 1998): 1.

743. "All Around the Towns," *Rochester Democrat & Chronicle,* June 28, 1957, 16. See also "Educator Receives Ph.D. at Syracuse," *Rochester Democrat & Chronicle,* June 10, 1958, 19.

744. "Two Administrative Changes Made at Sage," *Troy Record,* March 7, 1959, 8; "College Dean Promoted," *Rochester Democrat & Chronicle,* April 13, 1960, 14; "College Promotes Marion Native," *Rochester Democrat & Chronicle,* April 5, 1965, 46.

745. "Dr. Radley Named Dean at Nazareth," *Troy Times Record,* March 19, 1969, 25; "Baptist Named to Catholic College Post," *Albany Times-Union,* March 25, 1969, 5. See also "Non-Nun as Dean," *Rochester Democrat & Chronicle,* March 15, 1969, 8B; "New Type Dean Will Serve Nazareth College," *Rochester Democrat & Chronicle,* April 20, 1969, 131.

746. "Ex-Sage Teacher in State Post," *Troy Times Record,* March 30, 1973, 24; "Female Is New Provost," *Ithaca Journal,* March 29, 1973, 9; "Suny Trustees Choose Woman to Be Provost," *New Rochelle Standard-Star,* March 29, 1973, 26.

747. "Nazareth Dean Named SUNY Provost," *Rochester Democrat & Chronicle,* March 29, 1973, 18.

748. "Dr. Perdue Renamed College Head," *Watertown Daily Times,* June 28, 1974, 10; "Top Aides Appointed for SUC at Oswego," *Syracuse Post-Standard,* June 28, 1974, 36.

749. Ann Robson, "Dr. Virginia Radley," *Oswego Shopper,* October 30, 1974.

750. "Dr. Radley Ready to Step In," *Syracuse Post-Standard,* February 25, 1977, 36.

751. Russell Tarby, "SUNY Oswego President to be Named Wednesday," *Oswego Palladium-Times,* March 21, 1978, 3.

752. "Virginia Radley; Scholar Takes Helm at SUCO," *Oswego Palladium-Times,* March 23, 1978, 15–A. See also Greta Petry, "Virginia Radley: Ready When the Opportunity Came," *Oswego Palladium-Times,* November 15, 1978, 3.

753. "Virginia L. Radley, SUNY Administrator," *Rochester Democrat & Chronicle,* February 23, 1998, 17.

754. Petry, "Virginia Radley."

755. Brent Senft, "Budget Cuts Bleed SUNY System," *Oswego Palladium-Times,* September 25, 1980, 1.

756. Antone Clark, "An Impressive Public Figure," *Oswego Palladium-Times,* December 3, 1982, 4. See also Antone Clark, "Radley: SUNY in Trouble," *Oswego Palladium-Times,* December 2, 1982, 1; Joanne Berman, "SUNY President Issues Call to Arms," *Oswego Palladium-Times,* February 11, 1983, 1.

757. See, for example, Steve Yablonski, "Armed Officers Cause Drop in Crime Rate," *Oswego Palladium-Times,* September 15, 1982, 8; Sara Franklyn, "Security Can Do a 'Full Job,'" *Oswego Palladium-Times,* October 6, 1979, 2; "Confusion Surrounds Gun Issue," *Oswego Palladium-Times,* September 25, 1979, 1.

758. See "What People Say," *Palladium-Times,* April 29, 1977.

759. "Radley Brands Critics 'Yahoos,'" *Oswegonian,* April 8, 1982, 3.

760. Clark, "Radley."

761. "Special Edition," *Perspective,* April 25, 1984.

762. "Dr. Radley Resumes Teaching," *Oswego Alumni Bulletin* (Summer 1988): 2.

763. "'Yearning in desire to follow knowledge,' The Radley Era at Oswego," special issue, *Update* (July 1998): 1–2. See also "The Presidents at Oswego State University," *Oswego Palladium-Times,* September 7, 1998, 4.

764. "President Radley Addresses AIAA."

765. Kevin Dilworth," "Teachers to Blame, Educator Says," *Rochester Democrat & Chronicle,* July 20, 1978, 47.

766. Dr. Virginia Radley," Four Years in College Can't Make Up for 18," *Oswego Palladium-Times,* April 9, 1982, 4.

767. "Freedom, Responsibility Go Hand in Hand," *Oswego Palladium-Times,* May 12, 1982, 4.

768. Virginia L. Radley, *Samuel Taylor Coleridge* (Boston, MA: Twayne, 1966); Virginia L. Radley, *Elizabeth Barrett Browning* (Boston, MA: Twayne, 1972).

769. See, for example, "The Next One Hundred Years: Women and Work," New York State Association of Bankers, Oswego, Spring 1976; "How to Shrink Programs Effectively and Humanely," American Council on Education, October 1981.

770. Tricia Crisafulli, "Dr. Radley in Demand," *Oswego Palladium-Times,* November 29, 1979, 3.

771. "Dr. Radley Honored by Legislature," *Oswego Palladium-Times,* March 12, 1979, 2; "Chamber of Commerce Honors Dr. Radley," *Oswego Palladium-Times,* December 1, 1982, 1; "Virginia Radley Receives Honorary Degree," *Oswego Valley News,* June 2, 1981, 11; "Two Oswego County Women Cited," *Oswego Palladium-Times,* October 1, 1982, 2.

772. "Radley: College Ready to Meet Challenges," *Oswego Palladium-Times,* May 25, 1986, 3c.

773. "SUNY's First Woman President Resumes Teaching and Research," *Focus on Women* March 1988, 1.

774. "Radley Announces Resignation," *Oswego Palladium-Times,* September 4, 1987, 1.

775. Chris Brock, "Mixed Reviews Greet News," *Oswego Palladium-Times,* September 4, 1987, 1.

776. "Beyond the Presidency: A Leading Professorship for Virginia L. Radley," *Alumni Bulletin* (Spring 1989): 6.

777. "SUNY's First Woman President," 2.

778. "An Appreciative Eye," *Oswego* (Winter 1992): 7.

779. "Radley Named Scholar in Residence," *Sage Times,* January 29, 1993, 1.

780. See, for example, "Dr. Virginia L. Radley," *Oswego Palladium-Times,* December 22, 1998; "Virginia L. Radley, First Female SUNY President," *Stamford Advocate,* December 22, 1998, 9; "Virginia L. Radley, Ex-President and Professor at SUNY-Oswego," *Schenectady Daily Gazette,* December 22, 1998, 12; "Virginia L. Radley, SUNY Administrator," *Rochester Democrat & Chronicle,* December 23, 1998, 17; "SUNY's First Female College President Dies," *Watertown Daily Times,* December 22, 1998, 24; "Virginia L. Radley, 71, A SUNY President," *New York Times,* December 24, 1998. See also Natalie Woodall, "Beloved College Leader Fondly Remembered," *Oswego Palladium-Times,* April 29, 1999, 1.

781. Dorothy Rogers, *SUNY College at Oswego: Its Second Century Unfolds* (Oswego, NY: SUNY Oswego Press, 1988), 150.

Chapter 2

1. "Williamstown," *Camden Advance-Journal,* September 26, 1901; "Mrs. Mary Hanrahan Ballister," *Camden Advance-Journal,* June 4, 1942, 3. Mr. Ballister

succumbed to blood poisoning. Mary Hanrahan Ballister died after breaking her hip.

2. Advertisement for Dey Bros. Department Store, *Syracuse Journal,* May 10, 1919, 7.

3. "Former Williamstown Girl Dies Suddenly," *Camden Advance-Journal,* January 9, 1930, 8. See also "Williamstown," *Pulaski Democrat,* January 15, 1930, 6; "Miss Ballister Dies in Office," *Syracuse Journal,* January 4, 1930, 3; "Dey Floor Manager Suddenly Stricken," *Syracuse Herald,* January 4, 1930.

4. "Robert Gordon," *Oswego Daily Palladium,* September 28, 1891, 4; "Mrs. Sarah J. Gordon," *Oswego Daily Times,* December 20, 1901, 4.

5. "At Drexel Institute," *Philadelphia Times,* June 13, 1896, 3.

6. No headline, *Oswego Daily Times,* June 6, 1896, 4.

7. "Three First Prizes," *Oswego Daily Times,* October 3, 1896, 2.

8. "Personal," *Oswego Daily Times,* February 17, 1897, 4.

9. Pope, *History,* 257.

10. "Craft Show Is Opened," *Morning Oregonian,* April 15, 1910, 11.

11. "Art and Artists Pass in Review," *Philadelphia Inquirer,* November 21, 1915, 3. See also "Much Praise for Miss Gordon," *Oswego Daily Palladium,* January 2, 1924; "Pottery Exhibit Reviewed," *Fiat Lux,* January 19, 1932, 1.

12. "Miss Jessie Gordon," *Philadelphia Inquirer,* December 12, 1942, 11.

13. "Succeeds Dead Instructor," *Philadelphia Inquirer,* January 29, 1922.

14. "Gallery Grows at Art Alliance," *Philadelphia Inquirer,* October 18, 1936, 3.

15. "Miss Jessie F. Gordon," *Palladium-Times,* December 11, 1942; "Miss Jessie F. Gordon," *Philadelphia Inquirer,* December 12, 1942, 11. Her death was widely noted in short obituaries.

16. Pope, *History,* 259. See also "School Exercises," *Oswego Daily Times,* February 5, 1880.

17. "Miss Ida L. Griffin," *Oswego Daily Palladium,* November 3, 1887, 1.

18. Quoted in "Ida L. Griffin," *Oswego Daily Palladium,* November 18, 1887, 1.

19. See, for example, "The First Woman School Commissioner," *New York Daily Graphic,* December 29, 1887, 42; "Ida L. Griffin Holds the Fort," *New York Press,* February 9, 1888, 1; "Our Ida in Rome," *Oswego Daily Palladium,* May 9, 1888.

20. "Arbor Day Results," *Albany Argus,* November 1, 1889, 8.

21. See "An Educational Council," *Oswego Daily Palladium,* February 24, 1888; "Teachers' Association," *Sandy Creek News,* October 15 1888, 2.

22. "Oswego County Canvas," *Oswego Daily Times,* December 5, 1890.

23. "News Nuggets," *Sandy Creek News,* August 20, 1891, 8.

24. "Oswego County News," *Utica Weekly Herald,* December 1, 1891; "Personal," *Sandy Creek News,* December 3, 1891.

25. "Oswego Outings," *Sandy Creek News,* December 1, 1892; "We and Our Neighbors," *Brookfield Courier,* February 8, 1893.

26. "Mrs. Daniel Keating," *Pulaski Democrat,* December 29, 1897; "Oneida," *Utica Semi-Weekly Herald,* December 14, 1897, 5.

27. For the purpose of complete transparency, the author acknowledges that she was acquainted with Rhea C. Wilder LaVeck. Some information contained herein may be based upon personal recollection.

28. "Pvt. Marion LaVeck, Missing Two Months in Italy, Now Safe," *Syracuse Post-Standard,* December 18, 1944.

29. "Carpenter Killed When He Falls in Belfry of Church," *Oswego Palladium-Times,* May 13, 1948, 4; "Carpenter Killed in Belfry Fall," *Rome Daily Sentinel,* May 13, 1948, 26; "Marion LaVeck Killed," *Sandy Creek News,* May 18, 1948, 5.

30. See, for example, "Mrs. Lois Wilder of Pulaski O.E.S. District Deputy," *Oswego Palladium-Times,* October 18, 1952, 3; "OES District to Hold Honorary Tea," *Oswego Valley News,* June 7, 1971; "Tracy H. Wilder, Sr.," *Oswego Palladium-Times,* October 28, 1973.

31. "Mrs. LaVeck New Deputy for OES," *Oswego Palladium-Times,* October 11, 1960, 4.

32. "Mrs. LaVeck Honored by O.E.S. at Reception," *Pulaski Democrat,* October 27, 1960, 1; "Official Visits," *Oswego Palladium-Times,* February 23, 1961, 5. See also "Over 200 Here Tuesday Night for Reception Honoring District Officers," *Sandy Creek News,* March 91961, 5.

33. "Pulaski Woman Elected to State O.E.S. Office," *Oswego County Weeklies,* October 21, 1965, 26.

34. "Rhea LaVeck Heads OES," *Sandy Creek News,* October 26, 1967, 1; "Many Honor Mrs. LaVeck at Reception in Syracuse," *Pulaski Democrat,* October 26, 1967, 4; "OES Reception," *Binghamton Press and Sun-Bulletin,* November 17, 1967, 5.

35. See, for example, "26 Chapters of OES to Be Visited," *White Plains Reporter Dispatch,* February 29, 1968, 16; "Grand Matron to St. Johnsville," *Herkimer [NY] Evening Telegram,* March 21, 1968, 6; "State Head of OES Visits Area," *Troy Times Record,* April 8, 1968, 25; "OES Grand Officers Here April 18th," *Essex County Republican,* April 5, 1968, 1; "OES Grand Matron to Make Official Visit," *Andover News,* April 18, 1968, 1; "O.E.S. Grand Matron Visits District," *Oswego County Weeklies,* June 20, 1968, 34.

36. See, for example, "Chapter Receives Official Visit," *Kingston Daily Freeman,* March 27, 1968, 30. The headline is misleading. Clinton Chapter No. 445 was celebrating its fifty-ninth birthday.

37. "Grand Officers Dedicate Elizabeth Chapter O.E.S.," *Oswego Valley News,* October 31, 1968; "Personal Notes, Coming Events," *Palladium-Times,* September 10, 1968, 3.

38. See, for example, "Victoria Chapter Order of Eastern Star," *Mexico Independent,* May 9, 1968, 1.

39. "Mrs. LaVeck Recognized," *Syracuse Post-Standard,* April 25, 1969, 10; "Mrs. Rhea LaVeck Honored," *Watertown Daily Times,* May 14, 1969, 21.

40. For a contemporary perspective on Shakerism, see "Among the Shakers," *Sandy Creek News,* October 11, 1888, 3. The writer described life in the Mount Lebanon Community.

41. E-mail message from Roben Campbell dated March 27, 2021.

42. The hurricane that ravaged New England was the first ever to appear in Boston. See "Storm of 88 Miles an Hour, Wind Breaks Boston Records," *Boston Globe,* September 22, 1938, 6.

43. For more information on the McLean family, see Glenna Gorski and others, *Williamstown Military Veterans,* vol. 1 (Williamstown, NY: Williamstown Historical Society, n. d.), 173.

44. "Laguna Artists Tell Stories of Selves," *Santa Ana Daily Register,* March 28, 1921, 10. The large sum of money mentioned probably was the ten thousand dollars she loaned to her brother, William J., which was never repaid. She obtained a judgment in 1900 to recover her losses. So far as is known, her father was not an art dealer but he certainly might have been interested in art since he was a professional photographer.

45. "Fine Art Is Their Profession," *Syracuse Sunday Herald,* October 20, 1895, 6.

46. "Frank W. Oliver," *Oswego Daily Palladium,* November 13, 1882; "Funeral of the Late Frank W. Oliver," *Oswego Daily Palladium,* November 16, 1882.

47. Beulah Shares Schroeder, *Interments in Riverside Cemetery 1855–1910,* 148.

48. "Odds and Ends," *Oswego Daily Palladium,* September 14, 1889. The painting of Robert Oliver, Mary's father-in-law, still exists and is in the possession of Lake City Lodge No. 127 Free and Accepted Masons, Oswego, New York. Henry D. McCaffrey was mayor of Oswego City in 1888.

49. See advertisement for Mary A. Oliver's portrait studio, *Oswego Daily Palladium,* October 24, 1893, 6.

50. "Mrs. Oliver's Studio," *Oswego Daily Palladium,* November 22, 1894, 6. For information on Katherine E. "Kate" Miller, see "A Duo of Weddings," *Syracuse Standard,* April 17, 1895; "Syracuse behind Art 50 Years, Says Mrs. Cobb," *Syracuse American,* January 8, 1928, 15; "Mrs. Cobb Dies on Coast, Wife of Former Judge," *Syracuse Post-Standard,* April 4, 1956.

51. "Fine Art Is Their Profession," *Syracuse Sunday Herald,* October 20, 1895, 6.

52. "Mrs. Oliver's Miniature Work," *Oswego Daily Palladium,* January 28, 1895, 8. Professor Unni Lund was the first cousin of Madame Charlotte Lund, the opera singer. See Charlotte's story for details.

53. "Geneva Artist Honored," *Geneva Daily Times,* December 30, 1903; "Silver Medal for Paintings," *Syracuse Daily Journal,* January 4, 1904, 6. See also "Art," *Minneapolis Journal,* July 1, 1905, 12.

54. See Florence M. Freeman, "Traveling Art Exhibition in Local Gallery," *Long Beach Press,* February 2, 1921, 7.

55. Many references to Mary found online erroneously claim she died in 1948. Her gravestone provides exact birth and death dates.

56. "Mrs. Malvina Waugh," *Oswego Daily Times,* April 6, 1908, 5; "His Mother's Death," *Utica Saturday Globe,* April 18, 1908, 32.

57. "Honor to Whom Honor Is Due," *Missions,* May 1915, 401–402.

58. "Miss Carrie E. Waugh," *Oswego Daily Times,* August 23, 1921, 4; "Miss Carrie E. Waugh, Sister of Rev. H. E. Waugh, Succumbs," *Utica Daily Press,* August 24, 1921, 4; "Miss Carrie E. Waugh," *Lowville Journal and Republican,* November 10, 1921.

59. "A Loveful Life," *Missions,* November 1921, 620–621.

Bibliography

Newspapers

Albany Argus
Albany Evening Journal
Albany Times-Union
Altoona Tribune
Amherst (NY) *Bee*
Amsterdam Evening Recorder
Anaheim Gazette
Andover (NY) *News*
Atlanta Constitution
Attica News
Auburn Bulletin
Auburn Citizen
Auburn Citizen-Advertiser
Augusta Chronicle
Baldwinsville Gazette and Farmers' Journal
Batavia Daily News
Bayonne Herald and Greenville Register
Berkeley Daily Gazette
Billboard
Binghamton Press and Sun-Bulletin
Boston Evening Transcript
Boston Globe
Boston Journal
Boston Sunday Globe
Breckinridge News
Brooklyn Citizen
Brooklyn Daily Eagle

Brooklyn Times-Union
Buffalo Courier
Buffalo Evening News
Buffalo News
Buffalo Review
Buffalo Times
Buffalo Times-Herald
Butte Intermountain
Butte Miner
Canajoharie Courier
Carlisle Valley Sentinel
Cedar Rapids Evening Gazette
Charlotte News
Chatham Chat
Chicago Daily Inter Ocean
Chicago Daily News
Chicago Daily Tribune
Chicago Examiner
Chicago Sunday Tribune
Christian Leader
Christian Observer
Cincinnati Post
Cleveland Leader
Cleveland Plain Dealer
Coldwater Sentinel
Colorado Springs Gazette
Columbia State (South Carolina)
Daily Saratogian
Danville Advertiser
Day Book
Delineator
Denver Post
Detroit Free Press
Detroit News Tribune
Duluth News Tribune
Eagle River Review
Empire State Universalist
Endicott Bulletin
Enterprise and News
Escondido Times-Advocate
Essex County Republican
Fiat Lux

Flemington (NJ) *Republican*
FOCUS
Fort Wayne News and Sentinel
Fort Worth Star-Telegram
Fulton Patriot
Fulton Times
Geneva Daily Times
Gettysburg Times
Goshen Democrat
Goshen Herald
Harrisburg Daily Independent
Harrisburg Patriot
Harrisburg Telegraph
Hartford Courant
Herkimer Evening Telegram
Homer (LA) *Guardian-Journal*
Houston Chronicle and Herald
Huntington Herald
Ithaca Journal
Jefferson County Journal
Jersey Journal
Journal and Tribune
Juniata Herald
Kalamazoo Gazette
Kansas City Star
Kansas City Times
Kingston Daily Freeman
Knickerbocker Press
Knoxville Journal and Tribune
Knoxville Sentinel
Lakeland (FL) *Evening Telegram*
Lancaster Examiner
Lewiston Daily Sun
Lewiston Saturday Journal
Lexington Intelligencer
Liberator
Lincoln Evening News
Lincoln Star
Little Falls Herald
Little Falls Journal and Courier
Long Beach Press
Los Angeles Sunday Times

Los Angeles Times
Lowville Journal and Republican
Memphis Commercial Appeal
Mexico Deaf-Mutes Journal
Mexico Independent
Miami News
Middlebury Register
Milwaukee Journal
Minneapolis Journal
Minneapolis Star Tribune
Minneapolis Times
Montclair Times
Montgomery Advertiser
Morning Call
Morning Oregonian
Morning Pioneer
Mountain View Herald
Mount Vernon Daily Argus
Mower County Transcript
Muncie Times
Naples Record
Nassau Daily Review
National Reformer
Neenah Daily Times
Newark Advocate
Newark Star-Eagle
Newburg Daily Press
New Haven Morning Journal and Courier
Newton Journal
Newton Record
New York Clipper
New York Daily News
New York Daily Worker
New York Dramatic Mirror
New York Evening Express
New York Evening Post
New York Evening World
New York Herald
New York Press
New York Sun
New York Sunday Press

New York Times
New-York Tribune
New York Weekly Press
North Star
Ocean Grove Record
Ogdensburg Journal
Ogdensburg Republican-Journal
Omaha Daily Bee
Omaha Morning World-Herald
Ontario Repository-Messenger
Oswego Commercial Times
Oswego County Messenger
Oswego Daily Palladium
Oswego Daily Times
Oswego Morning Express
Oswego Morning Express and Times
Oswego Morning Post
Oswegonian
Oswego Palladium-Times
Oswego Shopper
Oswego Times-Express
Oswego Valley News
Otsego Farmer
Ottawa Citizen
Passaic Daily News
Passaic Herald-News
Paterson Evening News
Paterson Morning Call
Peekskill Highland Democrat
Philadelphia Inquirer
Philadelphia Times
Pittsburg Weekly Gazette
Port Jervis Evening Gazette
Portland (OR) *Daily Press*
Portsmouth (NH) *Herald*
Post-Star
Poughkeepsie Daily Eagle
Poughkeepsie Daily News
Poughkeepsie Eagle News
Poughkeepsie Evening Enterprise
Pulaski Democrat

Putnam County Courier
Racine Journal Times
Raleigh Morning Post
Red Wing Argus
Reno Gazette-Journal
Richmond (MO) *Democrat*
Richmond (IN) *Item*
Richmond Times-Dispatch
Rochester Daily Democrat
Rochester Democrat & Chronicle
Rockford Register-Republic
Rome Daily Sentinel
Sage Notes
Salt Lake Tribune
San Diego Union and Bee
Sandy Creek News
San Francisco Chronicle
Santa Ana Daily Register
Saskatoon Star-Phoenix
Selma Times
South Gate Press
Schenectady Daily Gazette
Scranton Tribune
Scranton Tribune-Republican
Scranton Truth
Southtown Economist
Spokane Chronicle
Springfield Daily News
Stamford Advocate
St. Johnsville Enterprise and News
St. Louis Post-Dispatch
St. Louis Republic
Sunberry Sun
Syracuse American
Syracuse Daily Journal
Syracuse Daily Standard
Syracuse Evening Herald
Syracuse Herald
Syracuse Journal
Syracuse Post-Standard
Syracuse Sunday Herald

Syracuse Weekly Express
Tampa Bay Times
Thrice-a-Week World
Times Record
Topeka Daily Capital
Topeka State Journal
Toronto Star
Troy Times Record
Uniontown (PA) *Morning Herald*
Utica Daily Press
Utica Daily Union
Utica Herald-Dispatch
Utica Morning Herald
Utica Observer-Dispatch
Utica Saturday Globe
Utica Semi-Weekly Herald
Utica Sunday Journal
Utica Sunday Tribune
Utica Weekly Herald
Valley Sentinel
Vermont Tribune
Virginia Pilot
Wanaque News
Warren Sheaf
Washington Evening Star
Washington Herald
Washington Sunday Star
Washington Times
Watertown Daily Standard
Watertown Daily Times
Watkins Express
Weekly Auburnian
Weekly Memphis Eagle
White Plains Reporter Dispatch
Wilkes-Barre Leader
Wilmington Morning Star
Winnipeg Tribune
Winona Daily Republican
Yonkers Statesman
Yonkers Statesman and News
York (PA) *Dispatch*

Periodicals

"A Loveful Life." *Missions*, November 1921, 620–631.

"Biographical." *Northern Christian Advocate*. March 1852, 52. [Minerva Ames's obituary.]

"Charlotte Lund Heads World's Smallest Opera Company." *Musical Observer* 24, no. 5, May 1925, 38.

"Charlotte Lund, Prima Donna Soprano." New York: J. B. Pond Lyceum Bureau, 1916.

Cunningham, Mary. "An Oswego Man Opens the Door of China." *Ninth Publication of the Oswego Historical Society*. Oswego, NY: Palladium-Times, 1945, 82–91.

"Dedication—Dorothy J. Mott." *Thirty-First Publication of the Oswego County Historical Society*. Phoenix: Phoenix Press, 1970, v.

"Dedication—Miss Grace E. Lynch." *Twenty-Eighth Publication of the Oswego County Historical Society*, 1966–1967, iv.

Doyle, Esther Ruttan. "The Columbian Doll Story." *Thirty-Third Annual Publication of the Oswego County Historical Society*. Oswego, NY: Beyer Offset, 1972, 71–74.

Gage, Dr. D. S. "A Remembrance of Julia MacNair Wright." *Christian Observer*, October 14, 1903.

Gray, S. P. "Rev. Wm. W. Rundell." *Minutes of the Fourth Session of the New York Conference of the Methodist Episcopal Church Held in Potsdam April 5th to 11th, 1876*. Watertown, NY: Kenyon & Holbrook, 1876, 30–31.

"Honor to Whom Honor Is Due." *Missions*, May 1915, 401–402.

"In Memoriam." *Empire State Universalist*, November 1927.

The Key. Vol. 17 (October 1900): 89.

Lane, Lunette Cooper. "The Story of Lieut. A. Cooper—Civil War Veteran, Author and Poet." *Thirtieth Publication of the Oswego Historical Society*. Oswego, NY: Palladium-Times, 1950, 62–71.

"Mrs. Armonella Devendorf." *Christian Leader*, November 5, 1927, 1438.

Myers, J. H. "Mrs. Harriet P. Rundell." *Minutes of the Twenty-Fifth Session Northern New York Conference, Methodist Episcopal Church . . . Held in Watertown, N.Y., April 14–19, 1897*. Published by the secretaries, n. d., 74–75.

"Obituary Notices [Luther W. Mott]." *Quarterly Journal of the New York Historical Association*, January 1924, 71.

Parker, Lottie. "My Most Successful Play." *Green Room Album*, July 1911, 879–881.

Penfield, Lida S. "Charlotte Blair Parker." *Ninth Publication of the Oswego Historical Society*. Oswego, NY: Palladium-Times, 1945, 43–51.

———. "Ned Lee—His Life and Times," *Seventh Publication of the Oswego County Historical Society*. Oswego, NY: Palladium-Times, 1943, 18–26.

"The Scandinavian Concert." *American Scandinavian Review* 1, November 6, 1913, 16.

Stanley, May. "Musical Critics Artist's Best Friends, Says Charlotte Lund." *Musical America*, June 17, 1916, 13.

Waterbury, Edwin M. "Oswego Historical Society Yet Strong after Fifty Active Years." *Tenth Publication of the Oswego Historical Society.* Oswego, NY: Palladium-Times, 1946, 112–155.

Woodall, Natalie J. "Charles H. Treadwell: Long-Time Educator and Masonic Leader." *Oswego Palladium-Times*, August 16, 2022, 1.

———. "Charlotte Lund: An Unforgotten Oswego Treasure." *Oswego Palladium-Times*, December 24, 2019, 1.

———. "Dr. Ernest Manwaren: A Masonic Scandal." *Oswego Palladium-Times*, October 22, 2022, 1.

———. "Harvey Irving Pratt: Oswego's Scholar Shoe Salesman." *Oswego Palladium-Times*, February 4, 2023, A-7.

———. "John D'Auby Higgins: Oswego's Mighty Mayor." *Oswego Palladium-Times*, March 4, 2023, A-7.

———. "John McNair: Plotting Oswego's Future." *Oswego Palladium-Times*, July 16, 2022, 1.

———. "She's the 'Mother' of Fulton." *Oswego Palladium-Times*, March 31, 1999, 7-A.

———. "Thomas Smith Mott: A Man 'Made of Sterner Stuff.'" *Oswego Palladium-Times*, May 6, 2023, 7.

———. "William Pierson Judson: Father of the Oswego County Historical Society." *Oswego Palladium-Times*, December 17, 2022, A-7.

———. "Willis Gaylord Chaffee: Business Education Pioneer." *Oswego Palladium-Times*, March 18, 2023, A-7.

Wright, Julia McNair. "The Life-Labor of Jean Garston." *Ladies' Repository*, November 1859, 679–683.

Online Sources

www.Ancestry.com

www.Familysearch.com

www.Findagrave.com

www.Fultonhistory.com

www.genealogybank.com

www.newspapers.com

www.NYSHistoricalNewspapers.com

"A Brief History of Delsarte." www.delsarteproject.com. Accessed January 17, 2024.

Duchan, Judy. "A History of Speech-Language Pathology." www.ascu.buffalo.edu. Accessed January 16, 2024.

"Muriel Allerton, 93." www.oswegocountytoday.com. July 26, 2013. Accessed January 19, 2024.

"Rhea W. LaVeck." www.obits.syracuse.com. Accessed January 14, 2024.
"Senate Honors Muriel Allerton as 2010 Woman of Distinction." www.nysenate.
    gov. Accessed January 2, 2024.

Books

Browne, Walter, and E. De Roy Koch. *Who's Who on the Stage.* New York: B. W.
    Dodge, 1908.
Churchill, John. *Landmarks of Oswego County, New York.* Syracuse, NY: D. Mason,
    1895.
DeMass, George R. *Images of America: Town of Oswego.* Charleston, SC: Arcadia, 2014.
Engel, Helen, and Marilynn Smiley, eds. *Remarkable Women in New York State
    History.* Charleston, SC: History Press, 2013.
Evans, Sara M. *Born for Liberty.* 2nd ed. New York: Free Press Paperbacks, 1997.
Gagne, Sarah Pullar. *Five Generations of an American Family.* Sarah Pullar Gagne,
    2017.
Gorski, Glenna, and others. *Williamstown Military Veterans.* Vol. 1. Williamstown,
    NY: Williamstown Historical Society, n. d.
Goss, Charles Frederic. *The Redemption of Peter Corson.* Indianapolis, IN: Bow-
    en-Merrill Company, 1900.
Herringshaw, Thomas William. *Herringshaw's National Library of America.* Vol. 5.
    Chicago, IL: American Publishers' Association, 1914.
*Historical Sketches Relating to the First Quarter Century of the State Normal and
    Training School at Oswego, N.Y.* Oswego, NY: R. J. Oliphant, 1888.
International Who's Who in Education. Edited by Ernest Kay. Cambridge: International
    Who's Who in Education, 1981.
International Who's Who in Music and Musical Gazetteer. 1st ed. New York: Current
    Literature Publishing Company, 1918.
Johnson, Crisfield. *History of Oswego County, New York, 1789–1877.* Philadelphia,
    PA: L. H. Everts., 1877.
Leonard, John W., ed. *The Woman's Who's Who of America.* Vol. 3. New York:
    Commonwealth, 1914.
Lund, Charlotte. *Opera Miniature Series.* 6 vols. Philadelphia, PA: Theodore Dresser,
    1923–1930.
Maxwell, W. S. *General Alumni Catalogue for Boston University, 1918.* Boston, MA:
    Boston University, 1918.
*Memorial Addresses Delivered in the House of Representatives in Memory of Luther
    Mott.* Washington, DC: Government Printing Office, 1925.
*Memorial Addresses on the Life and Character of Newton W. Nutting (A Representative
    from New York.)* Washington, DC: Government Printing Office, 1890.
Oswego City Directory.

Parker, Lottie Blair. *Homespun.* New York: Henry Holt, 1909.

Parrish, Diane Doyle. *The Story of the Columbian Dolls: How the Adams Sisters Saved the Family Farm.* New Haven, CT: CreateSpace, 2013.

Penfield, Lida Scovil. *Stories of Oswego: Tales of the Early Days Told to the Children of the Oswego Normal Training School.* Oswego, NY: Normal School Print Shop, 1919.

Pope, William A. *History of the First Half Century of the Oswego State Normal and Training School.* Oswego, NY: Radcliffe Press, 1913.

Rogers, Dorothy. *Oswego: Fountainhead of Teacher Education.* New York: Appleton-Century-Crofts, 1961.

———. *SUNY College At Oswego: Its Second Century Unfolds.* Oswego, NY: SUNY College at Oswego, 1988.

Schroeder, Beulah Shares. *Interments in Riverside Cemetery, Oswego, New York, 1855–1910.* Oswego, NY: n.p., 1972.

Seagraves, Anne. *Daughters of the West.* Hayden, ID: Wesanne, 1996.

Simpson, Elizabeth M. *Mexico Mother of Towns: Fragments of Local History.* Mexico, NY: Mexico Independent, 1949.

Strong, James, and John McClintock, eds. *The Cyclopedia of Biblical, Theological, and Ecclesiastical Literature.* Vol. 9. New York: Harper and Bros., 1894.

Treadwell, Harriette Taylor, and Margaret Free. *Reading-Literature Readers.* 6 vols. Evanston, IL: Row, Peterson, 1911–1914.

Velazquez, Rita C., ed. *Directory of American Scholars.* Vol. 2. Farmington Hills, MI: Gale, 1999.

Welch, Edgar Luderne. *Grip's Historical Souvenir of Mexico.* Syracuse, NY: Grip, 1904.

Who's Who in America. N.p.: Marqus Who's Who, 1998.

Who's Who in New York City and State. Vol. 11. New York: Lewis Historical Publishing, 1947.

Wickser, Josephine Wilhelm. *Pageant of Oswego: Commemorating Two Hundredth Anniversary of First Settlement in Oswego by the White Man.* Foreword and historical notes by Lida Penfield. Oswego, NY: Palladium-Times, 1925.

Willard, Frances, and Mary Livermore. *A Woman of the Century.* Buffalo, NY: Charles Wells Moulton, 1894.

Woodall, Natalie Joy. *Men of the 110th Regiment: Oswego's Own.* Denver, CO: Outskirts, 2016.

———. *Men of the 110th Regiment: Oswego's Own—A Biographical Supplement.* Rev. ed. Richland, NY: Half-Shire Historical Society, 2023.

———. *Notable Civil War Veterans of Oswego County, New York.* Albany: SUNY Press, 2023.

———. *Of Blood and Battles: Oswego's 147th Regiment.* Denver, CO: Outskirts, 2019.

Wright, Julia McNair. *The Complete Home: An Encyclopedia of Domestic Life and Affairs, Embracing All the Interests of the Household.* Philadelphia, PA: J. C. McCurdy, 1879.

———. *Sea-Side and Way-Side.* 4 vols. Boston, MA: D. C. Heath, 1888–1892.

Index

Abandoned Wives' Act of March 3, 1899, 9–10
Academy for Speech Correction, 132
Adams, Cornelia, 81, 225 note
Adams, Emma Eunice, 79–88
Alexander, James B., 77
Alexander, Mary I. Place, 56, 57, 242 note
Alger, Anna Slauson, 64
Allerton, Muriel Leola Jobst, 16, 175–181
American Association of University Women (AAUW), 105

Ballister, Cora M., 193–194
Baptist Home Mission, 209
Blackstone, William, 2
Brady, William A., 62, 63, 64–65
Bruce, Ellen M., 26–31

Catt, Carrie Chapman, 136
Chicago Political Equality Club, 125, 126
Chicago Woman's Club, 128
Christ Episcopal Church, 150, 156, 244 note
Clarke, Charlotte Ambler, xix
Clarke, Edwin Winslow, xix

Clayton, Una (Fanny Pearl Keyes), 108–116
Columbian Dolls, 81–85, 86
Cooter, Josiah and Lucy Parmiter, 9–10
Coverture, 2

Declaration of Sentiments, 3–6
Delsartre System of Expression, 41–44
Devendorf, Armonella "Nell" Marshall, 32–37
Devendorf, Henry Clay, 32–33, 34, 35
Divorce, 8

Eclectic Club, 68
Entail, 1
Equal Rights Amendment, 16

Fifteenth Amendment, 14–15
Fitch, Clyde, 65
Fort George, 71, 122
Fortnightly Club, 73
Fort Oswego Chapter, DAR, 70, 77, 119, 122, 135–136, 148
Fourteenth Amendment, 14
Frank, Nancy Mott, 141, 154, 157
Free, Margaret, 124
Freedmen's Aid Society, 208, 209

Glynn, George A., 139
Gordon, Jessie Fairfield, 194–196
Gould, Frank L., 150–151
Grace Presbyterian Church, 40, 56
Griffin, Herbert Lauris, 115, 116
Grismer, Joseph, 65

Halsey, John George, 108, 109
Hamilton Homes, 150–151
Home for the Homeless (Ladies'
    Home), 12–13, 55, 130
Horton, Elizabeth Richards, 84–85
Humane Society of Oswego City, 122

Illinois Equal Suffrage Association, 127
Illinois League of Women Voters, 127
Irwin, Louise, xxi, 12
Ithaca Reconstruction Home, 154

Keating, Daniel, 197
Keating, Ida Louise Griffin, 196–198

LaVeck, Marion Edward, 199
LaVeck, Rhea Claire Wilder, 198–201
Lee, Mary Victoria, xx, 16, 38–46, 54
Little, Mary E., 40
Low, Emma Dygert, 36–37
Lozier, Charlotte Denman, 39
Lunch, Unni Charlotte (Professor),
    88–89, 206–207
Lund, Unni Charlotte (Madame),
    88–100
Lynch, Grace E., 170–174, 176

MacFarlane, Louise, xxi–xxii, 13
Mackin, Marion C., 150
Macmillan, Isabel Taylor, 116,
    118–119
Macmillan, Newton, 118
Manwaren, Ernest, 10–11
Married Women's Property Act, 3

McLean, Semantha "Almira" Reynolds,
    201–203
McNair, John, 47
McNair, Matthew, 47, 50–51
Montcalm Park, 71–73
Moody, Dwight Lyman, 39, 54
Morey, Francis "Frank" Lee, 109–110,
    114, 115
Morton, Martha, 63
Mott, Bailey Elizabeth, 133, 154–157
Mott, Dorothy, 16, 132, 154–157
Mott, Lucretia, 3, 6, 13
Mott, Luther Wright, 56, 133, 134,
    140–141, 142
Mott, Ruth Woolsey Johnson, xx,
    133–143
Mott, Thomas Smith, 152–153, 154

Newkirk, Laura R., 54–55
New York League for Speech
    Improvement, 132
Nineteenth Amendment, 120, 127

Oliver, Francis "Frank," 204
Oliver, Mary Austen, 203–207
Order of the Eastern Star, xviii, 36–37,
    115, 161, 200, 201
Orphan and Free School Association,
    26
Oswego County [Historical] Society,
    73–74, 77, 86, 104–105, 143, 156,
    157, 170, 174
Oswego County Political Equality
    Club, 122
Oswego Hospital, xxi, 56
Oswego Housing Authority, 150
Oswego Normal School, 26, 31, 42,
    43, 45, 56, 60, 69, 76, 81, 89, 95,
    102, 104, 107, 121, 123, 170, 196

Pankhurst, Emily, 126–127

Parker, Charlotte "Lottie" Blair, 16, 60–69, 131
Parker, Harry Doel, 62, 65, 67, 68–69
Penfield, Lida Scovil, 62, 101–107
Pestalozzi, Johann Heinrich, 38–39
Primogeniture, 1
Purviance, Helen Gay, 16, 158–169

Radley, Virginia Louise, 16, 182–192
Raines, Thomas Raleigh, 97–98, 231 note
Rainier, Elvira Sarah, xx, 54–59, 118
Randall, Anna T. Fitch, 60–61
Roe v. Wade, 16
Rundell, Harriet Peck Ames, 19–25
Rundell, William W., 21–22, 24
Ruttan, Marietta Adams, 86

Salvation Army, 158, 159–160
Sanborn, Hazel Harriet Straight, 57–58
Sanborn, James Forrest, 58
Sheldon, Edward Austin, 26, 30, 39, 46, 69, 104
Simeon DeWitt Apartments, 151
Society for the Prevention of Cruelty to Children, 122
Soldiers' Aid Society, 23
Spencer, Elmina Pleiades Keeler, xix
Stanton, Elizabeth Cady, 3, 4, 15
Stevens, Harriet Elisabeth, 69–78
Straight, Emma Dickerman, 57
Straight, Henry, 57
Straight, Willard, 57–58
Sweet, Thaddeus C., 72, 142

Taylor, Grace Taft, 119–123
Taylor, Jane Bliss, 128–132

Tifft, Alice Mott, 133, 143–147
Tifft, Jr., Edwin C., 146
Tifft, Sr., Edwin C., 145, 147
Torchlight Ceremony, 102–103
Treadwell, Jr., Charles Humphrey, 127–128
Treadwell, Charles (Smith) Humphrey, 128
Treadwell, Harriet [Harriette] Fish Taylor, xx, 121, 123–128, 132
Trout, Grace Wilbur, 127

Van Buren, Catherine Pickens, 8–9
Van Buren, Martin Pieter, 8–9

Walker, Mary Edwards, xix, 12, 13
Waugh, Caroline "Carrie" E., 208–210
Waugh, William E., 64
Weaver, Almira Meachem, 9
Wilder, Lois Belle Parsons, 198
Wilder, Tracy Hartwell, 198
Wilson, Woodrow, 136, 139
Woman's Baptist Home Mission Society of Chicago, 209
Woman's Home Missionary Society, 81
Woman's Outlook Club, 55, 56, 57, 118
Woman's Relief Corps, 35
Woman's Suffrage, 6, 136
Women's Rights Convention at Seneca Falls, New York, 3–8
Woodward, Ronald L., 177
Wright, Julia McNair, 16, 47–54
Wright, William Janes, 47–48, 49–50, 53, 54

Zonta, 150, 156, 181